T0281653

Learn Kotlin for Android Development

The Next Generation Language for Modern Android Apps Programming

Peter Späth

Apress®

Learn Kotlin for Android Development: The Next Generation Language for Modern Android Apps Programming

Peter Späth
Leipzig, Germany

ISBN-13 (pbk): 978-1-4842-4466-1
https://doi.org/10.1007/978-1-4842-4467-8

ISBN-13 (electronic): 978-1-4842-4467-8

Copyright © 2019 by Peter Späth

This work is subject to copyright. All rights are reserved by the Publisher, whether the whole or part of the material is concerned, specifically the rights of translation, reprinting, reuse of illustrations, recitation, broadcasting, reproduction on microfilms or in any other physical way, and transmission or information storage and retrieval, electronic adaptation, computer software, or by similar or dissimilar methodology now known or hereafter developed.

Trademarked names, logos, and images may appear in this book. Rather than use a trademark symbol with every occurrence of a trademarked name, logo, or image we use the names, logos, and images only in an editorial fashion and to the benefit of the trademark owner, with no intention of infringement of the trademark.

The use in this publication of trade names, trademarks, service marks, and similar terms, even if they are not identified as such, is not to be taken as an expression of opinion as to whether or not they are subject to proprietary rights.

While the advice and information in this book are believed to be true and accurate at the date of publication, neither the authors nor the editors nor the publisher can accept any legal responsibility for any errors or omissions that may be made. The publisher makes no warranty, express or implied, with respect to the material contained herein.

Managing Director, Apress Media LLC: Welmoed Spahr
Acquisitions Editor: Steve Anglin
Development Editor: Matthew Moodie
Coordinating Editor: Mark Powers

Cover designed by eStudioCalamar

Distributed to the book trade worldwide by Springer Science+Business Media New York, 233 Spring Street, 6th Floor, New York, NY 10013. Phone 1-800-SPRINGER, fax (201) 348-4505, e-mail orders-ny@springer-sbm.com, or visit www.springeronline.com. Apress Media, LLC is a California LLC and the sole member (owner) is Springer Science + Business Media Finance Inc (SSBM Finance Inc). SSBM Finance Inc is a **Delaware** corporation.

For information on translations, please e-mail editorial@apress.com; for reprint, paperback, or audio rights, please email bookpermissions@springernature.com.

Apress titles may be purchased in bulk for academic, corporate, or promotional use. eBook versions and licenses are also available for most titles. For more information, reference our Print and eBook Bulk Sales web page at http://www.apress.com/bulk-sales.

Any source code or other supplementary material referenced by the author in this book is available to readers on GitHub via the book's product page, located at www.apress.com/9781484244661. For more detailed information, please visit http://www.apress.com/source-code.

Printed on acid-free paper

To Alina

Table of Contents

About the Author

Peter Späth graduated in 2002 as a physicist and soon afterward became an IT consultant, mainly for Java-related projects. In 2016 he decided to concentrate on writing books on various subjects, with a primary focus on software development. With a wealth of experience in Java-related languages, the release of Kotlin for building Android apps made him enthusiastic about writing books for Kotlin development in the Android environment.

About the Technical Reviewer

Ted Hagos is the CTO and Data Protection Officer of RenditionDigital International (RDI), a software development company based out of Dublin. Before he joined RDI, he had various software development roles and also spent time as a trainer at IBM Advanced Career Education, Ateneo ITI, and Asia Pacific College. He spent many years in software development, dating back to the days of Turbo C, Clipper, dBase IV, and Visual Basic. Eventually, he found Java and spent many years working on Java-related projects. Nowadays, he's busy with full-stack JavaScript and Android.

Introduction

Computer programs are for executing operations using input data to produce output data, sometimes by manipulating data taken from a database during that operation. The word *database* here is used in the most general sense: It could be a file, some memory storage, or a full-fledged database product.

Many different programming languages exist nowadays, each with its own merits and drawbacks. Some of them aim at execution stability, some at high performance, some are tailored to solve specific tasks, and some exist only because a company wants to establish a strong market position. Looking at the way programming languages have developed over time is an interesting subject in and of itself, and it has implications for various aspects of information technology. One could write a separate book about that, but for this book I simply want to stress one important fact about computer language development, which I think has a direct effect on the way modern computer programs are written. If you are looking at the historical development of computer languages, you will notice a substantial change in the *abstraction level* the languages exhibit. Whereas in the infancy of the industry a programmer needed to have a fairly good knowledge of computer hardware, now different levels of abstraction have been introduced into the languages, meaning an increased conceptional and linguistic distance from hardware features. This has increasingly alleviated the requirement that software developers know what is occurring in a computer's central processing unit (CPU).

Along with an increasing level of abstraction, modern computer languages— sometimes implicitly, sometimes explicitly—exhibit a prominent new feature: the *expressiveness* of language constructs. Let me try to illustrate this using an example written in pseudo-code. Let's say you have a list of items and want to perform an operation on each of the items. With some knowledge of the internal functioning of computers, a programmer might write a code snippet like this:

- `Create some array of data in the memory.`
- `Assign a pointer to the first element.`
- `Loop over the array.`

- Dereference the pointer, retrieving a list element.
- Do something with the element (example.g., print it).
- Increment the pointer, let it point to the next item.
- If we are beyond the last element, exit the loop.
- End loop.

Although this looks a little bit complex, it closely relates to what computers are doing under the hood, and early languages looked more or less like this. As a first abstraction and a way to improve readability, we can try to get rid of the "pointer" element and instead write:

- variable theList = [somehow create the list of items]
  - loop over "theList", assigning each item to an iteration variable "item":
  - do something with "item", for example print it
- end loop

This already looks more expressive compared to the first version, and a lot of current programming languages allow for this kind of programming style. We can do even better, though: You can see the definition of the list being written in one line, separated from the list processing in the loop. There's nothing preventing us from writing a lot of overly complex code between the list definition and the loop, and this is what you see quite often, making the program hard to read and understand. Wouldn't it be better to have it all in one statement? Using a more expressive snippet allows us to write such a combined statement. In pseudo-code, it could look like this:

```
[somehow create the list of items].
  [maybe add some filter].
  forEach { item ->
    do something with "item", for example print it
  }
```

This is about the maximum of expressiveness you can get, if you see the dot "." as some kind of "do something with it" command and "{ ... }" as a block of code doing something, with the identifier in front of the -> in this case designating a loop variable.

Note Making your code expressive from the very beginning will not only help you to write good code, it will also help you to develop your programming skills beyond average. Expressive code is easier to maintain and extend, easier to reuse, easier to understand for others, and easier to debug if the program shows some deficiencies.

The programming language Kotlin is capable of getting us to such an extent of expressiveness, and in this book I want to introduce Kotlin as a programming language for Android that allows you to accomplish things in an expressive and concise way. As a matter of fact, in Kotlin the little looping example, with a filter added, reads:

```
arrayOf("Blue", "Green", "Yellow", "Gray").
    filter { it.startsWith("G") }.
    forEach { item ->
      println(item)
    }
```

If you run this, it will print the text Green Gray on two lines of the console. With the notion of parameters being placed inside round brackets, you should be able to understand this snippet without knowing a single Kotlin idiom.

Note Don't worry if you don't know how to write and run this, we'll be getting our feet wet very soon in the first chapter of the book.

Once you reach the end of the book, you should be an advanced developer able to address problems in the Kotlin language, with particular attention on Android matters. Of course, you will not know all possible libraries that are out there in the wild for solving specific problems, as only experience will help you there. Knowing most of the language constructs and having good ideas concerning programming techniques, however, will set you on the way to become an expert programmer for Android.

The Kotlin version referred to in this book is 1.3. Most of the examples and most of what gets explained here is likely valid for later versions as well.

The Book's Target Audience

The book is for beginning software developers with little or no knowledge of programming, and for developers with knowledge of other languages who are interested in using Kotlin for future Android projects. The target platforms are Android devices. The book is not meant to present a thorough introduction into Android; instead, it uses Android as a platform as is and thoroughly introduces the Kotlin programming language and how it gets used for Android.

Basic knowledge of how to use a desktop or laptop computer, including the installation and starting of programs, is expected. The operating system you want to use plays no major role, but because we are using Android Studio as a development environment, you must choose an operating system able to run this integrated development environment (IDE). This is the case for Linux, Windows, and Mac OS. Screenshots are taken from an Ubuntu Linux installation.

In the end, you will be able to write and run Kotlin programs for Android of beginning to midlevel complexity.

Source Code

All source code shown or referred to in this book can be found at

```
https://github.com/Apress/learn-kotlin-for-android-development
```

How to Read This Book

Reading this book sequentially from the beginning to the end will provide the maximum benefit. If you already have some basic development knowledge, you can skip sections and chapters at will, and of course you can always take a step back and reread sections and chapters while you are advancing through the book.

CHAPTER 1

Your First Kotlin Application: Hello Kotlin

In this chapter we are going to learn how to use the Android Studio integrated development environment (IDE) to write and execute a first simple Kotlin program.

Setting Up an IDE: Android Studio

Although computer programs could be written in simple text editors and then prepared and executed by some system-level commands entered in a system terminal, using an IDE helps in keeping project files together and also simplifies various development-related activities.

Note Computer languages come in two flavors: Either you have some program code that by some execution engine gets interpreted while the program is running and then executed on the CPU, or you have a *compiling* language with a special preparatory system command first translating the program code into a *compiled* program that can be directly executed by the operating system or by some specially tailored execution engine. Kotlin is such a compiling language. If you use an IDE like Android Studio, the compilation step usually is automatically done for you.

In this book we use Android Studio as an IDE. It is developed by Google, Inc., and based on the community edition of the IntelliJ IDEA. You can freely download, install, and use it. As of this writing, the download page is hosted at `https://developer.android.com/studio/`. If that link is not functioning, you can easily find the download

1

© Peter Späth 2019
P. Späth, *Learn Kotlin for Android Development*, https://doi.org/10.1007/978-1-4842-4467-8_1

location by entering "android studio download" in your favorite search engine. To use Android Studio, you don't have to buy a license for private or commercial projects. To install Android Studio on your PC, follow these steps:

1. Download the installer for your operating system. There are installers for Linux (tested for Ubuntu 14.04; higher versions should work as well), Windows (starting from version 7), and MacOS (starting from MacOS X 10.10).

2. Start the installer. For Linux, unpack the installer ZIP, then navigate to the bin folder and start studio.sh in a terminal. On Windows systems, start the .exe file. On MacOS X systems, launch the .dmg file and then drag and drop Android Studio to the Applications folder. Launch it again from there.

Note   To open a terminal in Ubuntu Linux press Ctrl+Alt+T. Inside the terminal, commands need to be entered using the keyboard. To change to a directory enter cd /path/to/directory. To start a .sh file enter ./name.sh

---

The details of the installation depend on your operating system specifics, including the operating system version, and also the version of your Android Studio download. The page where you downloaded Android Studio will give you more details and even present videos for the installation procedure.

In any case the installer for Android Studio will download additional components. The same holds for the Project Wizard when you create new projects, depending on the features needed for the project and also depending on the components already installed. You thus need to have some patience before you can start your first project; subsequent startups will, of course, be faster.

Proceed with the installer up to the point where you are being asked whether you want to create a new project. For Linux this will look like Figure 1-1, and for other operating systems you will be presented something similar.

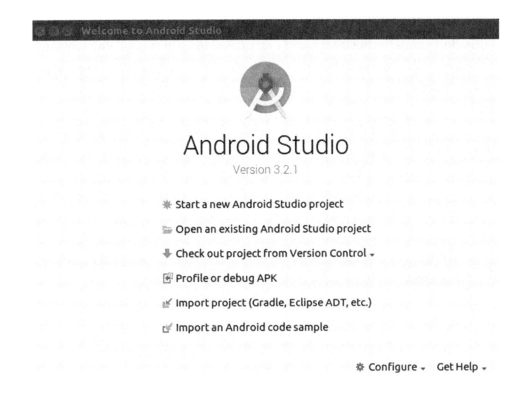

Figure 1-1. *The Project Creation Wizard*

Connecting Your Android Device

First it is important to say that for developing Android apps you don't necessarily need to have a real hardware device at hand. In the section "Setting Up and Using Emulators" later in this chapter, we talk about how to use emulators to simulate Android devices. For professional apps, however, it is a good idea to have at least one Android hardware device at hand.

Android Studio allows for working with both real and simulated devices. To work with only a real device like a smartphone obviously can give you the most profound assurance your app is running. However, it will tell you only your smartphone can operate your app; you cannot be sure other devices will be just as happy with it. You certainly don't want to buy dozens of different smartphones and other Android devices. Likewise, though, working only with simulated devices and not with a real device cannot give you 100 percent assurance your app works on any real devices.

The suggested development technique therefore is to use both real and simulated devices. You don't have to check each and every development step in both worlds, but once you reach a milestone you should do a double check. Of course, before you publish your app and make it available to a broader audience, you should test it on both real and simulated devices.

Your process to connect the studio to a real device might vary, but ideally all you have to do is connect your smartphone to the USB port of your PC or laptop and make sure your device is a debuggable device. Describing solutions for any problem that might come up doesn't make too much sense here, because any update of your operating system or Android Studio can easily change the picture. Therefore if you have problems, please consult the official Android and Android Studio documentation, and use your favorite search engine to find corresponding blog entries. The procedure for connecting hardware devices basically goes as follows:

1. To make your smartphone debuggable, for Android version 4.2 or higher, open the Settings dialog box, go to About phone, and tap seven times on the build number. For versions prior to that, you might instead have to go to Settings ➤ Develop Option ➤ Check "USB debugging."

2. Connect the smartphone to your laptop or PC via USB cable.

To see whether the studio actually got connected to the device, go to Tools ➤ Android ➤ Android Device Monitor. You should see your device listed in the devices section of the Device Monitor, as shown in Figure 1-2.

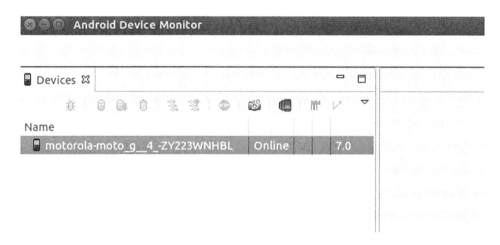

Figure 1-2. *A hardware Android device*

Starting Your First Kotlin App

It is now time to write our first Kotlin application inside Android Studio. From the installation step where you are being asked whether you want to create a project, or after you start an installed Android Studio instance the first time, or from inside a running Android Studio at File ➤ New ➤ New Project, inside the menu, proceed as follows:

1. Select or click Start a New Android Studio Project.

2. Inside the Project Wizard, as the application name, enter HelloKotlin. Although not strictly necessary, it is better to avoid space characters inside the name.

3. For company domain, enter example.com. Aside from not using spaces, what you enter here is up to you. It is, however, good practice to enter a real domain name you or your company owns. For projects you know you will never publish, choose whatever you like.

4. The project location that Android Studio suggests is decent enough, but if you like you can choose a different one.

5. Make sure Include Kotlin support is selected.

6. Choose Phone and Tablet as a form factor.

7. Choose API 19 as a minimum software development kit (SDK).

8. Choose Empty Activity. As Activity name, use the suggested MainActivity. Make sure Generate Layout File is selected, and as a layout name, accept the suggested activity_main. Make sure Backwards Compatibility is selected as well.

The first time you create a project Android Studio will automatically download and install any additional components it needs, and then it also performs an initial build. This will take several minutes, so be patient here.

At this point if everything worked well the Android Studio main window will appear as shown in Figure 1-3.

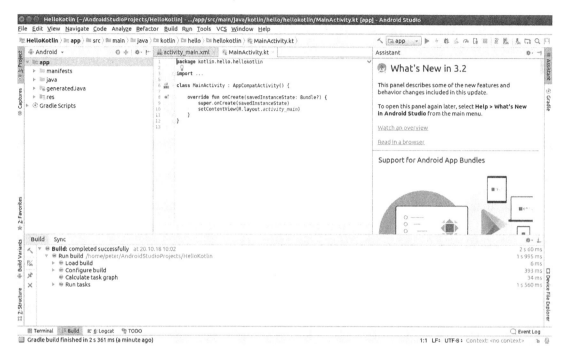

Figure 1-3. *The Android Studio main window*

Setting Up and Using Emulators

Now it is time to install a device emulator. Emulators are very handy, because they allow for developing Android apps without having to connect a real device. Emulators simulate Android devices on your computer's screen. To install one of the several available, go to Tools ➤ AVD Manager. The screen that appears shows the title Your Virtual Devices. Click Create Virtual Device. The following screen shows a device list, as shown in Figure 1-4.

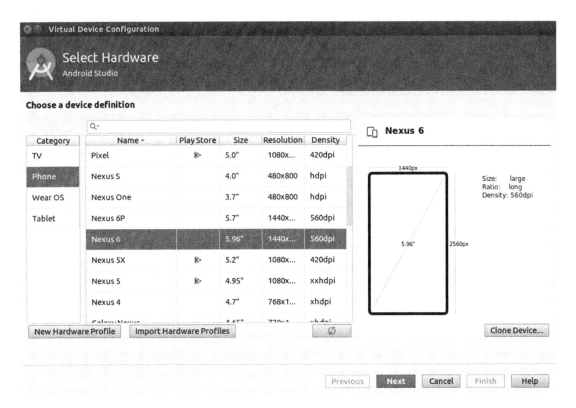

Figure 1-4. *Emulated devices*

Under Category, make sure you select Phone. In the middle pane, select the Nexus 6 entry. Click Next. On the next screen, click the Download link for Oreo, API 27. Go through the subwizard that then appears. Here a system image gets downloaded; this is something like the operating system for the emulator device. Back on the System Image screen, the Oreo, API 27 item now gets selected and it is possible to click Next. Click Next, and on the next screen click Finish.

The Your Virtual Devices screen now shows one entry, as displayed in Figure 1-5. You can now close that window.

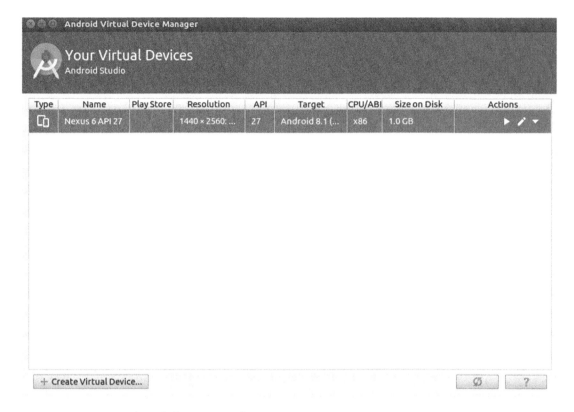

Figure 1-5. *Emulated devices with an entry*

Continuing with the HelloKotlin App

Back in the Android Studio main window, on the left side inside the app, by clicking on the small triangles next to the names you can navigate to the following files (see Figure 1-6):

```
app  →  java  →
    com.example.hellokotlin  →  MainActivity
app  →  res  →
    layout  →  activity_main.xml
```

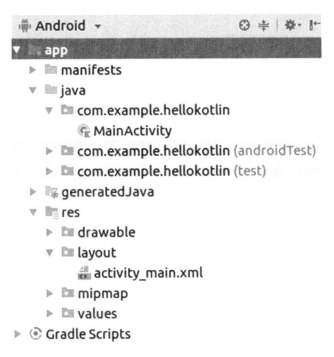

Figure 1-6. *The HelloKotlin app*

Double-clicking on any of the files will display them in the editor in the center pane of the window. The two files `MainActivity` and `activity_main.xml` are the central files we will need to adjust for our first simple Kotlin app. The file `activity_main.xml` defines the layout on the smartphone's screen. We will adapt it to show a button and a text area. For that purpose, open the file, switch to the text view of the editor by selecting the Text tab on the bottom of the pane, and then as its contents, write the following:

```
<?xml version="1.0" encoding="utf-8"?>
<android.support.constraint.ConstraintLayout
    xmlns:android=
      "http://schemas.android.com/apk/res/android"
    xmlns:tools=
      "http://schemas.android.com/tools"
    xmlns:app=
      "http://schemas.android.com/apk/res-auto"
    android:layout_width="match_parent"
    android:layout_height="match_parent"
    tools:context=".MainActivity">
```

```
    <LinearLayout
        android:layout_width="match_parent"
        android:layout_height="match_parent"
        android:orientation="vertical"
        app:layout_constraintBottom_toBottomOf="parent"
        app:layout_constraintLeft_toLeftOf="parent"
        app:layout_constraintRight_toRightOf="parent"
        app:layout_constraintTop_toTopOf="parent">
      <Button android:layout_width="wrap_content"
                android:layout_height="wrap_content"
                android:text="Go"
                android:onClick="go"/>
      <EditText
                android:id="@+id/text"
                android:layout_width="wrap_content"
                android:layout_height="wrap_content"
                android:inputType="textMultiLine"
                android:ems="10"
                tools:layout_editor_absoluteY="286dp"
                tools:layout_editor_absoluteX="84dp"/>
    </LinearLayout>
</android.support.constraint.ConstraintLayout>
```

So much for the graphical design. The program goes into the MainActivity.kt file.
Open this one in the editor by double-clicking the name.

As its contents, write the following:

```
package kotlin.hello.hellokotlin

import android.support.v7.app.AppCompatActivity
import android.os.Bundle
import android.view.View
import kotlinx.android.synthetic.main.activity_main.*
import java.util.*

class MainActivity : AppCompatActivity() {
```

```kotlin
override fun onCreate(savedInstanceState: Bundle?) {
    super.onCreate(savedInstanceState)
    setContentView(R.layout.activity_main)
}

fun go(v:View) {
    text.setText("Hello Kotlin!" + "\n" + Date())
}
}
```

Start the app by clicking the green triangle in the task button bar on top of the window. From the Available Virtual Devices list, choose Nexus 6 API 27, then click OK. The first time you might be asked whether you want to install a feature called *Instant Run*. If so, click Install and Continue.

Now the emulator window appears. The app gets built, sent to the emulator, and started there, as shown in Figure 1-7.

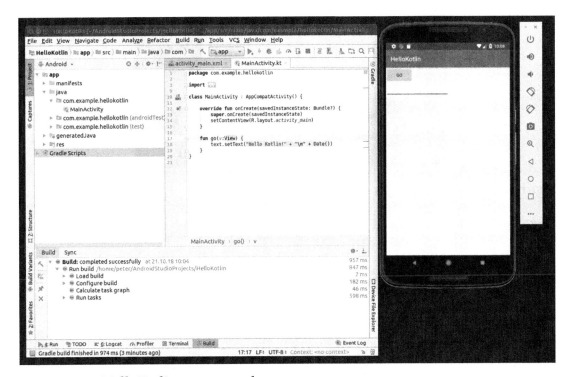

Figure 1-7. *HelloKotlin app started*

Click Go and the emulated devices screen gets updated to show the text "Hello Kotlin!" and the current date, as shown in Figure 1-8.

Figure 1-8. *HelloKotlin app on the device*

Congratulations! You just wrote, compiled, and ran your first Kotlin application!

Using the Command Line

Although you can continue using Android Studio for working on projects to any depth, it is also possible to use the command line in a terminal to build and run apps. If you want to continue using Android Studio, you can safely skip this section. For all others, I want to describe how to use a terminal to build apps, and more precisely the HelloKotlin app we created in the last section.

Note   Using the command line helps, for example, in cases where you don't have a desktop environment, like on servers. You can also use it in an automated build environment where developers provide the code, but the program to be executed on Android devices is generated automatically.

Interestingly, Android Studio helps us to get rid of itself. For any project you have successfully built inside Android Studio, the folder containing the project files also will contain specially tailored build scripts that you can use to build apps without using Android Studio.

First we need to open a terminal: In Ubuntu Linux, press Ctrl+Alt+T. In Windows you find a terminal by searching for CMD in the system menu. For Apple Mac OS, a terminal can be opened after you search for Terminal in Spotlight. Next we need to know where in the file system the project files reside. If you accepted the suggestion Android Studio gave while creating the project, the paths will be as follows:

```
/home/[USER]/AndroidStudioProjects/HelloKotlin
    for Linux
/Users/[USER]/AndroidStudioProjects/HelloKotlin
    for Mac OS X
C:\Users\[USER]\AndroidStudioProjects\HelloKotlin
    for Windows
```

where [USER] is your logon username. If you used a custom project location instead, you have to use that one.

Fluently using a terminal is an art and we won't go into details here. The following commands will, however, give you a starting point. Inside the terminal we change to the project folder as follows:

```
cd [PATH]        #for Linux and Mac OS X and Windows
```

where [PATH] is the project folder we just determined. From here we can build the app by entering

```
./gradlew app:build     #for Linux and Mac OS X
gradlew   app:build     #for Windows
```

Note   The gradlew command belongs to the Gradle build system. Gradle gets used throughout Android Studio for building executable apps.

The final app as an APK file with an .apk suffix will now show up inside app/build/outputs/apk/debug/. The APK comes from Android PacKage; such a file is a compressed collection of all the files Android needs to install an app on your device. The gradlew wrapper script actually allows for many more options to build and investigate projects. Enter -help or tasks as an argument to have them all listed.

```
./gradlew -help     #for Linux and Mac OS X
./gradlew tasks     #for Linux and Mac OS X
gradlew -help       #for Windows
gradlew tasks       #for Windows
```

For the tasks command to specifically show the app's tasks, you have to prepend app:, which we saw earlier for the build task.

Note   Describing what you can do with such an APK file resulting from a build is left to an Android book. As a hint to get you started, learn how to use the tools provided in the SDK, especially the adb platform tool.

CHAPTER 2

Classes and Objects: Object Orientation Philosophy

At the beginning of the book we said that computer programs are about processing some input and generating some output from it, possibly also altering the state of some data-holding instance like a file or a database. Although this is certainly true, it does not tell the whole story. In real-world scenarios, computer programs exhibit another characteristic: They are supposed to be of some practical use, and as a result of that, model real-world events and things.

Say, for example, you write a simple program for registering paper invoices and summing up the money amounts for each day. The input is clear: It is the paper invoices in electronic form. The output is the daily sum, and along the way a database keeps records for all registered invoices. The modeling aspect tells us that we deal with the following objects: an invoice in electronic form, a database for keeping the records, and some calculation engine for accessing the database and performing the summation operation. To be of practical use these objects need to exhibit the following features. First, depending on their nature, they might have a *state*. For the invoice object, for example, we have the name of the seller, the name of the buyer, the date, the name of the goods, and of course the monetary amount. Such state elements are commonly referred to as *properties*. The database obviously has the database contents as its state. The calculation engine, in contrast, doesn't need its own state, and it uses the state from the other objects to do its work. The second feature of objects is operations you can perform on them, commonly referred to as *methods*. The invoice object, for example, might have methods to set and tell us about its state, the database object needs methods for saving

15

© Peter Späth 2019
P. Späth, *Learn Kotlin for Android Development*, https://doi.org/10.1007/978-1-4842-4467-8_2

and retrieving data from its store, and the calculation engine obviously must be able to perform the summation calculation for each day.

Before we deepen our insights in that kind of real world to computer world mapping methodology, let us first sum up what we have seen so far.

- *Objects:* We use objects to identify things in the real world we want to model in a computer program.

- *State:* Objects often have a state, which describes the characteristics each object has to be able to handle the tasks it is supposed to perform.

- *Property:* The state of an object consists of a set of properties. Properties thus are elements of a state.

- *Method:* A method is a way to access an object. This describes the functional aspects an object needs to exhibit to handle the tasks it is supposed to perform, possibly including changing and querying its state.

Note   Depending on the terminology used, methods are also sometimes called *operations* or *functions*, and properties are sometimes referred to as *attributes*. Although we continue to use *property* we'll switch to using *function* for methods because the Kotlin documentation uses the term *function* and we want to keep things easy for you, including reference research in the Kotlin documentation.

One important concept to understand is that Invoice is not an object, nor is Person, nor is Triangle. How can that be? We just were talking of invoices as objects, and why are Person and Triangle not objects? This contradiction comes from some kind of linguistic fluffiness. Did you realize that we're talking of Invoice, but not of an invoice? There is a major difference between those: An invoice, or more precisely a particular invoice, is an object, but Invoice is a classification or class. All possible invoices share membership in the Invoice class, and all concrete persons share membership in the Person class, just as all possible triangles belong to the Triangle class. Does this seem theoretical or even nitpicking? Perhaps, but it has important practical implications and we really need to understand that class notion. Consider a thousand invoices arriving on a particular day. In some computer program, do we really want to write something like this:

```
object1 = Invoice(Buyer=Smith,Date=20180923,Good=Peas,Cost=$23.99), object2
= Invoice(...), ..., object1000 = Invoice(...)
```

That just doesn't make sense, because we don't want to write a huge new computer program every day. What instead makes sense is having an Invoice class that describes all possible invoices. From this class we must be able to create concrete invoices given some invoice style input. In pseudo-code:

```
data = [Some incoming invoice data]
```

This provides incoming invoice data for a particular paper invoice. Make sure the data can be represented by the abstract characteristics of the Invoice class, so it has a buyer, a date, goods or services, and so on. This is the same as saying that Invoice is a valid classification of all possible input data.

```
object = concrete object using that data
```

You can build a concrete invoice object, given the classification and the data. Another way of saying building a concrete invoice object from the Invoice class is constructing an object from the class or creating an Invoice instance. We will be using that instance and constructor notion in the rest of the book.

Our main subject of this chapter, object orientation, exactly is about classes, instantiation, and objects. Some details are still missing, but let us first summarize what we just learned and continue with our definition list:

- *Class:* A class characterizes all possible objects of some kind. It is thus an abstraction, and any such object characterized by the class is said to belong to that particular class.

- *Instance:* An instance of a class represents exactly one object belonging to that class. The process of creating an object from a class and concrete data is called instantiation.

- *Construction:* The process of creating an instance from a class is also called construction.

Equipped with these object orientation concepts we can now start looking at how Kotlin deals with objects, classes, and instantiation. In the following sections we also talk about some aspects of object orientation we haven't introduced yet. We could have done that here in a theoretical manner, but describing it with the Kotlin language at hand is a little easier to grasp.

Kotlin and Object-Oriented Programming

In this section we talk about the main characteristics of classes and objects in Kotlin. Some aspects are covered in greater detail in later sections, but here we want to give you the basics you need for Kotlin programming.

Class Declaration

> **Note**   The term *declaration* here is used for the description of the structure and the constituent parts of a class.

In Kotlin, to declare a class you basically write

```
class ClassName(Parameter-Declaration1, Parameter-Declaration2, ...) {
      [Class-Body]
   }
```

Let us examine its parts:

- ClassName: This is the name of the class. It must not contain spaces, and in Kotlin by convention you should use CamelCase notation; that is, start with a capital letter, and instead of using spaces between words, capitalize the first letter of the second word, as in EmployeeRecord.

- Parameter-Declaration: These declare a primary constructor and describe data that are needed to instantiate classes. We talk more about parameters and parameter types later, but for now we mention that such parameter declarations basically come in three varieties:

    - Variable-Name:Variable-Type: An example would be userName: String. Use this to pass a parameter usable for instantiating a class. This happens inside a special construct called an init{} block. We'll talk about that initialization later.

- `val Variable-Name:Variable-Type` (e.g., `val userName: String`): Use this to pass a usable parameter from inside the `init{}` block, but also define a nonmutable (unchangeable) property. This parameter is thus used to directly set parts of the object's state.

- `var Variable-Name:Variable-Type` (e.g., `var userName: String`): Use this to pass a usable parameter from inside the `init()` function, but also to define a mutable (changeable) property for setting parts of the object's state.

  For the names use CamelCase notation, this time starting with a lowercase letter, as in nameOfBuyer. There are lots of possibilities for a variable type. For example, you can use `Int` for an integer and the declaration then could look like `val a:Int`. In Chapter 3 we talk more about types.

- `[Class-Body]`: This is a placeholder for any number of functions and additional properties, and also `init { ... }` blocks worked through while instantiating a class. In addition, you can also have *secondary constructors* and *companion objects*, which we describe later, and inner classes.

Exercise 1

Which of the following appears to be a valid class declaration?

1.
```
class Triangle(color:Int) (
    val coordinates:Array<Pair<Double,Double>>
        = arrayOf()
)
```

2.
```
class Triangle(color:Int) {
    val coordinates:Array<Pair<Double,Double>>
        = arrayOf()
}
```

```
3.    class simple_rectangle() {
          val coordinates:Array<Pair<Double,Double>>
              = arrayOf()
      }

4.    class Colored Rectangle(color:Int) {
          val coordinates:Array<Pair<Double,Double>>
              = arrayOf()
      }
```

Property Declaration

We'll be talking about detailed characteristics of properties in Chapter 3. Here I provide just a brief summary for simple property declarations: They basically look like

```
val Variable-Name:Variable-Type = value
```

for immutable properties, and

```
var Variable-Name:Variable-Type = value
```

for mutable properties. The = value is not needed, however, if the variable's value gets set inside an init { } block.

```
class ClassName(Parameter-Declaration1,
        Parameter-Declaration2, ...) {
    ...
    val propertyName:PropertyType = [init-value]
    var propertyName:PropertyType = [init-value]
    ...
}
```

One word about mutability is in order: Immutable means the val variable gets its value at some place and cannot be changed afterward, whereas mutable means the var variable is freely changeable anywhere. Immutable variables have some advantages concerning program stability, so as a rule of thumb you should always prefer immutable over mutable variables.

Exercise 2

Which one of the following is a valid class?

1.  ```
    class Invoice() {
        variable total:Double = 0.0
    }
    ```

2.  ```
    class Invoice() {
        property total:Double = 0.0
    }
    ```

3.  ```
    class Invoice() {
        Double total =
        0.0
    }
    ```

4.  ```
    class Invoice() {
        var total:Double = 0.0
    }
    ```

5.  ```
    class Invoice() {
        total:Double = 0.0
    }
    ```

Exercise 3

What is wrong with the following class (not technically, but from a functional perspective)?

```
class Invoice() {
    val total:Double = 0.0
}
```

How can it be fixed?
```

Class Initialization

An init { } block inside the class body may contain statements that get worked through when the class gets instantiated. As the name says, it should be used to *initialize* instances before they actually get used. This includes preparing the state of an instance so it is set up properly to do its work. You can in fact have several init{ } blocks inside a class. In this case the init{ } blocks get worked through sequentially in the order in which they appear in the class. Such init{ } blocks are optional, however, so in simple cases it is totally acceptable to not provide one.

```
class ClassName(Parameter-Declaration1,
      Parameter-Declaration2, ...) {
   ...
   init {
       // initialization actions...
   }
}
```

Note   A // starts a so-called *end-of-line comment;* anything starting from that until the end of the current line is ignored by the Kotlin language. You can use it for comments and documentation.

If you set properties inside an init { } block, it is no longer necessary to write = [value] inside the property declaration.

```
class ClassName(Parameter-Declaration1,
      Parameter-Declaration2, ...) {
   val someProperty:PropertyType
   ...
   init {
       someProperty = [some value]
       // more initialization actions...
   }
}
```

If you specify a property value inside the property declaration and later change the property's value inside init { }, the value from the property declaration gets taken to initialize the property before init{ } starts. Later, inside init { } the property's value then gets changed by suitable statements:

```
class ClassName {
        var someProperty:PropertyType = [init-value]

        ...

        init {

            ...

            someProperty = [some new value]

            ...

        }
}
```

Exercise 4

What is wrong with the following class?

```
class Color(val red:Int,
            val green:Int,
            val blue:Int)
{
    init {
        red = 0
        green = 0
        blue = 0
    }
}
```

Exercise 5

What is wrong with the following class?

```
class Color() {
    var red:Int
    var green:Int
```

```kotlin
  var blue:Int
  init {
    red = 0
    green = 0
  }
}
```

An Invoice in Kotlin

That is enough theory; let us work out the Invoice class we already talked about. For simplicity, our invoice will have the following properties: the buyer's first and last name, the date, the name and amount of a single product, and the price per item. I know in real life we need more properties, but this subset will do here because it describes enough cases and you can easily extend it. A first draft of the actual Invoice class then reads:

```kotlin
class Invoice(val buyerFirstName:String,
      val buyerLastName:String,
      val date:String,
      val goodName:String,
      val amount:Int,
      val pricePerItem:Double) {
}
```

We talk about data types later in this chapter, but for now we need to know that String is any character string, Int is an integer number, and Double is a floating-point number. You can see that for all the parameters passed to the class I used the val ... form, so after instantiation all those parameters will be available as immutable (unchangeable) properties. This makes a lot of sense here, because the parameters are exactly what is needed to describe the characteristics, or *state*, of an invoice instance.

Note   In Kotlin it is permitted to omit empty blocks altogether. You could therefore remove the { } from the Invoice class declaration. Nevertheless, we leave it here, because we will add elements to the body soon.

More Invoice Properties

The class body is still empty, but we can easily think of properties we might want to add. For example, it could be interesting to have the full name of the buyer at hand, and the total price of all items. We can add the corresponding properties:

```
class Invoice(val buyerFirstName:String,
        val buyerLastName:String,
        val date:String,
        val goodName:String,
        val amount:Int,
        val pricePerItem:Double)
{
    val buyerFullName:String
    val totalPrice:Double
}
```

Did we forget to initialize the properties by adding values via = something? Well, yes and no. Writing it that way is actually forbidden, but because we will initialize those properties inside an init{ } block soon, it is allowable to not initialize the properties.

Invoice Initialization

No sooner said than done, we add a corresponding init{ } block:

```
class Invoice(val buyerFirstName:String,
        val buyerLastName:String,
        val date:String,
        val goodName:String,
        val amount:Int,
        val pricePerItem:Double)
{
    val buyerFullName:String
    val totalPrice:Double
    init {
        buyerFullName = buyerFirstName + " " +
            buyerLastName
```

```
            totalPrice = amount * pricePerItem
    }
}
```

By the way, there is a shorter way of writing such one-line initializers for properties:

```
...
val buyerFullName:String = buyerFirstName + " " + buyerLastName
val totalPrice:Double = amount * pricePerItem
...
```

This makes an init{ } block unnecessary. There is, however, no functional difference to using an init{ } block, and the latter allows for more complex calculations that do not fit into one statement.

Exercise 6

Write the Invoice class without the init{ } block, keeping its full functionality.

Instantiation in Kotlin

With the class declaration ready now, to instantiate an Invoice object from it, all you have to do is write this:

```
val firstInvoice = Invoice("Richard", "Smith", "2018-10-23", "Peas", 5, 2.99)
```

If you don't know how to put all that into a program, in Kotlin it is totally acceptable to write everything in one file, which then reads:

```
class Invoice(val buyerFirstName:String,
       val buyerLastName:String,
       val date:String,
       val goodName:String,
       val amount:Int,
       val pricePerItem:Double)
{
    val buyerFullName:String
    val totalPrice:Double
```

```
    init {
        buyerFullName = buyerFirstName + " " +
            buyerLastName
        totalPrice = amount * pricePerItem
    }
}

fun main(args:Array<String>) {
    val firstInvoice = Invoice("Richard", "Smith",
        "2018-10-23", "Peas", 5, 2.99)
    // do something with it...
}
```

The main() function is the entry point for Kotlin applications. Unfortunately, this won't work like that for Android, because Android has a different idea for how to start apps. Please be patient, as we will come back to that soon.

Note   Having said that, please do not write files containing a lot of different classes or long functions. We'll talk about program structure soon in the section "Structuring and Packages" later in this chapter. For now, just remember that having short identifiable pieces of code helps a great deal in writing good software!

Adding Functions to Invoices

Our Invoice class does not yet have explicit functions. I deliberately said explicit, because by virtue of both the constructor properties and the properties we added in the class body, Kotlin provides us implicit accessor functions in the form of objectName.propertyName. We can, for example, add inside any function:

```
...
val firstInvoice = Invoice("Richard", "Smith",
    "2018-10-23", "Peas", 5, 2.99)
val fullName = firstInvoice.buyerFullName
```

where `firstInvoice.buyerFullName` reads the full name of the buyer from the object. Under different circumstances we could also use accessors to write properties as in

```
...
val firstInvoice = Invoice("Richard", "Smith",
    "2018-10-23", "Peas", 5, 2.99)
firstInvoice.buyerLastName = "Doubtfire"
```

Do you see why we can't do that here? Remember, we declared buyer- LastName as an immutable `val`, so it cannot be changed. If we substituted for the `val` with `var`, the variable became mutable and the setting became an allowed operation.

As an example for an explicit function, we could create a means to let the object tell about its state. Let us call this function `getState()`. An implementation would be:

```
class Invoice( [constructor parameters] ) {
    val buyerFullName:String
    val totalPrice:Double
    init { [initializer code] }

    fun getState(): String {
        return "First name: ${firstName}\n" +
                "Last name: ${lastName}\n" +
                "Full name: ${buyerFullName}\n" +
                "Date: ${date}\n" +
                "Good: ${goodName}\n" +
                "Amount: ${amount}\n" +
                "Price per item: ${pricePerItem}\n" +
                "Total price: ${totalPrice}"
    }
}
```

where the `:String` in `fun getState(): String` indicates that the function returns a string, and the `return ...` actually performs the return action. The `${some- Name}` inside a string gets replaced by the value of `someName`, and the `\n` represents a line break.

Note   Developers use the term *implementation* quite often to describe the transition from an idea to the code performing the idea.

To invoke a function from outside the class, just use both the object name and the function name and write

```
objectName.functionName(parameter1, parameter2, ...)
```

Because we don't have any parameters for getState() this would be:

```
...
val firstInvoice = Invoice("Richard", "Smith",
    "2018-10-23", "Peas", 5, 2.99)
val state:String = firstInvoice.getState()
```

If, however, we find ourselves inside the class, say inside an init{ } block or inside any other function of the class, to call a function just use its name, as in

```
...
// we are inside the Invoice class
val state:String = getState()
```

Functions are going to be described in detail later in this chapter. For now, I only want to mention that functions might have a parameter list. For example, a method for the Invoice class calculating the tax with the tax rate as a parameter would read:

```
fun tax(taxRate:Double):Double {
    return taxRate * amount * pricePerItem
}
```

The :Double after the parameter list declares that the method returns a floating-point number, which the return statement actually does. For parameter lists with more than one element use a comma (,) as a separator. In case you didn't already realize it, the asterisk (*) is used to describe a multiplication operation.

To invoke that tax method, you write

```
...
val firstInvoice = Invoice("Richard", "Smith", "2018-10-23", "Peas", 5, 2.99)
val tax:Double = firstInvoice.tax(0.11)
```

Exercise 7

Add a method goodInfo() that returns something like "5 pieces of Apple." Hint: Use amount.toString() to convert the amount to a string.

The Complete Invoice Class

The Invoice class with all properties and methods we have talked about so far, and some code to invoke it, reads like this:

```
class Invoice(val buyerFirstName:String,
    val buyerLastName:String,
    val date:String,
    val goodName:String,
    val amount:Int,
    val pricePerItem:Double)
{
    val buyerFullName:String
    val totalPrice:Double

    init {
        buyerFullName = buyerFirstName + " " +
            buyerLastName
        totalPrice = amount * pricePerItem
    }

    fun getState():String {
        return "First name: ${buyerFirstName}\n" +
                "Last name: ${buyerLastName}\n" +
                "Full name: ${buyerFullName}\n" +
                "Date: ${date}\n" +
                "Good: ${goodName}\n" +
                "Amount: ${amount}\n" +
                "Price per item: ${pricePerItem}\n" +
                "Total price: ${totalPrice}"
    }
```

```kotlin
    fun tax(taxRate:Double):Double {
        return taxRate * amount * pricePerItem
    }
}

fun main(args:Array<String>) {
    val firstInvoice = Invoice("Richard", "Smith", "2018-10-23", "Peas",
                        5, 2.99)
    val state:String = firstInvoice.getState()
    val tax:Double = firstInvoice.tax(0.11)
    // do more things with it...
}
```

This works for an application style invocation you'd find if you built that class for a desktop or server application. It wouldn't run on Android, because there the procedures for starting up apps and communicating with the hardware differ substantially compared to such a simple main() method. Therefore, to get back to the subject, in the rest of this chapter we will develop a more Android-style app.

A Simple Number Guessing Game

In Android, applications circle around *Activities,* which are identifiable pieces of code corresponding to particular responsibilities from a user's workflow perspective. Each of these responsibilities can be handled by a distinct screen built up by graphical objects positioned in a screen layout. An app can have one or more activities that are represented by distinct classes, together with resource and configuration files. As we have already seen in Chapter 1, Android Studio helps in preparing and tailoring all the necessary files.

For the rest of this chapter and most of the following chapters we will be working on a simple game called the Number Guessing Game. Although extremely simple to understand, it is complex enough to show basic Kotlin language constructs and allows for extensions that help to illustrate most of the language features introduced during the course of the book. We thus neither start with the most elegant solution, nor do we show the most high-performance code from the beginning. The aim is to start with a working app and introduce new features step by step so we can improve our Kotlin language proficiency.

The game description goes as follows: At the beginning the user is presented some informational text and a Start button. Once started, the app internally chooses a random number between one and seven. The user is asked to guess that number and after each guess, the user is informed whether the guess matches, is too high, or is too low. Once the random number gets selected, the game is over and the user can start a new game.

To start app development, open Android Studio. If the last project you worked on is the HelloKotlin app from Chapter 1, the files from that app appear. To start a new project, from the menu select File ➤ New ➤ New Project. Enter `NumberGuess` as the application name, and `book.kotlinforandroid` as the company domain. Accept the suggested project location or choose your own. Make sure Include Kotlin support is selected. Click Next. Select Phone and Tablet as a form-factor, and API 19 as a minimum software development kit (SDK) version. Click Next again. Select Empty Activity and click Next. Accept the suggested activity name MainActivity and the suggested layout name activity_ main. Make sure Generate Layout File and Backwards Compatibility are both selected. Click Finish.

Android Studio will now generate all build files and basic template files for the game app. Inside the `res` folder you will find a couple of resource files, including images and text that are used for the user interface. We don't need images for now, but we define a couple of text elements that are used for both the layout file and the coding. Open the file `res/values/strings.xml` by double-clicking it. Let the file read:

```
<resources xmlns:tools="http://schemas.android.com/tools"
      tools:ignore="ExtraTranslation">
  <string name="app_name">
      NumberGuess</string>
  <string name="title.numberguess">
      NumberGuess</string>
  <string name="btn.start">
      Start</string>
  <string name="label.guess">
      Guess a number:</string>
  <string name="btn.do.guess">
      Do guess!</string>
  <string name="edit.number">
      Number</string>
```

```
<string name="status.start.info">
    Press START to start a game</string>
<string name="label.log">
    Log:</string>
<string name="guess.hint">
    Guess a number between %1$d and %2$d</string>
<string name="status.too.low">
    Sorry, too low.</string>
<string name="status.too.high">
    Sorry, too high.</string>
<string name="status.hit">
    You got it after %1$d tries!
    Press START for a new game.</string>
</resources>
```

The layout file is situated in res/layout/activity_main.xml. Open that file, switch to the text view by clicking the Text tab at the bottom of the center pane, and then as its contents write this:

```
<?xml version="1.0" encoding="utf-8"?>
<LinearLayout
    xmlns:android=
        "http://schemas.android.com/apk/res/android"
    xmlns:tools=
        "http://schemas.android.com/tools"
    xmlns:app=
        "http://schemas.android.com/apk/res-auto"
    android:orientation="vertical"
    android:layout_width="match_parent"
    android:layout_height="match_parent"
    android:padding="30dp"
    tools:context=
        "kotlinforandroid.book.numberguess.MainActivity">

    <TextView
            android:layout_width="wrap_content"
            android:layout_height="wrap_content"
```

```
        android:text="@string/title.numberguess"
        android:textSize="30sp" />

<Button

        android:id="@+id/startBtn"
        android:onClick="start"
        android:layout_width="match_parent"
        android:layout_height="wrap_content"
        android:text="@string/btn.start"/>

<Space android:layout_width="match_parent"
    android:layout_height="5dp"/>

<LinearLayout

        android:orientation="horizontal"
        android:layout_width="wrap_content"
        android:layout_height="wrap_content">
    <TextView android:text="@string/label.guess"
            android:layout_width="wrap_content"
            android:layout_height="wrap_content"/>
    <EditText
            android:id="@+id/num"
            android:hint="@string/edit.number"
            android:layout_width="80sp"
            android:layout_height="wrap_content"
            android:inputType="number"
            tools:ignore="Autofill"/>
    <Button
            android:id="@+id/doGuess"
            android:onClick="guess"
            android:text="@string/btn.do.guess"
            android:layout_width="wrap_content"
            android:layout_height="wrap_content"/>
</LinearLayout>

<Space android:layout_width="match_parent"
    android:layout_height="5dp"/>
```

```
<TextView
        android:id="@+id/status"
        android:text="@string/status.start.info"
        android:textColor="#FF000000" android:textSize="20sp"
        android:layout_width="wrap_content"
        android:layout_height="wrap_content"/>

<Space android:layout_width="match_parent"
    android:layout_height="5dp"/>

<TextView android:text="@string/label.log"
        android:textStyle="bold"
        android:layout_width="wrap_content"
        android:layout_height="wrap_content"/>
<kotlinforandroid.book.numberguess.Console
        android:id="@+id/console"
        android:layout_height="100sp"
        android:layout_width="match_parent" />

</LinearLayout>
```

You will get an error because the file refers to class kotlinforandroid.book. numberguess.Console, which does not exist yet. Ignore this for now; we are going to fix that soon. All the other elements of that layout file are described in depth in the Android developer documentation or an appropriate Android book. A few hints seem appropriate here, though.

- If you don't switch to the Text tab in the editor view for that file, the Design view type gets shown instead. The latter allows for graphically arranging user interface elements. We won't use the graphical design editor in this book, but you are free to try that one as well. Just expect some minor differences in the resulting XML.

- I don't use fancy layout containers; instead I prefer ones that are easy to write and easy to understand when looking at the XML code. You don't have to do the same for your projects, and in fact some other solutions might be better according to the circumstances, so you are free to try other layout approaches.

- Wherever you see @string/... in the XML code, it refers to one of the entries from the strings.xml file.

- The kotlinforandroid.book.numberguess.Console element refers to a custom view. You won't see that too often in tutorials, but custom views allow for more concise coding and improved reusability, which means you could easily use them in other projects. The Console refers to a custom class we will write soon.

The Kotlin code goes into the file java/kotlinforandroid/book/numberguess/MainActivity.kt. Open this, and as its contents write:

```kotlin
package kotlinforandroid.book.numberguess

import android.content.Context
import android.support.v7.app.AppCompatActivity
import android.os.Bundle
import android.util.AttributeSet
import android.util.Log
import android.view.View
import android.widget.ScrollView
import android.widget.TextView
import kotlinx.android.synthetic.main.activity_main.*

class MainActivity : AppCompatActivity() {
    var started = false
    var number = 0
    var tries = 0

    override fun onCreate(savedInstanceState: Bundle?) {
        super.onCreate(savedInstanceState)
        setContentView(R.layout.activity_main)

        fetchSavedInstanceData(savedInstanceState)
        doGuess.setEnabled(started)
    }

    override fun onSaveInstanceState(outState: Bundle?) {
        super.onSaveInstanceState(outState)
        putInstanceData(outState)
    }
```

```kotlin
fun start(v: View) {
    log("Game started")
    num.setText("")
    started = true
    doGuess.setEnabled(true)
    status.text = getString(R.string.guess_hint, 1, 7)
    number = 1 + Math.floor(Math.random()*7).toInt()
    tries = 0
}

fun guess(v:View) {
    if(num.text.toString() == "") return
    tries++
    log("Guessed ${num.text} (tries:${tries})")
    val g = num.text.toString().toInt()
    if(g < number) {
        status.setText(R.string.status_too_low)
        num.setText("")
    } else if(g > number){
        status.setText(R.string.status_too_high)
        num.setText("")
    } else {
        status.text = getString(R.string.status_hit,
            tries)
        started = false
        doGuess.setEnabled(false)
    }
}

//////////////////////////////////////////////////
//////////////////////////////////////////////////

private fun putInstanceData(outState: Bundle?) {
    if (outState != null) with(outState) {
        putBoolean("started",  started)
        putInt("number", number)
        putInt("tries", tries)
```

```kotlin
                putString("statusMsg", status.text.toString())
                putStringArrayList("logs",
                    ArrayList(console.text.split("\n")))
        }
    }

    private fun fetchSavedInstanceData(
            savedInstanceState: Bundle?) {
        if (savedInstanceState != null)
        with(savedInstanceState) {
            started = getBoolean("started")
            number = getInt("number")
            tries = getInt("tries")
            status.text = getString("statusMsg")
            console.text = getStringArrayList("logs")!!.
                    joinToString("\n")
        }
    }

    private fun log(msg:String) {
        Log.d("LOG", msg)
        console.log(msg)
    }
}

class Console(ctx:Context, aset:AttributeSet? = null)
        : ScrollView(ctx, aset) {
    val tv = TextView(ctx)
    var text:String
        get() = tv.text.toString()
        set(value) { tv.setText(value) }
    init {
        setBackgroundColor(0x40FFFF00)
        addView(tv)
    }
```

```kotlin
fun log(msg:String) {
    val l = tv.text.let {
        if(it == "") listOf() else it.split("\n")
    }.takeLast(100) + msg
    tv.text = l.joinToString("\n")
    post(object : Runnable {
        override fun run() {
            fullScroll(ScrollView.FOCUS_DOWN)
        }
    })
}
}
```

Don't worry if by now you don't understand everything in that file. In the rest of this chapter and in subsequent chapters we refer to this project a lot, and in the end you will understand all of it. For now here is what you need to know.

- The package ... at the top of the file both defines a namespace for elements declared in that file and indicates its position in the file hierarchy. We will be talking about project structure later; for now it is enough to know that the argument should reflect the file position inside the java folder, with the dot . as a separator.

- The file contains two classes. In other languages each class is supposed to go in its own file, and in fact you could move the declaration of the Console class to the file Console.kt. In Kotlin you can write as many declarations as you wish into one file. You should not overuse this feature, though, as writing too many things in one big file inevitably leads to messy code. For small projects and for simplicity's sake, however, it is acceptable to put several declarations in a file.

- The import ... statements refer to classes from other projects or classes built into Kotlin. Listing them in import statements allows us to address the imported elements using just their simple name. Otherwise you'd have to prepend their package name to use them. It is common practice to import as much as possible to keep the code readable.

- The import statement `kotlinx.android.synthetic.main.activity_main.*` is special insofar it imports user interface-related classes the studio derived from the layout file. This has nothing to do with Kotlin; it is some automation controlled by Android Studio.

- The properties `var started = false`, `var number = 0`, and `var tries = 0` seem to miss the property types. However, Kotlin can automatically infer the type from the right-hand side of the assignments: `false` belongs to a boolean and both of the others belong to an integer. The `:PropertyType` can thus be left out here.

- The `class MainActivity : AppCompatActivity() { ... }` declaration indicates that class `MainActivity` is derived from class `AppCompatActivity`, or *inherits* from it. We will be talking about inheritance in detail later; for now it is enough to know that `MainActivity` is kind of a copy of `AppCompatActivity` with some parts redefined.

- The function `onCreate()` gets called by Android when the user interface gets created. Its parameter of type `Bundle` might or might not contain saved data from a restart of the user interface. This is something that happens often in Android apps, so we use that parameter to rebuild the state of the activity whenever the activity is restarted.

- The `onSaveInstanceState()` gets called when the activity is suspended temporarily. We use it to save the state of the activity.

- Both functions `start()` and `guess()` get invoked when the user clicks a button in the user interface. You can see that in the layout file. We use them as game actions and accordingly update the user interface and the activity object state.

- Functions marked with `private` are only going to be used from inside the same class; they are not visible to the outside. We will be talking about visibility later. To stress that fact, I usually put all private functions at the end of a class and separate normal from private functions by a two-line comment `//////....`

- The Console is a custom view object. It can be placed in any layout just like all the other built-in views Android provides.

- For reasons of brevity, no in-line documentation was added. We return to documentation issues in later chapters.

You can now start the game. Click the green arrow in the top toolbar of Android Studio and choose an emulator or a connected hardware device to specify where to run the app.

Constructors

We already learned that parameters passed to a class when an instantiation happens get declared in parentheses after the class name:

```
class ClassName(Parameter-Declaration1,
        Parameter-Declaration2, ...) {
    [Class-Body]
}
```

We also know that parameters are accessible from inside any init{ } block and furthermore lead to creating properties if we prepend val or var to the parameter declaration:

Variable-Name:Variable-Type

for parameters that just are needed for the init{ } blocks,

val Variable-Name:Variable-Type

if you additionally want the parameter to be converted to an immutable property, and

var Variable-Name:Variable-Type

if you additionally want the parameter to be converted to a mutable property instead.

Such a parameter declaration list in Kotlin is called a *primary constructor*. As you might guess, there are secondary constructors as well. Let's talk about primary constructors first, though, because they exhibit features we haven't seen yet.

The full primary constructor declaration actually reads:

```
class ClassName [modifiers] constructor(
        Parameter-Declaration1,
        Parameter-Declaration2, ...)
{
    [Class-Body]
}
```

The constructor in front of the parameter list can be omitted (together with the space character) if there are no modifiers. As modifiers, you can add one of these visibility modifiers:

- public: The instantiation can be done from anywhere inside and outside your program. This is the default.

- private: The instantiation can be done only from inside the very same class or object. This makes sense if you use secondary constructors.

- protected: The setting is the same as private, but the instantiation can be done from subclasses as well. Subclasses belong to inheritance, which is discussed in Chapter 3.

- internal: The instantiation can be done from anywhere inside the module. In Kotlin, a *module* is a set of files compiled together. You use this modifier if you don't want other programs (from other projects) to access a constructor, but you otherwise want the constructor to be freely accessible from other classes or objects inside your program.

Note   In other languages, constructors contain statements, or code to be executed on instantiation. The Kotlin designers decided to only name the parameters in the (primary) constructor and move any class initialization code to the init{ } block.

In our NumberGuess game the activity class MainActivity does not have a constructor. Actually, it implicitly has the default no-operation constructor, which doesn't need to be declared. In fact, a specialty of Android is that activities should not have an explicit constructor. This has nothing to do with Kotlin, though; it is just the way Android handles the life cycles of its objects. The `Console` class instead does have a constructor. This is again a requirement of Android for its view elements.

Exercise 8

Create a class `Person` with constructor parameters: `firstName` (a `String`), `lastName` (a `String`), `ssn` (a `String`), `dateOfBirth` (a `String`) and `gender` (a `Char`). Make sure the parameters are later available as instance properties and are changeable afterward.

Constructor Invocation

In the previous section we already applied the main usage pattern: Given, for example, a class

```
class GameUser(val firstName:String,
      val lastName:String,
      val birthday:String,
      val userName:String,
      val registrationNumber:Int,
      val userRank:Double) {
}
```

you can instantiate the class via

...

```
val firstUser = GameUser("Richard", "Smith",
    "2008-10-23", "rsmith", 123, 0.0)
```

You can see that for this kind of instantiation you have to specify the parameters in exactly the same order as in the class definition.

Exercise 9

Instantiate the `Person` class from the previous exercise, using name `John  Smith`, date of birth 1997-10-23, SSN 0123456789, and gender M. Assign it to variable `val person1`. Hint: Use single quotation marks for `Char` literals, like `'A'` or `'B'`.

Exercise 10

Add the GameUser class we talked about in this section to the NumberGuess game. Just add the class for now; do not write code to include the user in the game logic.

Named Constructor Parameters

There is actually a way to construct objects in a more readable and less error-prone fashion, compared to just listing parameters in the same order as given in the declaration. For instantiation you can also explicitly specify the parameter names and then apply any order at will:

```
val instance = TheClass(
    parameterName1 = [some value],
    parameterName2 = [some value],
    ...)
```

For our GameUser from the last exercise you can write

```
...
val user = GameUser(
    lastName = "Smith",
    firstName = "Richard",
    birthday = "2098-10-23",
    userName = "rsmith",
    registrationNumber = 765,
    userRank = 0.5)
```

With the names given, the sort order of the call parameters no longer plays a role. Kotlin knows how to properly distribute the passed-in parameters.

Exercise 11

Rewrite the Person instantiation from Exercise 9 using named parameters.

Exercise 12

Add a var gameUser property to the MainActivity and initialize it with the name John Doe, username jdoe, birthday 1900-01-01, registration number = 0 and user rank = 0.0. Use named parameters. Hint: To initialize the property right in the declaration use var gameUser = GameUser(...).

Constructor Default Values

Constructor parameters can also have default values. We could, for example, use ""
as a default birthday, and 0.0 as a rank in case we wouldn't care. This simplifies the construction of game users who don't specify a birthday, and new users, for example, with an initial ranking of 0.0. To declare such defaults you write:

```
class GameUser(val firstName:String,
     val lastName:String,
     val userName:String,
     val registrationNumber:Int,
     val birthday:String = "1900-01-01",
     val userRank:Double = 0.0) {
}
```

If you use parameters with and without defaults, such default values go frequently to the end of the parameter list. Only then is the distribution of passed-in parameters during invocation unique. You can now perform the very same construction as before, but watch out for the changed order:

```
...
val firstUser = GameUser("Richard", "Smith", "rsmith", 123, "2008-10-23", 0.4)
```

Now, by virtue of the default parameters, it is possible to omit parameters. In

```
...
val firstUser = GameUser("Richard", "Smith", "rsmith", 123, "2008-10-23")
```

the value `0.0` would apply for the ranking, and in

```
...
val firstUser = GameUser("Richard", "Smith", "rsmith", 123)
```

additionally the default birthday of `1900-01-01` would be used.

To make things even easier and extend readability further you can also mix default and named parameters, as in

```
...
val firstUser = GameUser(firstName = "Richard",
    lastName = "Smith",
    userName = "rsmith",
    registrationNumber = 123)
```

this time with any parameter sort order you like.

Exercise 13

Update the `Person` class from the previous exercises: add the default value ”” (the empty string) to the `ssn` parameter. Perform an instantiation using named parameters, letting the SSN's default value apply.

Exercise 14

Update the `GameUser` class from the `NumberGuess` game: Add the default value ”” (the empty string) to `birthday`, and add `0.0` to the `userRank` parameter.

Secondary Constructors

With named parameters and default parameter values, we already have quite versatile means for various construction needs. If this is not enough for you, there is another way of describing different methods of construction: *secondary constructors*. You can have several of them, but their parameter list must differ from that of the primary constructor and they must also be different from each other.

Note   More precisely, primary and secondary constructors all must have different *parameter signatures*. A signature is the set of parameter types, with the order taken into account.

To declare a secondary constructor, inside the class body write

```
constructor(param1:ParamType1,

        param2:ParamType2, ...)
{
    // do some things...
}
```

If the class has an explicit primary constructor as well, you must delegate to a primary constructor call as follows:

```
constructor(param1:ParamType1,
        param2:ParamType2, ...) : this(...) {
    // do some things...
}
```

where inside this(...) the parameters for the primary constructor have to be specified. It is also possible here to specify the parameters for another secondary constructor, which in turn delegates to the primary constructor.

For our GameUser example, removing the default parameter values from the primary constructor, a secondary constructor could read like this:

```
constructor(firstName:String,
        lastName:String,
        userName:String,
        registrationNumber:Int) :
    this(firstName = firstName,
        lastName = lastName,
        userName = userName,
        registrationNumber = registrationNumber,
        birthday = "",
        userRank = 0.0
    )
```

```
{
    // constructor body
    // do some things...
}
```

and you can instantiate the class via

```
...
val firstUser = GameUser(firstName = "Richard",
    lastName = "Smith",
    userName = "rsmith",
    registrationNumber = 123)
```

Inside the secondary constructor's body you can perform arbitrary calculations and other actions, which is what secondary constructors can be used for except for different, maybe shorter parameter lists.

The construct `firstName = firstName`, `lastName = lastName`, `userName = userName`, `registrationNumber = registrationNumber` might seem a bit confusing. It is easy to understand, however, if you remember that the part to the left of the equals sign points to the name in the primary constructor's parameter list, whereas the right side is the value taken from inside the `constructor(...)` parameter list.

Note   If you can achieve the same thing using default values and secondary constructors, you should favor default values because the notation is more expressive and concise.

Exercise 15

In the `Person` class of the previous exercises, add a secondary constructor with parameters `firstName` (a `String`), `lastName` (a `String`), `ssn` (a `String`), and `gender` (a `Char`). Let it call the primary constructor, setting the missing `dateOfBirth` to 0000-00-00. Create an instance using the secondary constructor.

If Classes Are Not Needed: Singleton Objects

Once in a while objects don't need a classification because you know there will never be different states associated with them. Here is another way of saying this: If we have a class, there will never be more than one instance needed, because all instances would somehow be forced to carry the same state during the lifetime of the application and thus would be indistinguishable.

To make things clear, Kotlin allows for creating such an object using the following syntax:

```
object ObjectName { [Object-Body]
}
```

where the object body could contain property declarations, init{ } blocks, and functions. Neither primary nor secondary constructors are allowed. To distinguish this kind of object from objects that are the result of class instantiations for the rest of the section, I use the term *singleton object*.

To access a singleton object's properties and functions you use a similar notation as for objects that are the result of a class's instantiation:

```
ObjectName.propertyName
ObjectName.function([function-parameters])
```

You won't use singleton objects too often, because object orientation without classes wouldn't make too much sense, and using too many singleton objects quite often is an indication of poor application design. There are, however, some prominent examples where object declarations make sense:

- *Constants:* For your application you might want to have a single object containing all constants the application needs.

- *Preferences:* If you have a file with preferences you might want to use an object to read in the preferences once the application has started.

- *Database:* If your application needs a database and you think your application will never access a different database, you might want to move database access functions into an object.

- *Utilities:* Utility functions are functional in a sense that their output
  only depends on their input and no state is associated; for example,
  `fun degreeToRad(deg: Double) = deg * Math.PI / 180`. They
  also serve a common purpose and adding them to certain classes
  doesn't make sense from a conceptual point of view. Providing such
  utility functions in a singleton object, for example named `Utility`,
  thus is reasonable.

Other use cases are possible; just make sure your decision to use classes or singleton objects is based on sound reasoning. If in doubt, experience tells us that using classes makes more sense.

For our `NumberGuess` game, looking into the file `MainActivity.kt` we can see that we use numbers 1 and 7 for the lower and upper bounds of the game logic. The numbers get used in the function `fun start(...)` for the text shown in the user interface, and for the random number determination:

```
status.text = getString(R.string.guess_hint, 1, 7)
number = 1 + Math.floor(Math.random()*7).toInt()
```

It is better to extract such constants to their own file, so it can more easily be changed later or used from within other classes if necessary. A `Constants` singleton object seems to be a very appropriate place for it. To improve the code, we create a new file via right-click in the project view at package `kotlinforandroid.book.numberguess` ➤ New ➤ Kotlin File/Class. Enter `Constants` as a name and make sure File is selected on the drop-down list. Inside the file that is created, underneath the `package` declaration, write

```
object Constants {
    val LOWER_BOUND = 1
    val UPPER_BOUND = 7
}
```

We again omitted the property types because Kotlin can infer that 1 and 7 are Int types.

Note   This autoinferring works for other types as well, so a common practice is to leave out the type specification and add it only if it is needed or helps to improve readability.

There is one other thing you might have noticed: We deviated from the naming schema for the `val` inside the companion object. Using this all-capitals with underscore notation expresses that we have a real immutable instance-independent constant. Such constants are thus easier to identify from inside your coding.

Back in `MainActivity.kt,` inside the `start()` function, we can now write

```
status.text = getString(R.string.guess_hint,
      Constants.LOWER_BOUND,
      Constants.UPPER_BOUND)
val span = Constants.UPPER_BOUND -
      Constants.LOWER_BOUND + 1
number = Constants.LOWER_BOUND +
      Math.floor(Math.random()*span).toInt()
```

for the user interface text and the secret number. The function then reads in total:

```
fun start(v: View) {
    log("Game started")
    num.setText("")
    started = true
    doGuess.setEnabled(true)
    status.text = getString(R.string.guess_hint,
          Constants.LOWER_BOUND,
          Constants.UPPER_BOUND)
    val span = Constants.UPPER_BOUND -
          Constants.LOWER_BOUND + 1
    number = Constants.LOWER_BOUND +
          Math.floor(Math.random()*span).toInt()
    tries = 0
}
```

Exercise 16

Which of the following is true?

1. Using a lot of singleton objects helps to improve code quality.

2. It is possible to instantiate singleton objects.

3. To declare singleton objects, use any of `object`, `singleton`, or `singleton object`.

4. Singleton objects don't have a state.

5. Singleton objects may have a constructor.

Exercise 17

Create a `Constants` singleton object with the following properties: `numberOf- Tabs = 5`, `windowTitle = "Astaria"`, `prefsFile = "prefs.properties"`. Write some code to print out all constants for diagnostic purposes. Hint: For formatting you could use \n inside strings for a line break.

If State Doesn't Matter: Companion Objects

Quite often, perhaps without even noticing it, your classes will have two categories of properties and functions: state related and not state related. Not state related means for properties that their value will be the same for all possible instances. For functions it means they will do exactly the same thing for all possible instances. This is somehow related to singleton objects, which do not care about a distinguishable state at all, and for that reason Kotlin allows for a construct named the *companion object*. Such companion objects have an indistinguishable state for all instances of a particular class they accompany, and this is where the "companion" in the name comes from.

To declare a companion object inside the class body, write this:

```
companion object ObjectName {
    ...
}
```

where the `ObjectName` is optional; in most cases you can omit it. Inside the companion object's body you can add the same elements as for singleton objects (see the previous section).

Note   You need the companion object to have a name only if you want to address it from outside the class, using a dedicated name: `ClassName.ObjectName`. However, even with the name missing you can access it via `ClassName.Companion`.

A companion object is a really good place to declare constants used by the class. You can then use the constants from anywhere inside the class as if they were declared in the class itself:

```
class TheClass {
    companion object ObjectName {
        val SOME_CONSTANT: Int = 42
    }
    ...
    fun someFunction() {
        val x = 7 * SOME_CONSTANT
        ...
    }
}
```

In our `NumberGuess` game there are two constants in the `Console` class: Look at the `init{ }` function where we specify a color value `0x40FFFF00` for the background color (this is a pale yellow). Also, in the function `fun log(...)` you can see a `100`, which happens to specify a memorized line number limit. I intentionally left these out for the `Constants` companion object, as those two new constants can be considered to more closely belong to the `Console` class and maybe are misplaced in a common constants file.

It is, however, a good idea to move them to a companion object, because both the color and the line number limit values are shared by all instances of the `Console` class and are not subject to being changed from inside an instance. An accordingly rewritten `Console` class reads:

```
class Console(ctx:Context, aset:AttributeSet? = null)
    : ScrollView(ctx, aset) {
  companion object {
      val BACKGROUND_COLOR = 0x40FFFF00
```

```
        val MAX_LINES = 100
    }
    val tv = TextView(ctx)
    var text:String
        get() = tv.text.toString()
        set(value) { tv.setText(value) }
    init {
        setBackgroundColor(BACKGROUND_COLOR)
        ddView(tv)
    }
    fun log(msg:String) {
        val l = tv.text.let {
          if(it == "") listOf() else it.split("\n") }.
                takeLast(MAX_LINES) + msg
        tv.text = l.joinToString("\n")
        post(object : Runnable {
            override fun run() {
                fullScroll(ScrollView.FOCUS_DOWN)
            }
        })
    }
}
```

Companion object properties and functions can also be accessed from outside the class. Just write this:

```
TheClass.THE_PROPERTY
TheClass.someFunction()
```

to directly address a property or a function from the associated companion object. The function can, of course, also have parameters.

Exercise 18

Create a Triangle class. Add constructor parameters and properties at will, but also create a companion object with a constant NUMBER_OF_CORNERS = 3. Inside the class, create an info() function indicating the number of corners.

Exercise 19

Inside a `main()` function, instantiate the `Triangle` class from Exercise 18, then assign the number of corners to some `val numberOfCorners`.

Describing a Contract: Interfaces

Software development is about things that need to be done, and in object-oriented development, this means things that need to be done on objects that are described inside classes. Object orientation, however, unveils a feature we haven't talked about until now: the separation of intent and implementation.

Consider, for example, a class or a couple of classes gathering information on two-dimensional graphical objects, and another class or couple of classes providing such graphical objects. This introduces a natural separation of classes. We call the information collecting part of the classes the info collector module, and the part that provides the graphical objects the client module. We want to extend that idea by allowing several client modules, and in the end we want to make sure the info collector module wouldn't care how many clients there are (see Figure 2-1).

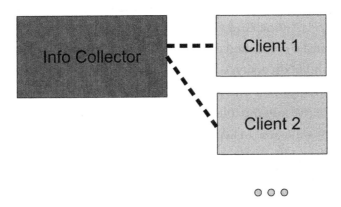

Figure 2-1. *Collector module and clients*

Note   We deviate from the usual path and temporarily leave the `NumberGuess` game. The concept of interfaces is a little easier to describe if we have several classes sharing some features, which the `NumberGuess` game doesn't have. I will, however, propose a possible extension to the `NumberGuess` game using an interface in one of the exercises.

The most important question now is this: How do the graphics objects get communicated between the modules? Here is one obvious idea: Because the clients produce the graphics objects, why not also let the clients provide the classes for them? At first that doesn't sound bad, but there is a major drawback: The info collector module needs to know how to handle each client's graphics object classes, and it also needs to be updated when new clients want to transfer their objects. Such a strategy is thus not flexible enough for a good program.

Let us try to turn it the other way around: The info collector module provides all graphics object classes and the clients use them to communicate data. Although this remedies the proliferation of different classes in the collector module, there is a different problem with this approach. Say, for example, the info collector gets a software update and provides an altered version for a graphics object class. If this happens, we must also update all clients, leading to a lot of work, including increased expenses in professional projects. So this approach is not the best either. What can we do?

We can introduce a new concept that does not describe how things are to be done, but only what needs to be done. This somehow mediates between the different program components and for this reason it is called an *interface*. If such an interface does not depend on the implementation and clients only depend on interfaces, the probability for a need to change clients is much lower if the info collector changes. You can also consider the interface as some kind of contract between the parties: Just like in real life, if the wording in a contract is satisfied the contract is fulfilled even when the way it is done is subject to some kind of diversity.

Before I can further explain this, let's work out the details of the graphics collector example a little more. We add the following responsibility to the graphics collector: The graphics collector must be able to take polygon objects that do the following:

- Tell about the number of corners they have.

- Tell us the coordinates of each corner.

- Tell about their fill color.

You are free to extend this at will, but for our aim those three characteristics are sufficient. We now introduce an interface declaration and write this:

```
interface GraphicsObject {
    fun numberOfCorners(): Int
```

```
    fun coordsOf(index:Int): Pair<Double, Double>
    fun fillColor(): String
}
```

The Pair<Double, Double> represents a pair of floating-point numbers for the x- and y-coordinate of a point. We let the graphics collector module define the interface, because the interface is what the clients need to know from the graphics collector module to communicate with it. The implementation of the three functions is, however, exclusively the clients' business, because for the graphics collector module the *how* of the contract fulfillment doesn't matter. The interface itself, though, is just a declaration of intent, so the client modules have to define what to do to fulfill the contract. Another way of saying this is the clients have to *implement* the interface functions. This new situation is depicted in Figure 2-2.

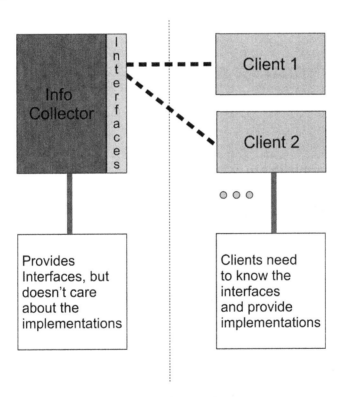

Figure 2-2. *Module communication with interfaces*

For example, for a triangle a client might provide this:

```
class Triangle : GraphicsObject {
    override fun numberOfCorners(): Int {
        return 3
    }
    override fun coordsOf(index:Int):
            Pair<Double,Double> {
        return when(index) {
            0 -> Pair(-1.0, 0.0)
            1 -> Pair(1.0, 0.0)
            2 -> Pair(0.0, 1.0)
            else throw RuntimeException(
                "Index ${index} out of bounds")
        }
    }
    override fun fillColor(): String {
        return "red"
    }
}
```

For Kotlin it is permissible to write " = ..." for functions if their result is calculable with a single expression, so the Triangle class can actually be written as follows:

```
class Triangle : GraphicsObject {
    override fun numberOfCorners() = 3
    override fun coordsOf(index:Int) =
        when(index) {
            0 -> Pair(-1.0, 0.0)
            1 -> Pair(1.0, 0.0)
            2 -> Pair(0.0, 1.0)
            else -> throw RuntimeException(
                "Index ${index} out of bounds")
        }
    override fun fillColor() = "red"
}
```

where we also used the fact that Kotlin can infer the return type automatically in many cases. The : GraphicsObject in the class declaration expresses that Triangle adheres to the GraphicsObject contract, and the override in front of each function expresses that the function implements an interface function. The Triangle class, of course, also might contain any number of noninterface functions; we just don't need one in this example.

Note   The : in the class header can be translated to "implements" or "is a ..." if there is an interface name to the right of it.

Inside the coordsOf() function we use a couple of new constructs we haven't seen yet. For now, the when(){ } selects one of the x -> ... branches depending on the argument, and the throw RuntimeException() stops the program flow and writes an error message to the terminal. We'll talk about those constructs in more detail in subsequent chapters.

Note   You can see that for the Triangle example we allow corner indexes 0, 1, and 2. It is common in many computer languages to start any kind of indexing at 0. Kotlin is no exception here.

We still need the accessor function inside one of the collector module's classes that a client needs to register a graphics object. We call it add() and it could read like this:

```kotlin
class Collector {
    ...
    fun add(graphics:GraphicsObject) {
        // do something with it...
    }
}
```

The clients now write something like this:

```kotlin
...
val collector = [get hold of it]
val triang:GraphicsObject = Triangle()
collector.add(triang)
...
```

We could have also written val `triang:Triangle` = `Triangle()` and the program would run without error. There is, however, a huge conceptual difference between those two. Can you tell why? The answer is this: If we write val `triang:Triangle` = `Triangle()` we express passing the `Triangle` class to the collector, which is what we actually didn't want to do. This is because we wanted to have a proper separation of the clients from the collector and use only the interface `GraphicsObject` for communication. The only acceptable way to express this is writing val `triang:GraphicsObject` = `Triangle()`.

Note   Internally the same object gets passed to the collector if we write either `triang:Triangle` or `triang:GraphicsObject`. But we don't only want to write programs that work; they must also properly express what they do. For that reason, `triang:GraphicsObject` is the much better option.

To get you started for your own experiments, in the following listings I provide a basic implementation of this interfacing procedure. First, in one file, we write a graphics object collector and also add the interface.

```
interface GraphicsObject {
    fun numberOfCorners(): Int
    fun coordsOf(index:Int): Pair<Double, Double>
    fun fillColor(): String
}

object Collector {
    fun add(graphics:GraphicsObject) {
        println("Collector.add():")
        println("Number of corners: " +
            graphics.numberOfCorners())
        println("Color: " +
            graphics.fillColor())
    }
}
```

You can see we use a singleton object here to simplify access. In another file we create a `GraphicsObject` and access the collector.

```kotlin
class Triangle : GraphicsObject {
    override fun numberOfCorners() = 3
    override fun coordsOf(index:Int) =
        when(index) {
            0 -> Pair(-1.0, 0.0)
            1 -> Pair(1.0, 0.0)
            2 -> Pair(0.0, 1.0)
            else -> throw RuntimeException(
                "Index ${index} out of bounds")
        }
    override fun fillColor() = "red"
}

fun main(args:Array<String>) {
    val collector = Collector
    val triang:GraphicsObject = Triangle()
    collector.add(triang)
}
```

You can see that it is possible to assign a singleton object to a val, although you could always also use the direct singleton object access notation described earlier in this chapter.

Although the concept of interfaces is not easy to grasp for a beginning developer, trying to understand interfaces from the very beginning and using them wherever possible is an invaluable aid for writing good software.

Exercise 20

Elementary particles have at least three things in common: a mass, a charge, and a spin. Create an interface ElementaryParticle with three corresponding functions to fetch: mass():Double, charge():Double, and spin():Double. Create classes Electron and Proton that implement the interface. An electron returns mass $9.11 \cdot 10^{-31}$, to be entered as 9.11e-31, charge −1.0, and spin 0.5. A proton returns mass $1.67 \cdot 10^{-27}$, to be entered as 1.67e-27, charge and spin 0.5.

61

Exercise 21

Taking the interface and the classes from Exercise 20, which one is true?

1. An `ElementaryParticle` can be instantiated:
    `var p = ElementaryParticle()`.

2. An `Electron` can be instantiated: `val electron = Electron()`.

3. A `Proton` can be instantiated: `val proton = Proton()`.

4. The initialization `var p:ElementaryParticle = Electron()`
    is possible.

5. The reassignment `p = Proton()` is possible.

6. The initialization `var p:Proton = Electron()` is possible.

Exercise 22

Imagine for the `NumberGuess` game we want to be able to try different functions of random number generation. Create an interface `RandomNumberGenerator` with one function `fun rnd(minInt:Int, maxInt:Int): Int`. Create a class `StdRandom` implementing that interface using the current code from the `MainActivity` class: `val span = maxInt - minInt + 1; return minInt + Math.floor(Math.random()*span). toInt()`. Create another class `RandomRandom` also implementing the interface, but with a property `val rnd:Random = Random()` (add `import java.util.*` to the imports) and using the code `minInt + rnd.nextInt( maxInt - minInt + 1 )`. Add a property of type `RandomNumberGenerator` to the activity, using either of the implementations. Alter the `start()` function from the activity to use that interface.

Structuring and Packages

For Kotlin applications it is possible to write all classes, interfaces, and singleton objects into a single file in the main folder `java`. Whereas for experiments and small projects this is totally acceptable, for larger projects you shouldn't do this. Midsize to larger projects will inevitably have classes, interfaces, and singleton objects that can be grouped into modules doing different things from a bird's-eye view perspective. Having large files implies some kind of conceptual flatness real projects don't actually have.

Note   To avoid always repeating the list, I henceforth use the term *structure unit* for classes, singleton objects, companion objects, and interfaces.

For this reason Kotlin allows us to put structure units into different *packages* corresponding to different folders and spanning different namespaces. The first thing we need to establish is a hierarchical structure. This means we assign structure units to different nodes in a tree. Each node thus contains a couple of structure units that show high cohesion, meaning they strongly relate to each other.

A Structured Project

Let's look at the NumberGuess example to find out what this structuring actually means. Up until now, including all the improvements and also the exercises, we have the following classes, interfaces, and singleton objects: the activity itself, a console class, a constants object, two classes and one interface for random numbers, and one class for user data. From this we identify the following packages:

- The root for the activity class.

- A package random for the random numbers. We put the interface right into the package, and the two implementations into a subpackage impl.

- A gui package for the Console view element.

- A model package for the user data class. Developers often use the term *model* to refer to data structures and data relations.

- A common package for the Constants singleton object.

We put this in corresponding directories and subdirectories under src and thus get the packages and folder structure depicted in Figure 2-3.

Figure 2-3. *Packaging*

As a convention, you must add a package declaration into each of the files reflecting this packaging structure. The syntax is:

```
package the.hierarchical.position
...
```

So, for example, the `RandomRandom.kt` file must start with

```
package kotlinforandroid.book.numberguess.random.impl

class RandomRandom {
    ...
}
```

Exercise 23

Prepare this structure in an Android Studio project. Start with empty files. Hint: Packages (i.e., folders), classes, interface, and singleton objects all can be initialized by right-clicking an item from the left side package structure in the Android Studio main window and selecting New.

Namespaces and Importing

As already mentioned, the hierarchical structure also spans namespaces. For example, the Console class lives by virtue of the `kotlinforandroid.book.numberguess.gui` package declaration in the `kotlinforandroid.book.numberguess.gui` namespace. This means there cannot be another Console class in the same package, but there can be Console classes in other packages, because they all have a different namespace.

Caution   Kotlin allows you to use a `package` declaration that differs from the hierarchical position in the file system. However, do yourself a favor and keep packages and file paths synchronized, otherwise you'll end up with a complete mess.

Structure units (i.e., classes, interfaces, singleton objects, and companion objects) can use other structure units from the same package by just using their simple names. If they use structure units from other packages, though, they must use their *fully qualified name*, which means it is necessary to prepend the package name with dots as separators. The fully qualified name for Console, for example, reads `kotlinforandroid.book.numberguess.gui.Console`. There is, however, a way to avoid typing lots of long names to refer to structure units from other packages: As a shortcut, you can *import* the referred-to structure unit by using an `import` statement. We have already seen that in a couple of examples, without further explaining it. To import the Console class, for example, you write directly under the `package` declaration:

```
package kotlinforandroid.book.numberguess

import kotlinforandroid.book.numberguess.gui.Console

class Activity {
    ...
}
```

In this case and anywhere in this file you can just use `Console` to address the `kotlinforandroid.book.numberguess.gui.Console` class. A file can have any number of such import statements. To also import the `Constants` class, write this:

```
package kotlinforandroid.book.numberguess

import kotlinforandroid.book.numberguess.gui.Console
import kotlinforandroid.book.numberguess.common.
      Constants

class Activity {
   ...
}
```

Note   IDEs like Android Studio provide help to do these imports for you. If you type a simple name Android Studio tries to determine what package might be intended. You can then press Alt+Enter with the mouse over the name to perform the import.

There is even a shortcut for importing all structure units from a package by using an asterisk (*) as a wildcard. So, for example, to import all the classes from package `kotlinforandroid.book.numberguess.random.impl`, you would write

```
package kotlinforandroid.book.numberguess

import kotlinforandroid.book.numberguess.
      random.impl.*

class Activity {
   ...
}
```

You can see the common root of all packages of the `NumberGuess` game reads `kotlinforandroid.book.numberguess`. Android Studio did that while we initialized the project. It is common practice to prepend a reverse domain name that points to you as a developer, or your educational institution or your company, plus a name for your project. For example, if you own a domain `john.doe.com` and your project is named `elysium`, you would use `com.doe.john.elysium` as your root package.

Note   There is no actual need for such a domain to exist. If you can't use an existing domain, you can use a made-up one. Just make sure the probability of clashes with existing projects is low. If you don't plan to ever publish your software, you can use what you want, including not using a domain root at all.

Exercise 24

Distribute all the code we have for the NumberGuess game into the files of the new structure from the previous section.

CHAPTER 3

Classes at Work: Properties and Functions

After reading Chapter 2 about classes and objects, it is now time shine more light on properties and their types, and also on the options we have to declare functions and what can be done from inside functions. This chapter talks about property and function declarations, but also about an important feature of object-oriented languages, *inheritance*, through which properties and functions of some class can be altered and redefined by other classes. We also learn about visibility and encapsulation, which help us to improve program structure.

Properties and Their Types

Properties are data holders or variables that define the state of an object. A property declaration inside a class uses the optional visibility type, optional modifiers, the keyword `val` for immutable (nonchangeable) variables or `var` for mutable (changeable) variables, the name, the type, and an initial value:

```
[visibility] [modifiers] val propertyName:PropertyType = initial_value
[visibility] [modifiers] var propertyName:PropertyType = initial_value
```

Apart from this, any property from a class's constructor prepended by `val` or `var` directly and automatically goes into a corresponding hidden property using the same name. In the following paragraphs we discuss all the possible options for properties given inside the class body.

© Peter Späth 2019
P. Späth, *Learn Kotlin for Android Development*, https://doi.org/10.1007/978-1-4842-4467-8_3

Simple Properties

Simple properties do not provide a visibility nor any modifiers, so their declaration reads

```
val propertyName:PropertyType = initial_value
var propertyName:PropertyType = initial_value
```

respectively, for immutable and mutable variables. Here are some additional rules:

- If inside the class or singleton object or companion object a value gets assigned inside the init{ } block, the = initial_value can be omitted.

- If Kotlin can infer the type by the initial value given, the :PropertyType can be omitted.

Such simple properties can be accessed from outside via instanceName.propertyName for classes and ObjectName.propertyName for singleton objects. Inside the class or singleton object, just use the propertyName to access it.

Let's add two simple properties to the GameUser class from the NumberGuess project from Chapter 2. We know the first and last name from the constructor, so it might be interesting to derive a property for initials and one for full name as follows:

```
class GameUser(val firstName:String,
           val lastName:String,
           val userName:String,
           val registrationNumber:Int,
           val birthday:String = "",
           val userRank:Double = 0.0) {
    val fullName:String
    val initials:String
    init {
        fullName = firstName + " " + lastName
        initials = firstName.toUpperCase() +
                    lastName.toUpperCase()
    }
}
```

Here you can see that for fullName and initials we have only vals, so it is not possible to reassign values to them. Because we first assign them inside init{ }, though, it is possible to omit the = initial value in the property declaration. Also, because all the constructor parameters have a val prepended, all of them get transported to corresponding properties, so all of them are properties: firstName, lastName, userName, registrationNumber, birthday, and userRank. To access them we use, for example:

```
val user = GameUser("Peter", "Smith", "psmith", 123, "1988-10-03", 0.79)
val firstName = user.firstName
val fullName = user.fullName
```

A user.firstName = "Linda" for assigning a value is not possible, though, because we have immutable vals. If we had vars instead this would be allowed:

```
class GameUser(var firstName:String,
          var lastName:String,
          var userName:String,
          var registrationNumber:Int,
          var birthday:String = "",
          var userRank:Double = 0.0) {
    var fullName:String
    var initials:String
    init {
        fullName = firstName + " " + lastName
        initials = firstName.toUpperCase() +
                   lastName.toUpperCase()
    }
}

// somewhere inside a function in class MainActivity
val user = GameUser("Peter", "Smith", "psmith",
       123, "1988-10-03", 0.79)
user.firstName = "Linda"
console.log(user.fullName)
```

Can you guess the output? This short program prints `Peter Smith`, although we changed the first name to `Linda`. The answer to the question of how this can be is that the full name gets calculated inside `init{ }`, and `init{ }` does not get invoked again after we alter the first name, so we'd have to take care of that.

Note   For example, you would introduce a new function like `setFirstName()` and update the first name, the full name, and the initials accordingly. A possibly cleaner variant is a function that calculates the full name on the fly, without using a separate property for it: `fun fullName() = firstName + " " + lastName`

This is one of the reasons you should prefer `vals` over `vars` wherever possible; it is just easier to avoid corrupted states.

Exercise 1

What is wrong with the following code?

```
class Triangle(color: String) {
    fun changeColor(newColor:String) {
        color = newColor
    }
}
```

Property Types

In the example code snippets, we've already seen a couple of types you can use for properties. Here is an exhaustive list.

- `String`: This is a character string. Each character from the Basic Multilingual Plane (the original Unicode specification) is of type `Char` (see later). Supplementary characters use two `Char` elements. For most practical purposes and in the majority of languages, assuming each string element to be a single `Char` is an acceptable approach.

- Int: This is an integer number. Values range from −2,147,483,648 to 2,147,483,647.

- Double: This is a floating-point number between 4.94065645841246544 · 10-324 and 1.79769313486231570 · 10+308 for both positive and negative signs. Formally it is a 64-bit floating-point value from the IEEE 754 specification.

- Boolean: This is a boolean value that can be true or false.

- *Any class:* Properties can hold instances of any class or singleton object. This includes built-in classes, classes from libraries (software built by others you use), and your own classes.

- Char: This is a single character. Characters in Kotlin use the UTF-16 encoding format (characters from the original Unicode specification) to store them.

- Long: This is an extended integer number with values between −9,223,372,036,854,775,808 and 9,223,372,036,854,775,807.

- Short: This is an integer number with a reduced value range. Values are from –32,768 to 32,767. You won't see this often, because for most practical use cases an Int is the better choice.

- Byte: This is an integer number from the very small range from –128 to 127. This type is frequently used for low-level operating system function calls. You will probably not use this type often, with the exception that it frequently gets used if you perform input/output (I/O) operations with files.

- Float: This is a lower precision floating-point number. Ranges are from $1.40129846432481707 \cdot 10^{-45}$ to $3.40282346638528860 \cdot 10^{+38}$ for both positive and negative signs. Formally it is a 32-bit floating-point value from the IEEE 754 specification. Unless storage space or performance is a major issue, you would usually prefer Double over Float.

- [Any class]: You can use any class or interface as a type, including those built in as provided by Kotlin, from other programs you use, and from your own programs.

- [Enumeration]: Enumerations are data objects with possible values from a set of unordered textual values. See Chapter 4 for further details.

Property Value Assignment

Properties can have values assigned at four places. The first place is at the property's declaration, as in

```
class TheClassName {
    val propertyName1:PropertyType1 = initial_value
    var propertyName2:PropertyType2 = initial_value
    ...
}

object SingletonObjectName {
    val propertyName1:PropertyType1 = initial_value
    var propertyName2:PropertyType2 = initial_value
    ...
}

class TheClassName {
    companion object {
        val propertyName1:PropertyType1 = initial_value
        var propertyName2:PropertyType2 = initial_value
        ...
    }
}
```

where initial_value is any expression or literal that can be converted to the expected property type. We will talk about literals and type conversion later in this chapter.

The second place where values can be assigned is inside init{ } blocks:

```
// we are inside a class, a singleton object, or
// a companion object
init {
    propertyName1 = initial_value
    propertyName2 = initial_value

    ...

}
```

This is only possible if the property was previously declared, either in the class, singleton object, or companion object, or as a var in the primary constructor declaration.

Only if properties have a value assigned to them inside an init{ } block can you omit the initial value assignment in the property declaration. It is therefore possible to write

```
// we are inside a class, a singleton object, or
// a companion object
val propertyName1:PropertyType1
var propertyName2:PropertyType2
init {
    propertyName1 = initial_value
    propertyName2 = initial_value

    ...

}
```

The third place where values can be assigned to properties is inside functions. Obviously this is only possible for mutable var variables. Those variables must have been previously declared using var propertyName:PropertyType = ..., and for the assignment you must omit the var.

```
// we are inside a class, a singleton object, or
// a companion object
var propertyName1:PropertyType1 = initial_value
...
fun someFunction() {
    propertyName1 = new_value

    ...

}
```

The fourth place where values can be assigned is from outside the class, singleton object, or companion object. Use `instanceName.` or `ObjectName.` and append the property name, as shown here:

```
instanceName.propertyName = new_value
ObjectName.propertyName = new_value
```

This is obviously possible only for mutable `vars`.

Exercise 2

Create a class A with one property `var a:Int`. Perform assignments: (a) set it to 1 inside the declaration, (b) set it to 2 inside an `init{ }` block, (c) set it to 3 inside function `fun b(){ ... }`, and (d) set it to 4 inside a `main` function.

Literals

Literals express fixed values you can use for property assignments and inside expressions. Numbers are literals, but so are strings and characters. Here are some examples:

```
val anInteger = 42
val anotherInteger = anInteger + 7
val aThirdInteger = 0xFF473
val aLongInteger = 700_000_000_000L
val aFloatingPoint = 37.103
val anotherFloatingPoint = -37e-12
val aSinglePrecisionFloat = 1.3f
val aChar = 'A'
val aString = "Hello World"
val aMultiLineString = """First Line
    Second Line"""
```

Table 3-1 lists all possible literals you can use for your Kotlin programs.

Table 3-1. *Literals*

Literal Type	Description	Enter
Decimal Integer	An integer 0, ± 1, ± 2, ...	0, 1, 2, ..., 2147483647, −1, −2, ..., −2147483648 If you like you can use underscores as the thousands separator, as in 2_012
Double Precision Float	A double precision floating-point number between $4.94065645841247.10^{-324}$ and $1.79769313486232.10^{+308}$ with a positive or negative sign	Dot notation: [s]III.FFF where [s] is nothing or a + for positive values, − for negative values; III is the integer part (any number of digits), and FFF is the fractional part (any number of digits)
		Scientific notation: [s]CCC.FFFe[t]DDD
		where [s] is nothing or a + for positive values, − for negative values, CCC.FFF is the mantissa (one or more digits; the .FFF can be omitted if not needed), [t] is nothing or a + for positive exponents, − for negative exponents, and DDD is the (decimal) exponent (one or more digits)
Char	A single character	Use single quotation marks, as in val someChar = 'A'. There are a number of special characters: write \t for a Tab, \b for a Backspace, \n for a newline, \r for a carriage Return, \' for a single quote, \\ for a backslash, and \$ for a dollar sign. In addition, you can write \uXXXX for any unicode character XXXX (hex values); for example, \u03B1 is an α

(continued)

Table 3-1. (*continued*)

Literal Type	Description	Enter
String	A string of characters	Use double quotation marks, as in `val someString = "Hello World"`. For the characters inside, the same rules as for `Chars` apply, except that for a single quotation mark you don't use a preceding backslash, but for a double quotation mark you use one: `"Don't say \"Hello\""`. In Kotlin there are also multiline *raw* string literals: Use triple double quotation marks as in `""" Here goes multiline contents"""`. Here the escaping rules for the characters inside no longer apply (that is where the name *raw* comes from).
Hexadecimal Integer	An integer 0, ± 1, ± 2, … using the hexadecimal basis	0x0, 0x1, 0x2, …, 0x9, 0xA, 0xB, 0xC, 0xD, 0xE, 0xF, 0x10, …, 0x7FFFFFFF, −0x1, −0x2, …, −0x80000000
Long Decimal Integer	A long integer 0, ± 1, ± 2, … with extended limits	0, 1, 2, …, 9223372036854775807, −1, −2, …, −9223372036854775808 If you like you can use underscores as thousands separator, as in 2_012L
Long Hexadecimal Integer	An integer 0, ± 1, ± 2, … with extended limits, using the hexadecimal basis	0x0, 0x1, 0x2, …, 0x9, 0xA, 0xB, …, 0xF, 0x10, …, 0x7FFFFFFFFFFFFFFF, −0x1, −0x2, …, −0x8000000000000000
Float	A single precision float	Same as double precision float, but add an f at the end; e.g., `val f = 3.1415f`

Note   Remember that in the decimal system 214 means $2 \cdot 10^2 + 1 \cdot 10^1 + 4 \cdot 10^0$. In the hexadecimal system we accordingly have 0x13D mean $2 \cdot 16^2 + 3 \cdot 16^1 + 13 \cdot 16^0$. The letters A, B, …, F correspond to 10, 11, …, 15.

As for type compatibility, you can assign normal integers to long integer properties, but not the other way around. You can also assign reduced precision floats to double properties, but not the other way around. Disallowed assignments require you use a conversion (see Chapter 5).

To assign literals to `Short` and `Byte` properties, use integers, but make sure the limits are not exceeded.

Both single and triple double quotation mark `String` literal representations exhibit a feature called *string templates*. That means that an expression starting with a dollar sign and followed by an expression surrounded by curly brackets gets executed and its result is passed to the string. Therefore `"4 + 1 = ${4+1}"` evaluates to the string `"4 + 1 = 5"`. For simple expressions built from just a single property name, the curly braces can be omitted, as in `"The value of a is $a"`.

Exercise 3

Find a shorter way to write

```
val a = 42
val s = "If we add 4 to a we get " + (a+4).toString()
```

avoiding the string concatenation `"..." + "..."`

Property Visibility

Visibility is about which parts of your program can access which functions and properties from other classes, interfaces, objects, or companion objects. We talk about visibility in depth in the section "Visibility of Classes and Class Members" later in this chapter.

Null Values

The special keyword `null` designates a value you can use for any nullable property. The `null` as value means something like uninitialized, not yet decided, or undefined. Any property can be nullable, but in the declaration you have to add a question mark to the type specifier:

```
var propertyName:PropertyType? = null
```

This is possible for any type, including classes, so you can write, for example:

```
var anInteger:Int? = null
var anInstance:SomeClass? = null
```

For mutable nullable `var` properties you can also assign `null` values at any time:

```
var anInteger:Int? = 42
anInteger = null
```

Other languages like Java allow nullability for any object type, which frequently leads to problems because `null` has neither any property nor function. Consider, for example, `someInstance.someFunction()`, which behaves nicely if `someInstance` points to a real object. If, however, you set `someInstance = null`, a subsequent `someInstance.someFunction()` is not possible and thus leads to an exceptional state. Because Kotlin draws a distinction between normal properties and nullable properties, such state inconsistencies can more easily be avoided by the Kotlin compiler.

We already used the so-called *dereferencing operator* (.) a lot to access functions and properties. To improve stability, Kotlin disallows the . operator for nullable variables (or expressions). Instead there is a safe-call variant "?." you have to use in this case—the dereferencing then happens only if the value on the left side of the operator is not `null`. If it is `null`, the operator calculates to `null` itself. Look at this example:

```
var s:String? = "Hello"
val l1 = s?.length() // -> 5
s = null
val l2 = s?.length() // -> null
```

Exercise 4

Which of the following is true?

1. You can perform an assignment `val a:Int = null`.

2. It is possible to write `val a:Int? = null; val b:Long = a.toLong()`.

3. It is possible to write `val a:Int? = null; val b:Long? = a.toLong()`.

4. It is possible to write `val a:Int? = null; val b:Long? = a?.toLong()`.

Property Declaration Modifiers

You can add the following modifiers to your property declaration:

- const: Add const as in

    ```
    const val name = ...
    ```

to the declaration to convert the property into a *compile time constant*. The property must be of type Int, Long, Short, Double, Float, Byte, Boolean, Char, or String for this to work. You can use this to avoid having to put a constant into the companion object. Other than that, concerning usage there is no difference between using and not using const.

- lateinit: If you add lateinit as in

  ```
  lateinit var name:Type
  ```

  where Type is a class, interface, or String (none of Int, Long, Short, Double, Float, Byte, Boolean, Char) you tell the Kotlin compiler to accept the var being or not being null. You can thus write

```kotlin
class TheClass {
    lateinit var name:String
    fun someFunction() {
        val stringSize = name.length
    }
}
```

This leads to a runtime error but not a compile time error, and thus thwarts the Kotlin nullability check system. Using lateinit makes sense if variables get initialized in a way the Kotlin compiler cannot detect (e.g., by reflection). Do not use lateinit unless you really know what you want do. By the way, it is possible to check whether a lateinit var has been initialized or not by using ::name.isInitialized.

Member Functions

Member functions are elements of classes, singleton objects, and companion objects responsible for accessing them. Inside functions, the state of the structure unit gets queried, altered, or both. A calculation based on the state could happen, by taking an input and producing an output dependent on that input and the state. Functions can also be purely functional without using the state, which means given some particular set of input parameters they always produce the same output. Figure 3-1 illustrates the various possibilities.

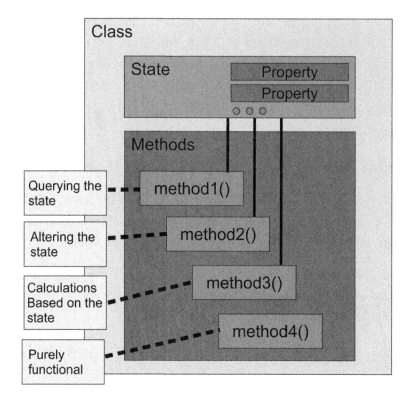

Figure 3-1. *Functions*

Depending on the terminology used, functions are also sometimes called *operations* or *methods*.

Functions Not Returning Values

To declare a function not returning anything, in Kotlin you write inside the body of a class, a singleton object, or a companion object.

```
[modifiers]
fun functionName([parameters]) {
    [Function Body]
}
```

Inside the function body, you can have any number of `return` statements exiting the function. A `return` at the end of the body is allowed as well, but not needed.

Functions might or might not have input parameters. If they don't, just write `fun functionName() { ... }`. If input parameters exist, they will be declared like this:

```
parameterName1:ParameterType1,
parameterName2:ParameterType2, ...
```

Note   In Kotlin, function arguments cannot be reassigned inside the function body. This is not a disadvantage, as reassigning function parameters inside the function is considered bad practice anyway.

Functions also can have variable argument lists. This feature is called *varargs* and we discuss it later. Another feature we cover later is *default arguments*. Such arguments allow for the specification of a default value that will be used if a parameter is not specified in the function invocation.

As an example, two simple function declarations with and without parameters look like this:

```
fun printAdded(param1:Int, param2:Int]) {
    console.log(param1 + param2)
}
fun printHello() {
    console.log("Hello")
}
```

Inside an interface—remember that we use interface to describe what needs to be done, but not how it needs to be done—functions do not have an implementation and thus declaring a body is not allowed. For functions not returning anything, the function declaration in interfaces thus reads like this:

```
fun functionName([parameters])
```

The optional [`modifiers`] you can prepend to the function declaration for fine-tuning a function's behavior are as follows:

- `private`, `protected`, `internal`, and `public`: These are visibility modifiers. Visibility is explained in the section "Visibility of Classes and Class Members" later in this chapter.

83

- open: Use this to mark a function in a class as overridable by subclasses. See the section "Inheritance" later in this chapter for details.

- override: Use this to mark a function in a class as overriding a function from an interface or from a superclass. See the section "Inheritance" later in this chapter for details.

- final override: This is the same as override, but indicates that further overwriting by subclasses is prohibited.

- abstract: Abstract functions cannot have a body, and classes with abstract functions cannot be instantiated. You must override such functions in a subclass to make them concrete (which means "unabstract" them). See the section "Inheritance" later in this chapter for details.

You cannot freely mix modifiers. Particularly for the visibility modifiers, only one is allowed. You can, however, combine any of the visibility modifiers with any combination of the other modifiers listed here. If you need more than one modifier, the separator to use is a space character.

Note that declarations in interfaces usually don't have and don't need modifiers. Visibility values other than public, for example, are not allowed here. Functions in interfaces are public by default, and because they have no implementations in the interfaces themselves, you can consider them abstract by default, so explicitly adding abstract is unnecessary.

Exercise 5

What is wrong with the following function?

```
fun multiply10(d:Double):Double {
    d = d * 10
    return d
}
```

Exercise 6

What is wrong with the following function?

```kotlin
fun printOut(d:Double) {
    println(d)
    return
}
```

Functions Returning Values

To declare a value-returning function in Kotlin inside a class, a singleton object, or a companion object, inside its body you add `: ReturnType` to the function header and write

```kotlin
[modifiers]
fun functionName([parameters]): ReturnType {
    [Function Body]
    return [expression]
}
```

The function parameters are the same as for functions not returning values, and so are the modifiers discussed previously. For the value or expression returned, Kotlin must be able to convert the expression's type to the function return type. An example for such a function would be as follows:

```kotlin
fun add37(param:Int): Int {
    val retVal = param + 37
    return retVal
}
```

It is possible to have more than one `return` statement inside the body, but they all must return a value of the anticipated type.

Note   Experience says that for improved code quality it is better to always use just one `return` statement at the end.

It is also possible to replace the body by a single expression if this is possible:

```
[modifiers]
fun functionName([parameters]): ReturnType = [expression]
```

The : ReturnType can be omitted here if the type the expression yields to is the anticipated function return type. Kotlin can therefore infer from

```
fun add37(param:Int) = param + 37
```

that the function return type is Int.

Again for interfaces, functions do not have an implementation and the function declaration in this case reads

```
fun functionName([parameters]): ReturnType
```

Note   Actually Kotlin internally lets all functions return a value. If a returned value is not needed, Kotlin assumes a special *void* type that it calls Unit. If you omit : ReturnType and the function does not return a value, or if the function body does not have a return statement at all, Unit is assumed. If, for whatever reason, it helps to improve the readability of your program, you can even write fun name(...) : Unit { ... } to express that a function does not return any interesting value.

Exercise 7

Is the following true?

```
fun printOut(d:Double) {
    println(d)
}
```

is the same as

```
fun printOut(d:Double):Unit {
    println(d)
}
```

Exercise 8

Create a shorter version of the following class:

```
class A(val a:Int) {
    fun add(b:Int):Int {
        return a + b
    }
    fun mult(b:Int):Int {
        return a * b
    }
}
```

Exercise 9

Create an interface AInterface describing all of class A from Exercise 8.

Accessing Masked Properties

In case of name clashes, function parameters may *mask* class properties. Say, for example, a class has a property *xyz* and a function parameter has the very same name *xyz*, as in

```
class A {
    val xyz:Int = 7
    fun meth1(xyz:Int) {
        [Function-Body]
    }
}
```

The parameter xyz is then said to mask the property xyz inside the function body. This means if you write xyz inside the function, the parameter gets addressed, not the property. It is still possible, though, to also address the property by prepending this. to the name:

```
class A {
    val xyz:Int = 7
    fun meth1(xyz:Int) {
```

```
        val q1 = xyz // parameter
        val q2 = this.xyz // property
        ...
    }
}
```

The this refers to *this current object*, so this.xyz means property xyz from this current object, not xyz as made visible by the function specification.

Note   Some people use the term *shadowed* instead of *masked* for such properties. Both mean the same thing.

Exercise 10

What is the output of

```
class A {
    val xyz:Int = 7
    fun meth1(xyz:Int):String {
        return "meth1: " + xyz +
               " " + this.xyz
    }
}
fun main(args:Array<String>) {
    val a = A()
    println(a.meth1(42))
}
```

Function Invocation

Given an instance, a singleton object, or a companion object, you invoke functions as follows:

```
instance.functionName([parameters]) // outside the class
functionName([parameters]) // inside the class
```

```
Object.functionName([parameters]) // outside the object
functionName([parameters]) // inside the object
```

To call the function of a companion object from inside the class you also just use functionName([parameters]). From outside the class, you'd use ClassName. functionName([parameters]) here.

Exercise 11

Given this class

```
class A {
    companion object {
        fun x(a:Int):Int { return a + 7 }
    }
}
```

describe how to access function x() with 42 as a parameter from outside the class in a println() function.

Function Named Parameters

For a function invocation you can use the argument names to improve readability:

```
instance.function(par1 = [value1], par2 = [value2], ...)
```

or

```
function(par1 = [value1], par2 = [value2], ...)
```

from inside the class or object. Here the parN are the exact function parameter names as in the function's declaration. As an additional benefit of using named parameters, you can use any parameter sort order you like, because Kotlin knows how to properly distribute the parameters provided. You can also mix unnamed and named parameters, but it is then necessary to have all named parameters at the end of the parameter list.

Exercise 12

Given this class

```
class Person {
    var firstName:String? = null
    var lastName:String? = null
    fun setName(fName:String, lName:String) {
        firstName = fName
        lastName = lName
    }
}
```

create an instance and use named parameters to set the name to John Doe.

Caution   Using named parameters in function calls greatly improves code readability. However, be careful if you use code from other programs, as with new program versions the parameter names might change.

Function Default Parameters

Function parameters might have defaults that apply if omitted in the function invocation. To specify a default you just use

```
parameterName:ParameterType = [default value]
```

inside the function declaration. A function parameter list may have any number of default values, but they all must be at the end of the parameter list:

```
fun functionName(
    param1:ParamType1,
    param2:ParamType2,
    ...
    paramM:ParamTypeM = [default1],
    paramM+1:ParamTypeM+1 = [default2],
    ...) { ... }
```

To let the defaults apply you then just omit them in the invocation. If you omit x parameters at the end of the list, the x rightmost parameters take their default values.

This sorting order dependency makes using default parameters a little cumbersome. If you mix named parameters and default parameters, though, using defaults adds versatility to functions.

Exercise 13

To the function declaration

```
fun set(lastName:String,
    firstName:String,
    birthDay?:String,
    ssn:String?) { ... }
```

add as defaults `lastName = ""`, `firstName = ""`, `birthDay = null`, `ssn = null`. Then invoke the function using named parameters, specifying just `lastName = "Smith"` and `ssn = "1234567890"`.

Function Vararg Parameters

We learned functions exist to take input data and alter an object's state from that, possibly producing some output data. So far we have learned about fixed parameter lists, covering a big subset of all possible use cases. What about lists of unknown, potentially unlimited size, though? Such lists are called *arrays* or *collections,* and any modern computer language needs to provide a way to handle such data in addition to types holding single data elements. We cover arrays and collections in greater detail in Chapter 9, but for now you should know that arrays and collections are fully fledged types and you can use them for single constructor and function parameters, as in ..., `someArray:Array<String>`, ...

There is, however, a construct that sits between using many different single-valued parameters and one array or collection parameter: *varargs.* The idea is as follows: As the last element in the parameter list of a function declaration, add a `vararg` qualifier as in

```
fun functionName(
    param1:ParamType1,
    param2:ParamType2,
    ...
    paramN:ParamTypeN,
    vararg paramV:ParamTypeV) { ... }
```

The result is a function that is able to take N + x parameters, where x is any number from 0 to infinity. This is provided, however, that all `vararg` parameters are of the type specified by `ParamTypeV`. Of course, N might be 0, so a function can have a single `vararg` parameter:

```
fun functionName(varargs paramV:ParamTypeV) {
    ...
}
```

Note   Kotlin actually allows `vararg` parameters to appear anywhere earlier in the parameter list. Kotlin then, however, can distribute passed-in parameters during function invocation only if the next parameter after the `vararg` has a different type. Because this complicates call structures, it is better to avoid such `vararg` constructs.

To invoke such a function, provide all non-`vararg` parameters in the call, then any number of `vararg` parameters (including zero):

```
functionName(param1, param2, ..., paramN,
    vararg1, vararg2, ...)
```

As a simple example we create a function that takes a date as `String`, then any number of names, again as `Strings`. The declaration reads:

```
fun meth(date:String, vararg names:String) {
    ...
}
```

The following invocations are now possible:

```
meth("2018-01-23")
meth("2018-01-23", "Gina Eleniak")
meth("2018-01-23", "Gina Eleniak",
      "John Smith")
meth("2018-01-23", "Gina Eleniak",
      "John Smith", "Brad Cold")
```

You can extend the name list at will.

The question is now this: How can we handle the `vararg` parameter inside the function? The answer is that the parameter is an array of the specified type, and it has all the features we describe in Chapter 9, including a `size` property and the access operator [] to get elements as in [0], [1], and so on. If we therefore use the example function with parameters `(date:String, vararg names:String)` and invoke it via

```
meth("2018-01-23", "Gina Eleniak",
     "John Smith", "Brad Cold")
```

inside the function you'll have `date = "2018-01-23"` and for the `vararg` parameter:

```
names.size = 3
names[0] = "Gina Eleniak"
names[1] = "John Smith"
names[2] = "Brad Cold")
```

Exercise 14

Build a `Club` class and add a function `addMembers` with the single `vararg` parameter `names`. Inside the function, use

```
println("Number: " + names.size)
println(names.joinToString(" : "))
```

to print the parameter. Create a `main(args:Array<String>)` function outside the class, instantiate a `Club`, and invoke its `addMembers()` function with three names "Hughes, John", "Smith, Alina", and "Curtis, Solange".

Abstract Functions

Functions inside classes can be declared without body and marked `abstract`. This transforms the class into an *abstract* class as well, and Kotlin requires the class to be marked `abstract` to be compilable.

```
abstract class TheAbstractClass {
    abstract fun function([parameters])
    ... more functions ...
}
```

Abstract classes are something between interfaces and normal classes: They provide implementations for some functions and leave other functions abstract (unimplemented) to allow for some variety. Abstract classes thus frequently serve for some kind of "basis" implementation, leaving the details to one or more classes implementing the abstract functions.

Abstract functions also make functions behave like interface functions, including the fact that classes with such functions cannot be instantiated. You have to create a subclass from such an abstract class implementing all functions to have something that can be instantiated.

```
abstract class TheAbstractClass {
    abstract fun function([parameters])
    ... more functions ...
}

// A subclass of TheAbstractClass ->
class TheClass : TheAbstractClass() {
    override fun function([parameters]) {
        // do something...
    }
}
```

Here TheClass can be instantiated, as it implements the abstract function. For more details about subclassing see the section "Inheritance" later in this chapter.

Polymorphism

Inside a class, a singleton object, a companion object, or an interface, you can have several functions using the same name with different parameters. There is no magic to that, but this feature in object orientation theory has its own name: *polymorphism*.

If you have several functions with the same name, Kotlin decides by looking at the parameters. An invoking code specifies which function to actually use. This dispatching procedure usually works and you won't see any problems, but with complicated classes and lots of possibilities for a certain class, perhaps including complex parameter lists with default arguments, interfaces, and varargs, the decision of which function to call is not unambiguous. In such cases the compiler issues an error message and you have to redesign the function call or your class for everything to work correctly.

Use cases for polymorphism are manifold; as a simple example consider a class with several `add()` functions allowing for an `Int` parameter, a `Double` parameter, or a `String` parameter. Its code could read:

```kotlin
class Calculator {
    fun add(a:Int) {
        ...
    }
    fun add(a:Double) {
        ...
    }
    fun add(a:String) {
        ...
    }
}
```

If you now call `calc.add(...)` with some argument, Kotlin takes the argument's type to find out which of the functions to call.

Caution   Be careful with function naming: Polymorphism (i.e., several functions with the same name) should not happen by accident or for just technical reasons. Instead, all functions using one particular name should serve the same purpose from a functional perspective.

Local Functions

In Kotlin, functions can be declared inside functions. Such functions are called *local functions* and they can be used from the point of their declaration until the end of the enclosing function.

```kotlin
fun a() {
    fun b() {
        ...
    }
    ...
```

```
    b()
    ...
}
```

Inheritance

In real life, inheritance means leaving one's belongings to someone else. In object-oriented computer languages like Kotlin, the idea is similar. Given a class A, writing class B : A indicates that we give all the assets from class A to class B. What is this good for, beyond having some kind of renamed copy of A? The magic is that class B can overrule or *override* parts of the assets it inherits from class A. This can be used to alter some aspects of the class it inherits from to introduce new behavior.

Although this overriding of functions and properties somewhat deviates from the real-life analogy of inheritance, inheriting classes and overriding particular functions and properties is one of the central aspects of any object-oriented language.

Classes Inheriting from Other Classes

The precise syntax for inheritance is

```
open class A { ... }
class B : A() {
    [overriding assets]
    [own assets]
}
```

if A has an empty default constructor, and

```
open class A([constructor parameters]) { ... }
class B : A([constructor parameters]) {
    [overriding assets]
    [own assets]
}
```

otherwise. Class B may, of course, have its own constructor:

```
open class A([constructor parameters]) { ... }
class B([own constructor parameters]) :
      A([constructor parameters])
{
    [overriding assets]
    [own assets]
}
```

The open in the class declaration is a Kotlin specialty. Only classes marked with open can be used for inheritance.

Note   This is a somewhat odd design decision from the makers of Kotlin. It basically disables inheritance unless you add open to all possible classes that could be used for inheritance. In real life, developers will likely forget to add open to all their classes or even refuse to add open everywhere because it feels like a nuisance, so inheritance most likely is broken if your program uses classes from other programs or libraries. Unfortunately, there is no way out, so we have to live with that. You can, of course, add open wherever needed in your own classes.

In relation to each other, the class used as a basis for inheritance is also called a *superclass* and the class inheriting from it is a *subclass*. In the preceding code, therefore, A is the superclass of B, and B is the subclass of A.

In our NumberGuess example you can see, for instance, that our MainActivity class inherits from AppCompatActivity. This subclassing of built-in activity classes is important for any app to work with Android.

Constructor Inheritance

At the very beginning of the subclass construction the superclass's constructor including the init{ } block will be called. If the superclass provides secondary constructors, for a subclass it is also possible to call one of the secondary constructors instead. This happens by simply using the secondary constructor's parameter signature:

```
open class A([constructor parameters]) {
    constructor([parameters2]) { ... }
}
class B : A([parameters2]) {
    ...
}
```

Because we know that secondary constructors always also invoke the primary constructor, inheritance by design in any case always invokes the superclass's primary constructor and init{ } block. This is also true if the subclass provides its own init{ } block, which then gets called second in line. Beginners tend to forget this fact, but if you keep this in mind you could avoid some difficulty.

In Kotlin, subclasses can steal properties from the superclass's constructor. To do so, the val or var needs to be prepended with open, as in this example:

```
open class A(open val a:Int) {
}
```

A subclass can then override the parameter in question:

```
open class A(open val a:Int) {
}
class B(override val a:Int) : A(42) {
    ...
}
```

Such an overridden property will then be addressed by any code from the superclass that formerly used its own original version of the property.

Exercise 15

What will be the output of

```
open class A(open val a:Int) {
    fun x() {
        Log.d("LOG",
            "A.x() -> a = ${a}")
    }
```

```
    fun q() {
        Log.d("LOG",
                "A.q() -> a = ${a}")
    }
}
class B(override val a:Int) : A(37) {
    fun y() {
        Log.d("LOG",
                "B.y() -> a = ${a}")
        q()
    }
}

// inside some activity function:
val b = B(7)
b.y()
```

Note that Log.d("TAG", ...) prints the second argument to the console.

Overriding Functions

To override functions of a superclass, in the subclass you have to use the override modifier and write

```
open class A {
    open fun function1() { ... }
}
class B : A() {
    override
    fun function1() { ... }
}
```

Again we have to add open to the function in the superclass to make it eligible for inheritance. The function could, of course, have a parameter list and parameter types must be the same in the superclass and in the subclass for overriding to work correctly.

The overridden function gets a new version in the subclass, but the original version is not lost altogether. It is possible to address the original function by writing

```
super.functionName(param1, param2, ...)
```

in the subclass.

Overriding Properties

Kotlin has a special feature not found in other object-oriented languages. Not only is it possible to override functions, but properties can also be overridden. For this to work, such properties need to be marked open in the superclass, as in

```
open class A {
    open var a:Int = 0
}
```

A class that inherits from this superclass can then override the property by declaring

```
class B : A() {
    override var a:Int = 0
}
```

Using this notation, any usage of the property from inside class B and A is then covered by the property as declared in class B. The property behaves as if the declaration in class A didn't exist any longer, and functions in A formerly using "their" version of this property will use the property from class B instead.

Exercise 16

What will be the output of

```
open class A() {
    private var g:Int = 99
    fun x() {
        Log.d("LOG", "A.x() : g = ${g}")
    }
    fun q() {
```

```
        Log.d("LOG", "A.q() : g = ${g}")
    }
}

class B : A() {
    var g:Int = 8
    fun y() {
        Log.d("LOG", "B.y() : g = ${g}")
        q()
    }
}

// inside some activity function:
val b = B()
b.x()
b.y()
```

Note that Log is provided by the Android libraries automatically included in your project. If you first get an error, place the cursor over it and then press Alt+Enter for a resolution. Can you guess why property g in class A has to be declared private, meaning no other class can see it or use it?

Exercise 17

In Exercise 16, remove the private from the property declaration and make class B override property g from class A. What will be the output?

Accessing Superclass Assets

Even with functions or properties overridden in some subclass, you can access the original versions from the superclass if you prepend a super. So, for example, in

```
open class A() {
    open var a:Int = 99
    open fun x() {
        Log.d("LOG", "Hey from A.x()")
    }
}
```

```
class B : A() {
    override var a:Int = 77
    override fun x() {
        Log.d("LOG", "Hey from A.x()")
    }
    fun show() {
        Log.d("LOG", "Property: " + a)
        Log.d("LOG", "Formerly: " + super.a)
        Log.d("LOG", "Function: ")
        x()
        Log.d("LOG", "Formerly: ")
        super.x()
    }
}

// inside some activity function:
val b = B()
b.show()
```

the output shows that from the subclass B we can use both the overridden and the
original properties and functions:

```
Property: 77
Formerly: 99
Function:
Hey from B.x()
Formerly:
Hey from A.x()
```

Local Variables

Local variables are val or var variables that get declared and used inside some function;
for example:

```
class TheClass {
    fun function() {
        ...
```

```
        var localVar1:Int = 7
        val localVar1:Int = 8

        ...

    }
}
```

Such local variables are valid from the place of their declaration to the end of the function; that is why they are called *local*. They are, of course, allowed to calculate any expression that is necessary to return something from the function, as they will not be destroyed before the return happens.

Local variables should not mask function parameters for code quality reasons. If you have a function parameter xyz of any type, you should not declare a local variable inside the function using the name xyz. The compiler allows that, but it will issue a warning about that shadowing.

Exercise 18

Which of the following classes is valid? For any invalid class, describe what the problem is.

1.
```
    class TheClass {
        var a:Int = 7

        fun function() {
            val a = 7
        }
    }
```

2.
```
    class TheClass {
        fun function(a:String) {
            val a = 7
        }
    }
```

3.
```
    class TheClass {
        fun function() {
            println(a)
            val a = 7
        }
    }
```

4.    ```kotlin
class TheClass {
    fun function():Int {
        val a = 7
        return a - 1
    }
}
```

5.    ```kotlin
class TheClass {
    fun function1():Int {
        val a = 7
        return a - 1
    }
    fun function2():Int {
        a = 8
        return a - 1
    }
}
```

Visibility of Classes and Class Members

We have mainly talked about classes, singleton objects, and companion objects (structure units) and their properties and functions thus far in a literally free manner:

```kotlin
class TheName { // or object or companion object
    val prop1:Type1
    var prop2:Type2
    fun function() {
        ...
    }
}
```

Literally free here means structure units, functions, and properties declared this way can be freely accessed from everywhere. In Kotlin, this kind of accessibility is called *public visibility*. You can even add the keyword public to all of them this way to describe this public visibility explicitly.

```
public [class or (companion) object] TheName {
    public val prop1:Type1
    public var prop2:Type2
    public fun function() {
        ...
    }
}
```

For conciseness, however, you would usually omit that, because public is the default visibility in Kotlin.

In Kotlin, it is possible to impose restrictions on visibility. At first sight it might appear easier if we keep the default public visibility everywhere because anything can be accessed from everywhere and you don't have to think about restrictions. For any nontrivial project, though, there are good reasons to consider drawing distinctions concerning visibility. The key term connected with that is *encapsulation*. What do we mean by that? Consider for example an analog clock. It shows the time and it provides a means to adjust the time by some clock control. We could model this by two functions, time() and setTime():

```
class Clock {
    fun time(): String {
        ...
    }
    fun setTime(time:String) {
        ...
    }
}
```

From a user's point of view, this is all that is needed to "talk" to a clock. What happens inside the clock is a different story: First, to adjust the time the clock needs to add or subtract some amount of time from the time currently shown. This is done by turning the control dial of the clock. Second the current state of the clock is more thoroughly described by the angles of the hour, minute, and second indicators. There is also a technical device that reacts to each second tick. This corresponds to the gear of the clock. We also need a timer that fires events every second, like the spring inside an analog clock does. Finally we also need to add some timer initialization code into an init{ } block. Taking all that into account, we'd have to rewrite our class to read like this:

105

```
class Clock {
    var hourAngle:Double = 0
    var minuteAngle:Double = 0
    var secondsAngle:Double = 0
    var timer:Timer = Timer()

    init {
        ...
    }

    fun time(): String {
        ...
    }

    fun setTime(time:String) {
        ...
    }

    fun adjustTime(minutes:Int) {
        ...
    }

    fun tick() {
        ...
    }
}
```

We now have two types of classes accessing assets: external ones the user cares about, and internal ones the user doesn't need to know about. Encapsulation precisely takes care of hiding internals from clients by introducing a new visibility class, private. As the name suggests, private properties and functions are private to the structure unit and nobody from outside needs to be concerned with them, or is even allowed to access them. To indicate that a property or function is private, just add the `private` keyword in front of it. For our `Clock` class we thus write

```
class Clock {
    private var hourAngle:Double = 0
    private var minuteAngle:Double = 0
    private var secondsAngle:Double = 0
    private var timer:Timer = Timer()

    init {
        ...
    }

    fun time(): String {
        ...
    }

    fun setTime(time:String) {
        ...
    }

    private fun adjustTime(minutes:Int) {
            ...
    }

    private fun tick() {
            ...
    }
}
```

Separating functions and properties this way has the following benefits:

- The client doesn't need to know details of the internal functioning of a class or an object. It can just ignore anything that is marked private, reducing distractions and making it easier to understand and use the class or object.

- Because the client only needs to know about public properties and functions, the implementation of the private functions together with all private properties is freely changeable at any time, provided the public properties and functions keep functioning in the expected way. It is thus easier to improve classes or fix deficiencies.

Back in the NumberGuess game, we already used private as a visibility specifier. If you look at just the function signatures of the activity class, you will see this:

```
class MainActivity : AppCompatActivity() {
    override fun onCreate(savedInstanceState: Bundle?)
    override fun onSaveInstanceState(outState: Bundle?)
    fun start(v: View)
    fun guess(v:View)

    ////////////////////////////////////////////////////
    ////////////////////////////////////////////////////

    private fun putInstanceData(outState: Bundle?)
    private fun fetchSavedInstanceData(
            savedInstanceState: Bundle?)
    private fun log(msg:String)
}
```

Here you also clearly see that we need onCreate() and onSaveInstanceState() to be public, because the Android runtime needs to access them from outside for life cycle handling. Furthermore, start() and guess() need to be public as well, because they get accessed from outside as a result of button presses. The remaining three functions are accessed from only inside the class, hence the private visibility for those.

Apart from public and private, there are two more visibility modifiers: internal and protected. Table 3-2 describes them together with the two we already know.

Table 3-2. *Visibility*

Visibility	Asset	Description
public	Function or property	(Default) The function or property is visible from everywhere inside and outside the structure unit.
private	Function or property	The function or property is visible only from inside the same structure unit.
protected	Function or property	The function or property is visible from inside the same structure unit, and from inside any direct subclass. Subclasses get declared via class TheSubclass-Name : TheClassName { ... } and they inherit all the public and protected properties and functions of the class from which they inherit.

(continued)

Table 3-2. (*continued*)

Visibility	Asset	Description
`internal`	Function or property	Functions and properties are public only for structure units from the same program. For programs from other compilations, especially for programs from others you include in your software, `internal` gets treated like `private`.
`public`	Class, singleton object, or companion object	(Default) The structure unit is visible from everywhere inside and outside the program.

`private`	Class, singleton object, or companion object	The structure unit is visible only from inside the same file. For inner classes the structure unit is only visible from an enclosing structure unit. For example
		
		`class A {`
		`    private class B {`
		`    ... }`
		`    fun function() {`
		`        val b = B()`
		`    }`
		`}`

`protected`	Class, singleton object, or companion object	The structure unit is visible only from an enclosing structure unit or a subclass of it. For example
		
		`class A {`
		`    protected class B {`
		`    ... }`
		`    fun function() {`
		`        val b = B()`
		`    }`
		`}`
		`class AA : A {`
		`// subclass of A`
		`    fun function() {`
		`        val b = B()`
		`    }`
		`}`

Note   For small projects, you wouldn't care about any visibility modifiers apart from the default `public` one. For larger projects, adding visibility restrictions helps to improve software quality.

Self-Reference: This

Inside any class's function, the keyword `this` refers to the current instance. We know that from inside the class, we can refer to functions and properties from the same class by just using their names. If visible, from outside the class we'd instead have to prepend the instance name. You can consider `this` as the instance name that could be used from inside the class, so, if we are in a function, to refer to a property or function from the same class we could equivalently use

```
functionName()      -the same as-      this.functionName()
propertyName        -the same as-      this.propertyName
```

If a function's argument uses the same name as a property of the same class, we already know that the parameter *masks* the property. We also know that we still could access the property if we prepend `this`. In fact, this is the primary use case for using `this`. Under some circumstances it could also help to improve the readability if you prepend `this.` to function or property names. For example, in functions that set instance properties, using `this` helps to express that setting properties is the primary purpose of the function.

Consider this:

```
var firstName:String = ""
var lastName:String = ""
var socialSecurityNumber:String = ""
...
fun set(fName:String, lName:String, ssn:String) {
    this.lastName = lName
    this.firstName = fName
    this.socialSecurityNumber = ssn
}
```

It technically also works without the three `this.` instances, but in that case it is less expressive.

Converting Classes to Strings

In Kotlin, any class automatically and implicitly inherits from the built-in class Any. You don't have to explicitly state it, and there is no way to prevent it. This super-superclass already provides a couple of functions, one of which has the name and return type toString():String. This function is kind of a multipurpose diagnostic function that frequently gets used to let an instance tell about its state in a textual representation. The function is open, so any class can override this function to let your classes indicate instance state in an informal way.

You are free to do whatever you want inside an overridden toString(), but most of the time one or the other property gets returned, as for example in this case:

```kotlin
class Line(val x1:Double, val y1:Double,
          val x2:Double, val y2:Double) {
{
    override fun toString() =
        "(${x1},${y1}) -> (${x2},${y2})"
}
```

Often you don't want to miss what superclasses do in their own toString() implementation, so you might prefer to write something like this:

```kotlin
class Line(val x1:Double, val y1:Double,
          val x2:Double, val y2:Double) {
{
    override fun toString() = super.toString()
        " (${x1},${y1}) -> (${x2},${y2})"
}
```

Remember the super. addresses unoverridden properties and functions.

Exercise 19

Can you guess what happens if you write this?

```
class Line(val x1:Double, val y1:Double,
           val x2:Double, val y2:Double) {
{
    override fun toString() = toString() +
        " (${x1},${y1}) -> (${x2},${y2})"
}
```

Many built-in classes in their toString() implementation already provide some useful output, so in most cases you don't have to override built-in classes just for the sake of providing a sensible toString() output. What happens for some of the other built-in classes and for any of your classes without their own toString() implementation is that toString() indicates the memory position of the instance. For example:

```
class A
val a = A()
println(a.toString())
```

will print something like A@232204a1, which, depending on the circumstances, is not very informative. Therefore for diagnostic output, providing a toString() implementation is a good idea.

CHAPTER 4

Classes and Objects: Extended Features

This chapter covers some extended object orientation features that are not necessary for a program to work, but nevertheless improve readability and expressiveness. The chapter presumes that you have read Chapter 2. We also use the NumberGuess sample app from Chapter 2.

Anonymous Classes

Inside your coding in some instances you might want to create a one-time implementation of an interface or a one-time subclass of some class. While in Kotlin, it is possible to write

```kotlin
class A : SomeInterface {
    // implement interface functions ...
}
val inst:SomeInterface = A()
// use inst ...
```

or

```kotlin
open class A : SomeBaseClass() {
    // override functions ...
}
val inst:SomeBaseClass = A()
// use inst ...
```

113

© Peter Späth 2019
P. Späth, *Learn Kotlin for Android Development*, https://doi.org/10.1007/978-1-4842-4467-8_4

Inside functions, there is a more concise way to create and use such one-time instances:

```
val inst:SomeInterface = object : SomeInterface {
    // implement interface functions ...
}
// use inst ...
```

or

```
val inst:SomeBaseClass = object : SomeBaseClass() {
    // override functions ...
}
// use inst ...
```

If you extend some superclass as in the latter listing, this one might also be abstract. It is then necessary, however, to implement all abstract functions, as is usually the case for an instantiation to be possible. Because the name of the interface implementation or subclass is neither specified nor needed, such classes are called *anonymous* classes. Inside the class body between the curly braces you can write anything that you could also write inside a named class's body.

Note   The object : inside the declaration suggests that there is just a one-time instantiation. It is not possible to have several instances of anonymous classes.

We know that this refers to the actual instance. This is also the case from inside anonymous classes, where this refers to the one instance of the anonymous class. There is an extension of this that allows us to get the instance of the *enclosing* class: Just append @ClassName to this. For example in

```
interface X {
    fun doSomething()
}
class A {
    fun meth() {
        val x = object : X {
            override doSomething() {
```

```
                println(this)
                println(this@A)
            }
        }
    }
}
```

the first this refers to the anonymous class, and this@A refers to the instance of class A.

Inner Classes

Classes and singleton objects can also be declared inside other classes or singleton objects, and even inside functions. They then can be accessed from inside their scope, so if a class or singleton object gets declared inside some class A, it can be instantiated inside A. If it is declared inside a function, it can be used from the point of its declaration until the end of the function.

```
class A {
    class B { ... }
    // B can now be instantiated from
    // everywhere inside A
    fun meth() {
        ...
        class C { ... }
        // C can now be used until the end of
        // the function
        ...
    }
}
```

Classes and objects inside other classes or other objects can be addressed from outside using a path specification similar to packages: If X as a class or an object gets declared inside A (a class or a singleton object), you can write A.X to access it from outside. You should probably do this, however, only if the inner class provides some kind of interface to the enclosing class, to avoid breaking encapsulation principles.

```kotlin
class A {
    class B { ... }
}
fun main(args:Array<String>) {
    val ab = A.B()
    // do something with it ...
}
```

Functions and Properties Outside Classes

In your project you can have Kotlin files that do not contain a single `class`, `interface`, or `object` declaration but nevertheless show `val` and `var` properties and functions. Whereas at first sight we seem to work outside object orientation if we use such files, in fact the Kotlin compiler implicitly and secretly creates a singleton object based on the *package* name and puts such properties and functions into this object.

Note   For very small projects it is acceptable to not use explicit classes and singleton objects. If a project gets bigger, it is still possible to only use such nonclass files, but you'll then risk having chaotic and unreadable code in the end.

Derived from that fact, the following rules apply for such properties and functions:

- It does not matter where in the file you declare `val` and `var` properties and functions; they will be usable from everywhere in the file.

- Such properties and functions are visible to other classes or singleton objects you write in other files using `import the.package.name.name` where the last `name` refers to the property or function name.

- You can have several files of that type inside a package. The Kotlin compiler then just sequentially parses all the files and gathers all the functions and properties that are neither from inside a class nor a singleton object. The file names play no role here.

- If you have several such files in different packages (as defined by the package declarations at the top of the files), name clashes do not cause a problem. You could have properties and functions using the same name. Nevertheless, you should avoid this to keep your code readable.

- It is possible to add classes, interfaces, and singleton objects to such files. You can use such structure units from the place of their declaration until the end of the file.

Additionally, it is possible to import properties and functions from all files of that kind inside a particular package using the wildcard notation `import the.package.name.*`. This comes in very handy to avoid a lengthy `import` list.

Exercise 1

You have a utility singleton object

```
package com.example.util

object Util {
    fun add10(a:Int) = a + 10
    fun add100(a:Int) = a + 100
}
```

and a client

```
package com.example

import com.example.util.Util

class A(q:Int) {
    val x10:Int = Util.add10(q)
    val x100:Int = Util.add100(q)
}
```

Could you think of a way to rewrite the `Util.kt` file to not use the `object {}` declaration? What will the client code look like?

Importing Functions and Properties

Functions and properties from singleton objects can be imported via import statements like these

```
import package.of.the.object.ObjectName.propertyName
import package.of.the.object.ObjectName.functionName
```

at the top of the file, after the `package` declaration and together with the other `import` statements for importing classes and singleton objects. It is then possible to directly use the function or property by using just its name, without a prepending `ObjectName`.

Note   There is no wildcard for importing all properties and functions of a singleton object. You have to put each of them into its own `import` line.

Exercise 2

Given that `Math.log()` calculates the logarithm of a number, and with `Math` residing inside package `java.lang`, rewrite

```
package com.example
class A {
  fun calc(a:Double) = Math.log(a)
}
```

such that `Math.` is no longer needed.

Data Classes

Classes that only contain properties and no or very few functions most likely are *data classes*, the purpose of which is to provision a bracket around a couple of properties. They thus serve as a kind of container gathering a range of properties. Think of a `Person` class which for a person gathers the name, birthday, place of birth, SSN, and so on. Kotlin has a special notation for such classes: Prepend `data` as in

```
data class ClassName([constructor])
```

This doesn't look very different from normal classes, but in contrast to them, prepending data leads to the following outcomes:

- The class automatically gets a specially tailored toString() function based on the properties; you don't have to write your own.

- The class automatically gets sensible equals() and hashCode() functions based only on the properties. We'll talk about object equality later; for now, this is what you need to know: The equality check relation a == b for two instances of data classes yields true only if the instances belong to the same data class, and all their properties need to be equal as well.

Data classes come handy if you need a function to return structured or compound data. In other languages you'd frequently have to use full-fledged classes, arrays, or lists for that purpose, which makes this task feel a little bit clumsy. In Kotlin you can instead concisely write, for example:

```
data class Point(val x:Double, val y:Double)

fun movePoint(pt:Point, dx:Double, dy:Double):Point =
    Point(pt.x + dx, pt.y + dy)

// somewhere in a function ...
val pt = Point(0.0, 1.0)
val pt2 = movePoint(pt, 0.5, 0.5)
```

You can see that with the single data class line at the top, we can make the function movePoint() return a structured datum.

Exercise 3

With the data classes

```
data class Point2D(val x:Double, val y:Double)
data class Point3D(val x:Double, val y:Double, val z:Double)
```

at hand, which of the following is true (the == stands for equals)?

1. `Point2D(0, 1) == Point2D(1, 0)`

2. `Point2D(1, 0) == Point3D(1, 0, 0)`

3. `Point2D(1, 0).x == Point3D(1, 0, 0).x`

4. `Point2D(1, 0) == Point2D(1.0, 0)`

5. `Point2D(1, 0) == Point2D(1, 0)`

Describe why or why not.

Exercise 4

Which classes of the `NumberGuess` game are considered data classes? Perform the conversion.

Enumerations

The enumeration type is basically a nonnumeric data type with values from a given set. Basically here means that internally the type gets handled by an integer by default, but in basic usage scenarios you don't have to be concerned about that. The term *set* is used in a mathematical sense, which means that values must be unique and do not have a sort order.

Enumerations in Kotlin are a specialized form of a class:

```
enum class EnumerationName {
    VALUE1, VALUE2, VALUE3, ...
}
```

where for `EnumerationName` you can use any camelCase name and VALUEx is any string from the character set A-Z0-9_ starting with a letter or _.

Note   For the values, technically more characters are available, but by convention you should use a combination of the characters shown here.

To declare a type of an enumeration you write, as for any other class,

```
val e1: EnumerationName = ...
var e2: EnumerationName = ...
```

where for the right side of the assignment you use EnumerationName. appending any of the enumeration values. For example, an enumeration with fruits as values would be declared and and used with this result:

```
enum class Fruit {
    BANANA, APPLE, PINEAPPLE, GRAPE
}

val f1 = Fruit.BANANA
val f2 = Fruit.BANANA
val f3 = Fruit.APPLE
var fx:Fruit? = null

// you can check for equality:
val b1:Boolean = f1 == f2  // -> true
val b2:Boolean = f1 == f3  // -> false

// you can reassign vars:
fx = Fruit.APPLE
fx = Fruit.BANANA

// toString() gives the textual value name
val s = fx.toString() // -> "BANANA"
```

Note that == is the equivalent of equals. This is a boolean expression we have not yet formally introduced. If you like, you can define the internal data type of enumeration values yourself: Just add a primary constructor to the enum class and use it for the values:

```
enum class Fruit(val fruitName:String) {
    BANANA("banana"),
    APPLE("apple"),
    PINEAPPLE("pineapple"),
    GRAPE("grape")
}
```

You can then use the name of the property you introduced to fetch this custom internal value:

```
val f1 = Fruit.BANANA
var internalVal = f1.fruitName // -> "banana"
```

An interesting built-in function for enumeration classes is the dynamic lookup function valueOf(): If you need to get a value dynamically from a string, write

```
val f1 = Fruit.valueOf("BANANA")
//      <- same as Fruit.BANANA
```

Use

```
EnumerationName.values()
```

to fetch all values for an enumeration (e.g., for loops). The enumeration values themselves also have two built-in properties:

- Use enumVal.name to get the value's name as a string.

- Use enumVal.ordinal to get the value's index in the enumeration values list.

Exercise 5

Add a Gender enumeration to the GameUser class from the NumberGuess game app. Allow values M, F, and X. Add a corresponding constructor parameter gender to the GameUser constructor parameters with default value X.

Custom Property Accessors

We know that a var property basically gets declared by writing

```
var propertyName:PropertyType = [initial_value]
```

We also know that to get the var we write object.propertyName and to set it we write object.propertyName =...

In Kotlin it is possible to change what is happening when you get or set the property. To adapt the getting process, you write this:

```
var propertyName:PropertyType = [initial_value]
    get() = [getting_expression]
```

Inside the [getting_expression] you can write what you like, including accessing functions and other properties. For more complicated cases you can also provide a body, as in

```
var propertyName:PropertyType = [initial_value]
    get() {
        ...
        return [expression]
    }
```

To instead change the setting process that applies for propertyName = ... you write

```
var propertyName:PropertyType = [initial_value]
    set(value) { ... }
```

Inside the set body you can access all the functions and all the other properties of the object. In addition, you can use the special field identifier to refer to the datum corresponding to the property.

You can, of course, do both; that is, adapt the getting and the setting processes:

```
var propertyName:PropertyType = [initial_value]
    get() = [getting_expression]
    set(value) { ... }
```

You can fine-tune the visibility of both the getters and setters of a property. Just write

```
[modifier] var propertyName:PropertyType = ...
    private get
    private set
```

or any of the other visibility modifiers. To make the getter private, though, the property itself must be declared to be private as well. Making the setter private for a public property is a valid option instead.

Interestingly, it is possible to define properties that do not have corresponding data in the class or singleton object. If you define both the setter and getter of a property and specify neither an initial value nor use `field` inside the setter code, no data field will be generated for that property.

Exercise 6

Can you guess what can be done with `val` instead of `var` properties?

Exercise 7

Write an `str` property that does the same as the `toString()` function (so it is possible to write `obj.str` instead of `obj.toString()`).

Exercise 8

Recall the `NumberGuess` game app:

```
data class GameUser(var firstName:String,
            var lastName:String,
            var userName:String,
            var registrationNumber:Int,
            var gender:Gender = Gender.X,
            var birthday:String = "",
            var userRank:Double = 0.0) {
    enum class Gender{F,M,X}

    var fullName:String
    var initials:String
    init {
      fullName = firstName + " " + lastName
      initials = firstName.toUpperCase() +
                lastName.toUpperCase()
    }
}
```

We had the problem that with a later `firstName` change the `fullName` gets corrupted.

```
val u = GameUser("John", "Smith", "jsmith", 123)
u.firstName = "Linda"
val x = u.fullName // -> "John Smith" WRONG!
```

Find a way to avoid such corrupted states. Hint: Afterward an `init{ }` block is no longer needed. Update your code accordingly.

Kotlin Extensions

In Kotlin, it is possible to "dynamically" add extensions to classes. We need to put that dynamically in quotation marks because the usage of such extensions must be defined in your code prior to execution. It is not possible in Kotlin to decide during runtime whether or not, and if so, which extensions get used. Computer language designers usually refer to such features as *static* features.

Here is what we mean by extensions: Wouldn't it be nice if we could add functions and custom properties to any class? This could be very useful, for example, if we want to add extra functionality to classes and functions provided by others. We know we can use inheritance for that purpose, but depending on the circumstances, this might not be possible or the implementation could feel clumsy.

Caution   The extension mechanism is extremely powerful. Be cautious not to overuse it. You can write very elegant code using extensions that no one understands without time-consuming research of the extension definitions.

Extension Functions

Consider we'd like to have a `hasLength(l:Int): Boolean` function inside the built-in `String` class. You might think that this is what inheritance is used for. However, it is not possible to extend the `String` class, because it is forbidden to extend `String` by design, so we can't use inheritance for that aim. Still, the Kotlin extension mechanism helps us here. We can write

```
package the.ext.pckg

fun String.hasLength(len:Int) = this.length == len
```

inside some file `fileName.kt` (the file name doesn't play a role here, so use whatever you like) inside some package `the.ext.pckg`. Remember the == checks for equality.

We can now use that extension function inside any class or singleton object and write

```
import the.ext.pckg.*

// anywhere inside a function ...
val hasLen10:Boolean = someString.hasLength(10)
```

The same process is possible for any other class, including your own classes, and companion objects. For the latter case write `fun SomeClass.Companion.ext() { }` to define a new extension function `ext`. The `Companion` here is a literal identifier used to address the companion object.

Note   If extension functions have the same name and function signature (parameter set) as already existing functions, the latter take priority.

Extension Properties

A similar procedure works for properties. Say you want to add an `l` property to `String` that does the same as `.length()` and calculates the string length. You can do that via some construct like this:

```
package the.ext.pckg

val String.l get() = this.length
```

Note that we can't use `val String.l = this.length` because for technical reasons extension properties are not allowed to actually create real data fields. An initialization is thus not possible, because in fact there is nothing that can be initialized. As for getters we can write what we want, so we can directly refer to `.length`. Now it is possible to write

```
import the.ext.pckg.*

// anywhere inside a function ...
val len1 = someString.length
val len2 = someString.l // this is the same
```

Extensions with Nullable Receivers

Note   *Receiver* refers to the class or singleton object that is being extended.

It is possible to catch `null` values for the extension. If you prepend a question mark as in

```
fun SomeClass?.newFunction(...) { ... }
```

you can check whether `this == null` inside the body and appropriately react in such cases to do the right thing. You can then write `instance.newFunction(...)` even if `instance` is `null` and even then get into the extension function.

Encapsulating Extensions

If you want to encapsulate extensions inside particular classes, singleton objects, or companion objects, it is possible to write something like this:

```
class SomeClass {
    fun SomeOtherClass.meth() {
        ...
    }
}
```

Here `SomeOtherClass` receives the extension function, but that function can only be used from inside `SomeClass`. For the `hasLength()` extension for the `String` class, the encapsulated version thus reads

```
class SomeClass {
    fun String.hasLength(len:Int) = this.length == len
    fun function() {
        ...

        // we can use hasLength() here
        val len10:Boolean = someString.hasLength(10)
        ...
    }
}
```

```
class SomeClass2 {
    // we can't use String.hasLength() here
}
```

A similar procedure allows us to encapsulate extension properties. The notation for such properties reads

```
class SomeClass {
    val SomeOtherClass.prop get() = ...
}
```

and the encapsulated version of the `String.l` extension for the string length is thus

```
class SomeClass {
    val String.l get() = this.length
    fun function() {
        ...
        // we can use .l here
        val len = someString.l
        ...
    }
}
```

The obvious advantage of encapsulated extensions is that we don't have to import extension files. If we want to define extensions that are usable for many classes, the nonencapsulated variant would be the better choice.

Functions with Tail Recursion

Recursive functions call themselves. This happens once in a while for certain algorithms. For example, the factorial function $n! = n \cdot (n-1) \cdot (n-2) \cdot \ldots 2 \cdot 1$ can be implemented as

```
fun factorial(n:Int):Int {
    return if(n==1) n else n * factorial(n-1)
}
```

Note that the `if()` expression returns the part before or after the `else`, depending on whether the argument evaluates to `true` or `false` (we'll be talking about branching later in the book).

For proper application functioning, the runtime engine needs to keep track of function calls, so internally a call to factorial() will look like factorial(factorial(factorial (...))) If this recursion depth is not too high, this is not a problem. If it gets really high, though, we'll run into trouble concerning memory usage and performance. However, provided the recursion happens in the last statement of such a function, it can be converted to a *tail recursion* function and then internally an overuse of system resources won't happen.

To convert a function to a tail recursion function, just prepend tailrec to fun, as in

```
tailrec fun factorial(n:Int) {
    return if(n==1) n else n * factorial(n-1)
}
```

Infix Operators

Infix operators are used for operations notated by

```
operand1    OPERATOR    operand2
```

We know a lot of such infix operators: Think of multiplication (3 * 4), addition (3 + 4), and more. In Kotlin, many such infix operators are predefined, but it is also possible to define your own infix operators. To do so, write

```
infix operator
fun SomeClass1.oper(param:SomeClass2) = ...
```

where oper is the name of the operator (use your own) and the ... performs any calculation using this (the instance of SomeClass1) and param. You can then write

```
[expression1] oper [expression2]
```

where the type of [expression1] is SomeClass1 and the type of [expression2] is SomeClass2. For more complicated calculations you can also use a function body as usual:

```
infix operator
```

```
fun SomeClass1.oper(param:SomeClass2):ResultType {
    ...
    return [result_expression]
}
```

For example, to allow a string to be repeated *n* times using a new operator TIMES, we write

```
infix operator fun String.TIMES(i:Int) =
    (1..i).map { this }.joinToString("")
```

(The second line is a functional construct; we'll be talking about functional design later.) We can then write

```
val s = "abc" TIMES 3 // -> "abcabcabc"
```

We can do this more cleverly if we take account of Kotlin having textual counterparts of the standard operators. The textual representation of *, for example, is times, so we can write

```
operator fun String.times(i:Int) =
    (1..i).map { this }.joinToString("")
```

which then allows us to use the asterisk for the same operation:

```
val s = "abc" * 3 // -> "abcabcabc"
```

The infix could be omitted here, because Kotlin knows that * belongs to an infix operation.

Using the standard operators for defining custom calculation is called *operator overloading*. In the following section we learn more about that, using a list and the textual representation of all the standard operators.

Operator Overloading

Operators take one or two expressions and produce a single output from that using the following notation:

```
[OPER] expression
[expression] [OPER] [expression]
```

Handling one expression is referred to as a *unary* operation and the operator accordingly gets called a *unary operator*. Likewise, handling two expressions gives us *binary* operations and *binary operators*.

From math we know a lot of operators like –a, a + b, a * b, a / b, and so on. Kotlin, of course, has many such operators built in for its data types, so 7 + 3 and 5 * 4 and so on do the expected things. We'll be talking about operator expressions in detail later in this book, but for now we want to pay some attention to operator overloading, the capability of Kotlin that lets you define your own operators using standard operator symbols for your own classes.

Say, for example, you have a `Point` class designating a point (x, y) in space, and a `Vector` class designating the direct connection between two points. From what we have already learned, we know that we can declare both of them concisely via

```
data class Point(val x:Double, val y:Double)
data class Vector(val dx:Double, val dy:Double)
```

Now from math we know it is possible to write for the vector from point P_1 to point P_2 the expression $\vec{v} = P_2 - P_1$. The calculation goes $dx = p2.x - p1.x$ and $dy = p2.y - p1.y$. Wouldn't it be nice if we could just write $v = p2 - p1$ to perform that operation, as in

```
val p1 = Point(1.0, 1.0)
val p2 = Point(4.0, -2.0)
val v:Vector = p2 - p1
```

Using operator overloading we can do exactly that. It is easy: First, we need the textual representation of the – operator, which happens to be minus. Second we write

```
data class Point(val x:Double, val y:Double) {
  operator fun minus(p2:Point) =
      Vector(p2.x-this.x, p2.y-this.y)
}
```

That is it. The `val v:Vector` = p2 - p1 now works, so whenever the compiler sees a - between two `Point` instances it calculates the vector combining them.

For unary operators the procedure is the same, but you don't specify a parameter in the operator function. For example, if you want -Vector(1.0, 2.0)) to work, giving the reversed vector, you just add

```
operator fun unaryMinus() = Vector(-this.dx, -this.dy)
```

to the `Vector` class.

131

You can do the same for all operators Kotlin knows. The textual representation for all of them is shown in Table 4-1.

Table 4-1. *Operators*

Symbol	Arity	Textual	Standard Meaning
+	U	unaryPlus	Reproduces data (e.g., +3).
−	U	unaryMinus	Negates data (e.g., −7).
!	U	not	Logically negates data (e.g., !true == false).
++	U	inc	Increments data (e.g., var a = 6; a++; // -> a == 7). The operator must not change the object on which it gets invoked! The assignment of the incremented value happens under the hood.
−−	U	dec	Decrements data (e.g., var a = 6; a−−; // -> a == 5). The operator must not change the object on which it gets invoked! The assignment of the decremented value happens under the hood.
+	B	plus	Adds two values.
−	B	minus	Subtracts two values.
*	B	times	Multiplies two values.
/	B	div	Divides two values.
%	B	rem	Remainder of a division (e.g., 5 % 3 = 2).
..	B	rangeTo	Creates a range (e.g., 2..5 -> 2, 3, 4, 5)
in !in	B	contains	Checks whether the right side is contained or not contained in the left side.
[]	B+	get / set	Indexed access. If on the left side of an assignment like q[5] = ... the set() function gets used with the last parameter designating the value to set. The get() and set() functions allow more than one parameter, which then corresponds to several comma-separated indexes inside []; for example, q[i] →q.get(i), q[i,j] →q.get(i, j), and q[i,j] = 7 →q.set(i, j, 7)

(continued)

Table 4-1. (*continued*)

Symbol	Arity	Textual	Standard Meaning
( )	B+	invoke	Invocation. Allows more than one parameter, which then corresponds to several comma-separated parameters inside ( ); for example, q(a) →q.invoke(a) and q(a, b) →q.invoke(a, b).
+ =	B	plusAssign	Same as plus(), but assigns the result to the instance at which the operator is invoked.
— =	B	minusAssign	Same as minus(), but assigns the result to the instance at which the operator is invoked.
* =	B	timesAssign	Same as times(), but assigns the result to the instance at which the operator is invoked.
/ =	B	divAssign	Same as div(), but assigns the result to the instance at which the operator is invoked.
% =	B	remAssign	Same as rem(), but assigns the result to the instance at which the operator is invoked.
==	B	equals	Checks for equality. The ! = stands for unequals and corresponds to equals() returning false.
< > <= >=	B	compareTo	Compares two values. The compareTo() function is supposed to return −1, 0, +1, depending on whether the argument is less than, equal to, or greater than the value to which the function is applied.

Note   Because in the operator function body or expression you can calculate what you want, you can let the operator do strange stuff. Just bear in mind that your class users expect a certain behavior when operators are used, so be reasonable with what you calculate there.

By the way, if you prefer to overload operators in an extension file, there is no magic required. Just write `operator fun TheClass.[operator_name]( [parameters] ) = ...` For the earlier points and vectors example, this reads

```
operator fun Point.minus(p2:Point) =
    Vector(p2.x-this.x, p2.y-this.y)
```

Don't forget to import the extension file, just like you would for any other extension.

Exercise 9

Add - and + operators to the `Vector` class. The calculation consists of adding or subtracting the `dx` and `dy` members: `Vector(this.dx + v2.dx, this.dy + v2.dy)` and `Vector(this.dx - v2.dx, this.dy - v2.dy)` if `v2` is the operator function parameter.

Delegation

We learned that inheritance via `class TheClass : SomeInterface { ... }` lets `TheClass` implement functions the interface only declares in an abstract manner. The implementation code enters the overridden functions in `TheClass`. Delegation is similar to inheritance; it starts the same way: `class TheClass : SomeInterface ...`. The difference is where the implementing code resides: For delegation it is presumed that an object is at hand that already implements the interface and `TheClass` primarily delegates the work to this object. Using the constructs we already know, this could be written as:

```
interface TheInterface {
    fun someMethod(i:Int):Int
    ...more functions
}

class Implementor0 : SomeInterface {
    override fun someMethod(i:Int):Int = i*2
    ...implement the other functions
}
```

```
class Implementor : TheInterface {
    val delegate = Implementor0()
    override fun someMethod(i:Int):Int = delegate(i)
    ...do the same for the other functions
}
```

The method someMethod() in the Implementor class delegated to the delegate, but it could also add some extra work, as in

```
override fun someMethod(i:Int):Int = delegate(i-1) + 1
```

Kotlin has a concise notation for the delegation basic pattern. You simply write

```
class Implementor : TheInterface by Implementor0()
// or
val impl0 = Implementor0()
class Implementor : TheInterface by impl0
```

The Kotlin compiler then automatically implements all the interface methods by forwarding the work to the delegate. You still can change any function by overriding it:

```
class Implementor : TheInterface by Implementor0() {
    override fun someMethod(i:Int):Int = i * 42
}
```

If you explicitly need the delegate object, you must add it to the constructor as in

```
val b = Implementor0()
class Implementor(val b:TheInterface) :
        TheInterface by b {
    override
    fun someMethod(i:Int):Int = b.someMethod(i-1) + 1
}
val instance = Implementor(b)
```

CHAPTER 5

Expressions: Operations on Data

We already used expressions a couple of times. Whenever you need to assign a value to a variable, need function call parameters, or need to provide a value to some kind of language construct, you need an expression. Expressions also show up where you don't expect them, and they can be ignored if we don't need them.

Expression Examples

Expressions can be subdivided into different types: numerical expressions, boolean expressions, string and character expressions, expressions acting on bits and bytes, and a few more unclassified expressions. Before we start explaining them in detail, here are some examples:

```
4 * 5         // multiplication
3 + 7         // addition
6 - 1         // subtraction
"a" + "b"     // concatenation
( 1 + 2 )     // grouping
-5            // negation
a && b        // boolean a AND b
"Hello"       // constant (String)
78            // another constant (Int)
3.14          // another constant (Double)
'A'           // another constant (Char)
arr[43]       // index access
funct(...)    // function invocation
```

© Peter Späth 2019
P. Späth, *Learn Kotlin for Android Development*, https://doi.org/10.1007/978-1-4842-4467-8_5

```
Clazz()        // instantiation
Obj            // singleton instance access
q.a            // dereferencing
q.f()          // another dereferencing
if(){ }        // language construct
when(){ }      // another language construct
```

Ubiquity of Expressions

In Kotlin, unlike many other computer languages, almost everything is an expression. Look, for example, at the function invocation funct(). You might think that a function not declared returning a value as in fun funct() { ... } is not an expression, because it seemingly cannot be assigned to a variable. Try it and write

```
fun a() {
}

val aa = a()
```

Surprisingly the compiler does not mark this code as erroneous. In fact, such a function actually does return a value; it is the instance of the Unit class and gets called Unit itself. You cannot do anything interesting with it, but it is a value and it makes a function not explicitly returning anything implicitly return something.

In the rest of this chapter we cover different expression types and conversions between them.

Numerical Expressions

Numerical expressions are constructs built of elements like literals, properties, and subexpressions, possibly combined by operators and resulting in a number. The set of commonly known operators referring to addition, subtraction, multiplication, and division are usually called *arithmetics*. In computation, this set of standard operators usually gets augmented by an increment and decrement operator ++ and −−, and an integer division remainder operator %. For the full list of possible elements that are usable for numerical expressions inside Kotlin, see Table 5-1.

Table 5-1. *Numerical Expression Elements*

Symbol	Meaning	Examples
literal	A literal	`3` or `7.5`
variable	A property	`val a = 7; val b = a + 3`
funct()	The value of a function, if it returns a number	`fun a() = 7; val b = 3 + a()`
[ ]	Access to an element in an array or a list of numbers	`arr[0]` `list[7]`
( )	Replaced by the result of the inside expression	`7 * ( a + b )`
+	If used in front of an expression, reproduces data	`val a = +3` `val a = +7.4`
-	If used in front of an expression, negates data	`val a = -(7+2)`
++	Can be used in front of or behind a `var`; if used in front of it, evaluates to the current value of the `var` + 1; if used behind it, evaluates to the current value of the `var`; as a side effect, increments the `var`	`var a = 7` `val b = 7 + ++a` `val c = 7 + a++`
--	Can be used in front of or behind a `var`; if used in front of it, evaluates to the current value of the `var` - 1; if used behind it, evaluates to the current value of the `var`; as a side effect, decrements the `var`	`var a = 7` `val b = 7 + --a` `val c = 7 + a--`
+	Adds two values	`7 + 6`
-	Subtracts two values	`7 - 6`
*	Multiplies two values	`7 * 6`
/	Divides two values; if between two non-floating-point values, returns a non-floating-point value; otherwise returns a `Double` or a `Float`	`7 / 6` (gives 1) `7.0 / 6.0` (gives 1:16667)
%	Remainder of a division of two integer values	`5 % 3` (gives 2)
subexpr	Any expression used as a subexpression, returning a number	In `5 + a / 7` the a/7 can be considered a subexpression

If you mix different types of numbers in an expression, the one with the larger value range gets used for the returned value's type, so dividing a Long by an Int returns a Long:

```
val l1:Long = 234567890L
val i1:Int = 37
val x = l1 / i1 // -> is a Long
```

Likewise, if you mix normal precision Float elements and double precision Double elements in an expression, Double wins:

```
val f1:Float = 2.45f
val d1:Double = 37.6
val x = f1 / d1 // -> is a Double
```

Mixing integer numbers with floating-point number elements will result in a floating-point number:

```
val i1:Int = 33
val d1:Double = 37.6
val x = i1 * d1 // -> is a Double
```

In case we need to combine three values (or subexpressions) and have two operators in a row, as in

$$expr1 \degree expr2 \degree expr3$$

the question is which operator gets evaluated first. This is called *operator precedence*, and the Kotlin rules for that are shown in Table 5-2.

Table 5-2. *Arithmetic Operators' Precedence*

Priority	Operators	Example
1	++ -- as a postfix	a++
2	- (in front of an expression) + (in front of an expression) ++ -- as a prefix	-(3 + 4) --a
3	* / %	7 * a
4	+ -	7 - a

You can always use round brackets (...) to prescribe any operator evaluation order. Just as used in math, the values within the brackets are calculated first before the bracketed solution is used.

Exercise 1

With `Math.sqrt(...)` designating the square root $\sqrt{}$, write this in Kotlin code:

$$\sqrt{\dfrac{a + \dfrac{b-x}{2}}{b^2 - 7 \cdot x}}$$

Assume `a`, `b`, and `x` are existing properties.

Boolean Expressions

Boolean expressions are expressions that evaluate to one of the boolean values `true` or `false`. We use boolean expressions often if we need to decide which parts of a program participate in the program flow. Objects and operators that participate in boolean expressions are listed in Table 5-3.

Table 5-3. *Boolean Expression Elements*

Symbol	Meaning	Examples
literal	A literal	`true` or `false`
variable	A property	`val a = true; val b = a`
`funct()`	The value of a function, if it returns a boolean	`fun a() = true;` `val b = a()`
`[ ]`	Access to an element in an array or a list of booleans	`arr[0]` `list[7]`
`( )`	Replaced by the result of the inside expression	`b1 && ( a || b )` (Note: && = AND, || = OR)

(*continued*)

Table 5-3. (*continued*)

Symbol	Meaning	Examples
&&	AND operation; a && b is true only if both a and b are true; note that the right side of && never gets evaluated if the left side evaluates to `false`	`true && true` (yields → `true`)
||	OR operation; a || b is true only if at least one of a and b is true; note that the right side of || never gets evaluated if the left side evaluates to `true`	`true || false` (yields → `true`)
!	Negates the following boolean expression	`val b = true;` `val r = !b` (yields r is false)
a == b	Yields `true` if a and b are equal; a and b are any objects or subexpressions; boolean or numerical subexpressions are equal if their values are the same; objects a and b are equal if their `hashCode()` functions return the same value and `a.equals(b)` returns `true`; two strings are equal if they both contain the same characters; two instances of a particular data class are equal if all their properties are equal	`a == 3` (`true` if a has the value 3) `a == "Hello"` (`true` if a is the string "Hello")
a != b	Unequals, same as `!( a == b )`	`7 != "XYZ"` (→ `true`) `7 != 7` (→ `false`)
a < b	True if a number a is less than a number b; also evaluates if on objects a and b the interface `Comparable` is defined	`a < 7` (→ `true` if a is less than 7)
a > b	True if a number a is greater than a number b; also evaluates if on objects a and b the interface `Comparable` is defined	`a > 3` (→ `true` if a is greater than 3)

(*continued*)

Table 5-3. (*continued*)

Symbol	Meaning	Examples
a <= b	True if a number a is less than or equal to a number b; also evaluates if on objects a and b the interface `Comparable` is defined	`a <= 7` (→ `true` if a is less than or equal to 7)
a >= b	True if a number a is greater than or equal to a number b; also evaluates if on objects a and b the interface `Comparable` is defined	`a >= 3` (→ `true` if a is greater than or equal to 3)
a is b	True if an object a implements class or interface b	`val a = 7; val b = a is Int` (→ `true`)
a !is b	Same as `!(a is b)`	`val a = 7; val b = a !is String` (→ `true`)
a === b	Checks for referential equality; returns `true` if objects are the `same` and is thus stronger than the `==` comparison; normally not used very often, because the semantic check using the `==` operator in most cases makes more sense	`class A` `val a = A();` `val b = A()` `val c = a === b` (→ `false`)

Similar to the numeric expressions from the previous section, boolean expression operators have a precedence if you use expressions with more operators. The Kotlin rules for boolean operator precedence are shown in Table 5-4.

Table 5-4. *Boolean Operators' Precedence*

Priority	Operators	Example
1	! (in front of an expression)	`val a = true; val b = !a`
2	is, !is	`a in b && c`
3	<, <=, >=, >	`a < 7 && b > 5`
4	==, !=	`a == 7 && b != 8`
5	&&	`a == 4 && b == 3`
6	||	`a == 4 || a == 7`

As for numeric expressions, you can use round brackets to force a different order of precedence:

```
val b1 = a == 7 && b == 3 || c == 4
val b2 = a == 7 && (b == 3 || c == 4)
```

As you can see, they are different. In the first line, the && wins and gets calculated first, because it has a higher priority compared to the ||. In the second line the || wins because it is inside a bracket.

String and Character Expressions

There are not too many expression elements for strings. You can, however, concatenate strings and perform string comparisons. See Table 5-5 for the full list of string expression elements.

Table 5-5. *String Expression Elements*

Symbol	Meaning	Examples
literal	A literal	"Hello world" or """Hello world"""
variable	A property	val a = "abc"; val b = a
funct()	The value of a function, if it returns a string	fun a() = "abc"; val b = a()
[ ]	Access to an element in an array or a list of strings	arr[0] list[7]
str[ ]	Extracts a character from a string	"Hello" [1] (yields "e")
( )	Replaced by the result of the inside expression	"ab" + ("cd" + "ef")
+	String concatenation	val a = "Hello " + "world" (yields → "Hello world")

(continued)

Table 5-5. (*continued*)

Symbol	Meaning	Examples
a == b	Checks for equality; two strings are equal if they both contain the same characters	a == "Hello" (true if a is the string "Hello")
a != b	Unequals, same as !(a == b)	"abc" != "XYZ" ($\rightarrow$ true)
a < b	True if a string a is lexicographically less than a string b	"abc" < "abd" ($\rightarrow$ true)
a > b	True if a string a is lexicographically greater than a string b	"cd" > "ad" ($\rightarrow$ true)
a <= b	True if a string a is lexicographically less than or equal to a string b	"abc" <= "abc" ($\rightarrow$ true) "abc" < "abc" ($\rightarrow$ false)
a >= b	True if a string a is lexicographically greater than or equal to a string b	"abc" >= "abc" ($\rightarrow$ true)
a in b	If a is a Char, true if b contains a; if a is a string itself, true if a is part of the string b	'e' in "Hello" ($\rightarrow$ true) 'lo' in "Hello" ($\rightarrow$ true)
a !in b	Same as !(a in b)	'x' !in "Hello" ($\rightarrow$ true)

String literals have a couple of special cases.

- String literals using three sets of double-quotation marks are called *raw strings*. They can contain everything, including line breaks and special characters like the backslash (\\). Writing "Hello\n world" yields "Hello world" separated by a line break. If you write """Hello\n world""", however, the output will be literally "Hello \n world". An exception is $; you have to write ${'$'} to get it.

- In both raw and normal ("escaped") strings you can use templates: A ${} gets replaced by the toString() representation of whatever is included inside the curly brackets. For example: "The sum of 3 and 4 is ${3+4}" yields the string "The sum of 3 and 4 is 7". If it is a single identifier like the name of a property, you can also omit the brackets and write $propertyName, as in "And the value of a is $a".

Characters have an integer representation because they correspond to an index inside a character table. This allows for a few arithmetic and comparison operators to work with characters. The list of character expression elements is shown in Table 5-6.

Table 5-6. *Character Expression Elements*

Symbol	Meaning	Examples
literal	A literal	`'A'` or `'7'`
variable	A property	`val a = 'x';` `val b = a`
`funct()`	The value of a function, if it returns a character	`fun a() = 'x';` `val b = a()`
`[ ]`	Access to an element in an array or a list of characters	`arr[0]` `list[7]`
`-`	Distance in the character table	`val d = 'c' - 'a'` (yields → 2)

`a == b`
`a != b`
`a < b`
`a > b`
`a <= b`
`a >= b`
	Character comparison; compares the indexes inside the character table	`'c' > 'a'`
		(yields → `true`)

Bits and Bytes

A byte is a more hardware-oriented data storage unit. We know that there is a `Byte` type and that it has values between −128 and 127. A byte corresponds to some hardware storage and processing element that can be accessed and used in an extremely fast manner. In your app you use bytes only once in a while, especially when it comes to using some low-level system functions or addressing connected hardware elements like the camera or the speaker.

You know that when you write down a number in the decimal number system like 125, what you actually mean is $5 \cdot 1 + 2 \cdot 10 + 1 \cdot 100$. Computers internally don't like the decimal numbering system, because if they used it, the difference between, for example, 7 and 8 could not reliably be represented by some technical property like the voltage between two contacts. What computers can do really well is find out whether something is switched on or not, represented by the ciphers 0 and 1. For that reason, they internally use the binary numbering system. If we need a 125 it actually gets represented by the binary number 01111101, which means $1 \cdot 1 + 0 \cdot 2 + 1 \cdot 2^2 + 1 \cdot 2^3 + 1 \cdot 2^4 + 1 \cdot 2^5 + 1 \cdot 2^6 + 0 \cdot 2^7$. The digits inside this number are called *bits*, and as it happens, we need eight bits to represent all possible values of a byte.

Because a byte is a number, you can do all the things with it we already talked about earlier regarding numeric expressions. A byte is also a collection of eight bits, however, and there are a couple of special operations you can do on the bit level (see Table 5-7). Note that Short, Int, and Long values correspond to two, four, and eight bytes and thus 8, 16, and 32 bits. Bit-level operations cannot only be performed on bytes, therefore, but on the other integer types as well.

Table 5-7. *Bit Expression Elements*

Symbol	Meaning	Examples
a and b	An AND on the bit level; each bit of a gets paired with the corresponding bit of b, and if both are 1, the bit in the result number will be set to 1, too	13 and 11 (evaluates to 9: 00001101 and 00001011 → 00001001)
a or b	An OR on the bit level; each bit of a gets paired with the corresponding bit of b, and if either or both are 1, the bit in the result number will be set 1, too	13 or 11 (evaluates to 15: 00001101 or 00001011 → 00001111)
a xor b	An XOR on the bit level; each bit of a gets paired with the corresponding bit of b, and if exactly one of them is 1, the bit in the result number will be set 1, too	13 xor 11 (evaluates to 6: 00001101 xor 00001011 → 00000110)
inv a	Switches all bits from some number a from 0 to 1 and vice versa	inv 13 (evaluates to 114: inv 00001101 → 11110010 = 114)

(continued)

Table 5-7. (*continued*)

Symbol	Meaning	Examples
a shl b	Shifts all bits from a by b bit positions to the left	13 shl 2 (evaluates to 52: 00001101 → 00110100 = 52)
a ushr b	Shifts all bits from a by b bit positions to the right; the name is an abbreviation for unsigned right shift, and means the leftmost bit gets no special treatment	13 shr 2 (evaluates to 3: 00001101 → 00000011 = 3)
a shr b	Shifts all bits from a by b bit positions to the right; if the leftmost bit is set to 1, the leftmost bit after each bit shift gets set to 1 as well	-7 shr 2 (evaluates to -2: 11111001 → 11111110 = -2)

Note that the shr operator for a signed shift-right operation refers to negative numbers in bit representation. Such negative numbers are built as follows: Make sure that the bits from the negative number and the bits from its arithmetical inverse added together lead exactly to an overflow. The representation of −3 as a byte thus gives 11111101, because this plus 00000011 (for +3) gives 100000000. The last number with nine digits for a byte leads to an overflow and the uppermost ninth bit gets lost, resulting in a zero. This eventually gives us the desired +3 + −3 = 0 also in the binary representation.

Other Operators

Kotlin has a few more operators we can use in expressions. They don't fit well into the distinction among numeric, boolean, string and character, and bit expressions, so we present them on their own in Table 5-8.

Table 5-8. *Other Expression Elements*

Symbol	Meaning	Examples
a in b	Checks whether some a is contained in b, with b maybe being an array or a collection; in general the in operator is applicable for any object that defines a operator fun contains(other:SomeClass): Boolean function, even for your own classes	class B class A { operator fun contains(other:B):Boolean { ... } } val b = B() val a = A() val contained = b in a
a !in b	The opposite of a in b; works also if operator fun contains(other:SomeClass): Boolean is defined for a's class	See a in b; add val notContained = b !in a
::	If used like ClassName::class it creates a reference to a class; if used like ClassName::funName or ClassName::propertyName it creates a reference to a function or a property	val c = String::class val f = String::length
a .. b	Creates a range from an integer (literal, Byte, Short, Int, Long, or Char) a to another integer b	1..100
a ?: b	The Elvis operator; if a is not null, take it; otherwise take b	var s:String? = ... var ss = s?:"default" (if s is null, take "default" instead)
a ?. b or a ?. b()	Safe dereferencing or safe call operator; for some object a, retrieves property b or the result from function b() invocation (can have parameters) only if a is not null; otherwise evaluates to null itself	var i:Int? = ... var ss:String? = i?.toString()
a!!	Makes sure a is not null; otherwise throws an exception	var s:String? = ... var ss = s!!.toString()

The !! operator at the end of an expression not only checks that it is not null, it also converts it to a non-nullable type:

```
val c:Int? = ...     // an int or null
val b = c!!          // b is non-nullable!
// the same: val b:Int = c!!
```

Even better, Kotlin remembers that we checked for c not being null and for the rest of the function considers c as a non-nullable property.

Caution   Even if the !! seems to be a versatile tool to simplify coding, you should not use it often. The operator somewhat thwarts Kotlin's way of handling nullability. The !! breaks non-nullability and hides the advantages we have by differentiating between nullable and non-nullable types and expressions.

Exercise 2

Create a class Concatenator that allows string concatenation via a function add(s:String). Add another function such that it is possible to write the following to see whether the concatenated string contains some substring.

```
val c = Concatenator()
c.add("Hello")
c.add(" ")
c.add("world")
val contained = "ello" in c
```

Conversions

If you have a val or var property or a function parameter of some type, the question is what happens if in an assignment we provide an expression of a different type. If this type mismatch is substantial, for example if we need an Int number and a String gets provided, the compiler will fail and we need to fix it. In other cases, for example providing an Int if we actually needed a Long, a simple conversion between the types would be nice.

Kotlin helps us here by providing several functions that can be used to perform type conversions manually. In the following list we investigate the options we have if types don't match.

- An Int is needed.

  - Byte, Short, Int, Long: All these provide a toInt() function that performs a direct conversion.

  - Char: Has a toInt() function that gives the index of the character in the character table.

  - Float, Double: Provide a toInt() function that for positive numbers returns the closest Int below the given floating-point number. For negative numbers the closest Int above the given floating-point number gets returned. In addition, they have a roundToInt() function that provides a half-up rounding to the next integer.

  - String: Provides a toInt() function that parses the given string and tries to convert it to an Int. This will fail if the string provided does not contain an integer number, as only an optional sign and the ciphers 0 to 9 are allowed. In addition, there is a toIntOrNull function that handles the same conversion but will not fail and will instead return null if the conversion is not possible. Variants toInt(radix:Int) and toIntOrNull(radix:Int) use a different numbering system (radix) for the conversion. For the hexadecimal radix (use 16 as a radix parameter), for example, the ciphers 0 to 9 and the letters A to F are allowed.

  - Boolean: No conversion from a boolean to an integer number is possible.

- A Long, Byte,or Short is needed.

  All types Byte, Short, Int, Long, Char, Float, Double, and String provide toLong(), toByte(), and toShort() functions, which follow the same rules as for the Int target type, except that different number ranges apply. Note that for strings an L suffix for long literals is not allowed.

- A Char is needed.

  All integer types Byte, Short, Int, and Long provide a toChar()
  function that uses the number provided to perform an indexed
  lookup in the character table. A Char.toChar() returns the argument
  untouched. The types Float and Double provide a toChar() function
  that first applies a toInt() and then performs the character table
  lookup. A string does not provide a conversion to a Char, but you can
  use a toCharArray() and then the index operator [] to access the
  array elements (e.g., "123".toCharArray()[0] gives '1').

- A Double or a Float is needed.

  - Byte, Short, Int, and Long: All these provide toFloat() and toDouble()
    functions that perform the obvious conversion.

  - Char: Characters have toFloat() and toDouble() functions as well, but
    those return the index in the character table converted to a floating-point
    number.

  - Float, Double: These provide toFloat() and toDouble() functions that
    perform a precision conversion if necessary.

  - String: This has toFloat() and toDouble() functions that try to parse the
    string provided to convert it to a Float or a Double. The String could use an
    English format floating-point number representation or scientific notation;
    for example, 27.48, -3.0, 1.8e4. This process will fail if the conversion is not
    possible. Variants toDoubleOrNull() and toFloatOrNull() will try the
    same conversion, but instead return null if a conversion error occurs.

  - Boolean: No conversion from a boolean to a floating-point number is
    possible.

- A String is needed.

  Any object in Kotlin provides a toString() conversion, which
  translates it to a human-readable representation. For integer
  numbers including characters, the conversion is obvious; for
  floating-point numbers the English format will be chosen; and
  booleans translate to true or false. The types Byte, Short, Int,
  and Long also have a toString(radix:Int) function that uses the
  provided numbering system (radix) for the conversion.

A couple of automatic conversions apply, so is it possible to write val l:Long = 7, which looks like an automatic Int to Long conversion.

Note As a rule of thumb during coding, you can test whether automatic conversions are possible, but in most cases it is better to explicitly declare the conversion.

In expressions where operators work, another kind of conversion rules applies. For any operator

$$a \circ b$$

where a is of type AType and b is of type BType, the operator implementation decides what the operation outcome type is. An important case is

```
[Number]    ∘    [Number]
```

where [Number] is out of Byte, Short, Int, Long, Float, or Double, and the operator is any numeric operator (+ - / * %). Here the type returned by the expression in most cases is the type with the higher precision. The precision ranking is Byte < Short < Int < Long < Float < Double. For example:

```
7 + 10_000_000_000L -> Long
34 + 46.7           -> Double
```

Another type of operator-induced conversion you'll see quite often in Kotlin programs is

```
String + [Any]
```

Here a concatenation of the string and the outcome of .toString() on [Any] will happen. For example:

```
"Number is "  +  7.3              ->    "Number is 7.3"
"Number is "  +  7.3.toString()   ->    "Number is 7.3"
"Hell" + 'o'                      ->    "Hello"
```

Comments in Kotlin Files

Comments in computer language files are text that does not belong to the computer language itself and thus have no influence over the program execution, but provide a textual description of elements and constructs used in the program. Comments help the reader to understand your program.

From a technical point of view comments are easy to generate and differentiate from the program syntax itself.

- Everything starting with a double slash // (not inside a string literal) to the end of the line is a comment.

- Everything starting with a /* and ending with a */ (both not inside a string literal) is a comment, no matter how many lines are spanned by this.

At first glance, comments might seem like a nice-to-have feature in programs, and adding or omitting them seems to be a personal decision of each developer. There is more to commenting, though. Looking a bit closer at the matter, comments are handled in the realm between two limits:

- *Writing no comments at all:* For short programs and those that are extremely well structured and self-explanatory, it is a valid, although arguable position to write no comments at all. The advantages of such an approach are obvious: You have to write less, there is no danger of confusing comments and source code, and following the approach properly will result in comprehensive code of high quality. There are disadvantages as well, though: You might be wrong in your assessment of whether your code is self-explanatory, tools depending on comments do not provide output, or your company's quality assurance guidelines might get violated.

© Peter Späth 2019
P. Späth, *Learn Kotlin for Android Development*, https://doi.org/10.1007/978-1-4842-4467-8_6

- *Verbose commenting:* On the other hand, if you verbosely comment each and every bit of your program, you will have to write a lot, and you might neglect code quality because ambiguous or confusing constructs in the program are clarified by the comments.

The best approach lies somewhere between these limits. As a rule of thumb, you should write comments for classes, interfaces, and singleton objects, explaining what they are good for, and you should comment public functions in them, including description of their parameters.

Note I owe you a confession here. The `NumberGuess` game app from the previous chapters did not contain any comments in the sources I provided. Comments were left out to keep the listings small, and the floating text around those listings serves as a substitute for the reader. After you've read this chapter, feel free to remedy this and add appropriate comments to the classes, interfaces, and singleton objects there.

In this chapter we cover exactly how comments should be added to Kotlin files, including what can be done with them.

Package Comments

We learned that packages correspond to files with a strong cohesion of their purpose and functioning. From a technical point of view, each package also corresponds to a directory in the operating system's file hierarchy.

It makes sense to describe packages through appropriate commenting, and the way we do this in Kotlin is as follows: For each package, that is to say inside each folder, create a file `package-info.md`. To do this inside Android Studio, you must switch to the Project Files view type in the project explorer (see Figure 6-1). Click the small gray downward-pointing rectangle next to Android to switch the view type. You can then right-click on one of the packages and from the shortcut menu select New ➤ File. Enter the complete file name `package-info.md`.

Files with the suffix `.md` are *Markdown* files. Markdown is a styling language similar to HTML, but with its own simplified syntax. We are going to describe Markdown soon, but first we must teach Android Studio how to handle Markdown files. To do so, double-click one of the new `package-info.md` files. The Studio opens the file in its standard text editor, but it displays a warning message on top of the edit pane, as shown in Figure 6-2.

Figure 6-1. *Project Files view*

Plugins supporting *.md files found.	Install plugins Ignore extension

```
1    package kotlinforandroid.book.numberguess
2
3    # Package org.jetbrains.kotlin.demo
```

Figure 6-2. *The Android Studio trying to open a Markdown file*

Click the Install plugins link. On the subsequent screens accept any license declaration, and if asked, select Use markdown support by JetBrains.

Inside each `package-info.md` file, let the first line read

```
# Package full.name.of.the.package
```

where for `full.name.of.the.package` you substitute the name of each package. The line starting with a single # actually stands for a level 1 heading.

The rest of the file contains Markdown styled text. For example, the `package-info.md` file inside the package `kotlinforandroid.book.numberguess.random` could read

```
# Package kotlinforandroid.book.numberguess.random

This package contains *interfaces* and *classes* for generating random numbers.

In your code you will write something like this:

    val rnd:RandomNumberGenerator = [ one of the 'impl' classes instantiated ]

For example,

    val rnd:RandomNumberGenerator = StdRandom()
    // or
    val rnd:RandomNumberGenerator = RandomRandom()
```

These `package-info.md` files and all the other documentation constructs we will talk about here then can be used to generate documentation for your project. During this process the *interface* will be translated to emphasized text, and passages with four spaces at the beginning of the line will have a code style format applied. Text inside backtick quotes (') will be marked as inline code. This particular Markdown file, for example, will be translated into a piece of documentation like the one shown in Figure 6-3. These and all the other standard Markdown syntax elements are described in the next section.

kotlinforandroid.book.numberguess.random

Package kotlinforandroid.book.numberguess.random

This package contains *interfaces* and *classes* for generating random numbers.

In your code you will write something like

```
val rnd:RandomNumberGenerator = [ one of the 'impl' classes instantiated ]
```

For example

```
val rnd:RandomNumberGenerator = StdRandom()
// or
val rnd:RandomNumberGenerator = RandomRandom()
```

Figure 6-3. *Translated Markdown code*

Markdown

Both Markdown files as used for package descriptions and inlined documentation inside your Kotlin code files use a common syntax for styling issues. These Markdown syntax elements are described in Table 6-1.

Table 6-1. *Markdown Syntax*

Style	Markdown Syntax	Hints
Heading Level 1	`# Heading`	The `package-info.md` file must not contain more than one level 1 heading. You can add a # at the end of the header line.

Heading Level 2–6	`## Heading`
	`### Heading`
	...
		The number of # determines the level. You can improve readability by appending the same number of # at the end of the header.

Unordered List	`- Item1`
	`- Item2`
	...
		You could also use + or * as an item indicator.

Ordered List	`1. Item1`
	`2. Item2`
	...
		The consecutive numbering will be assured automatically, so you could write any number (write always "1." or whatever).

(*continued*)

Table 6-1. (*continued*)

Style	Markdown Syntax	Hints
Emphasis	*some text* or _some text_	If you need an asterisk (*) or underscore (_) in your text, write * or _.
Strong Emphasis	**some text** or _ _some text_ _	If you need an asterisk (*) or underscore (_) in your text, write * or _.
Block Quote	> some text	You can increase the level by using more > characters at the line beginnings. Block quotes can contain other Markdown elements.
Paragraph Delimiter	<empty line>	A line break at the end of some text will not end a paragraph.
Link	See below	—
Inlined Code	'some text' (backticks)	If you need a backtick (') in your text, write \'.
Block Code	⊔⊔⊔⊔ code line 1 ⊔⊔⊔⊔ code line 2 ...	This must be surrounded by empty lines. ⊔ is a space character (you could also use one tab character instead).
Rules	- - - * * *	You can also use more of these, and use space characters as delimiters.
Escapes	Prepend a "\"	Use this to avoid characters doing something special, as described earlier in the table. Eligible characters are \ * _ [ ] ( ) # + - . ! '

You have several options for inserting links. First you can create an inlined link as follows:

```
[link text](link-URL)
or
[link text](link-URL "Title")
```

where the optional "Title" goes to the title attribute in case the documentation gets transformed to HTML. Then the title attribute, for example, gets shown to the user once the mouse hovers over the link (this behavior depends on the browser used). Here is an example for such an inlined link:

```
Find the link here:
[Link](http://www.example.com/somePage.html "Page")
```

Reference links use a reference ID so you can refer to the same link several times in a text. The syntax is

```
[link text][link ID]
```

where the link ID can contain letters, spaces, numbers, and punctuation, but is otherwise case insensitive. Somewhere else in the text the link definition itself needs to be provided, on a line on its own:

```
[link ID]: link-URL
or
[link ID]: link-URL "Title"
```

For long URLs or long titles, the optional "Title" can also be put in the next line. Note that the link definitions do not produce any output, they just make the text in the Markdown file easier to read.

As an abbreviation the link text can serve as both the text and the ID, if you write

```
[link text][]
```

and for the definition

```
[link text]: link-URL
or
[link text]: link-URL "Title"
```

If you don't need a link text but just want to tell the URL, you should convert the links to *automatic* links by surrounding them with angle brackets as in <http://www.apress.com>. The URL then gets printed as is, but is clickable in addition.

As an extension to links as just described, you can refer to classes, properties, and methods as if they were implicit links:

```
[com.example.TheClass]
[com.example.TheClass.property]
[com.example.TheClass.method]
```

You can do this the same way for interfaces and singleton objects. If you want to provide your own link text, write this:

```
[link text][com.example.TheClass]
[link text][com.example.TheClass.property]
[link text][com.example.TheClass.method]
```

If the element being documented might address classes, interfaces, or singleton objects by their simple name because they have been imported, the package specifier can be omitted and you can directly write [TheClass], [TheClass.property], and [TheClass.method].

Class Comments

We know that multiline comments can be written as /* ... */. As a slight modification, for documenting code elements the convention is to add another asterisk (*) to the left comment bracket: /** ... */, and in addition every line inside the comments is supposed to start with an asterisk as shown here:

```
/**
 *The comment ...
 * ...
 */
```

This is still a multiline comment that happens to start with an asterisk, but the tool that knows how to extract the documentation from the code recognizes this as something that needs to be handled. You can still use normal multiline comments /* ... */ at will, but the documentation tool will just ignore them.

Class comments are written just in front of the class ... declaration, as such an adapted multiline comment /** ... */. The content of the class description comment is Markdown code, as described earlier.

The first paragraph of such documentation should provide a short summary, as tools might use it for listings. In addition to standard Markdown elements, in the documentation you can add elements as follows:

- @param <name> description: Describes a type parameter <name> of the class. Class type parameters are described later in the book. You can also write @param[name] description.

- `@constructor description`: Describes the primary constructor of a class.

- `@property <name> description`: Describes a parameter of the primary constructor.

- `@sample <specifier>`: Inserts the specified function's code.

- `@see <specifier>`: Adds a link to the specified identifier (a class, interface, singleton object, property, or method).

- `@author description`: Adds authoring information.

- `@since description`: Adds information about how long the documented element has existed (version info, etc.).

- `@suppress`: Excludes the class, interface, or singleton object from the documentation.

An example of documentation for class `MainActivity` of the `NumberGuess` game reads like this:

```
/**
 * The main activity class of the NumberGuess game app.
 * Extends from the
 * [android.support.v7.app.AppCompatActivity]
 * class and is thus compatible with earlier
 * Android versions.
 *
 * The app shows a GUI with the following buttons:
 * - **Start**: Starts the game
 * - **Do Guess**: Used for guessing a number
 *
 * Once started, the game secretly determines a random
 * number the user has to guess. The user performs
 * guesses and gets told if the guessed number is too
 * low, too high, or a hit.
 *
 * Once hit, the game is over.
 *
```

```
 * @see Constants
*
 * @author Peter Späth
 * @since 1.0
 */
class MainActivity : AppCompatActivity() {
    ...
}
```

The corresponding output, once converted by a documentation tool, would look like Figure 6-4.

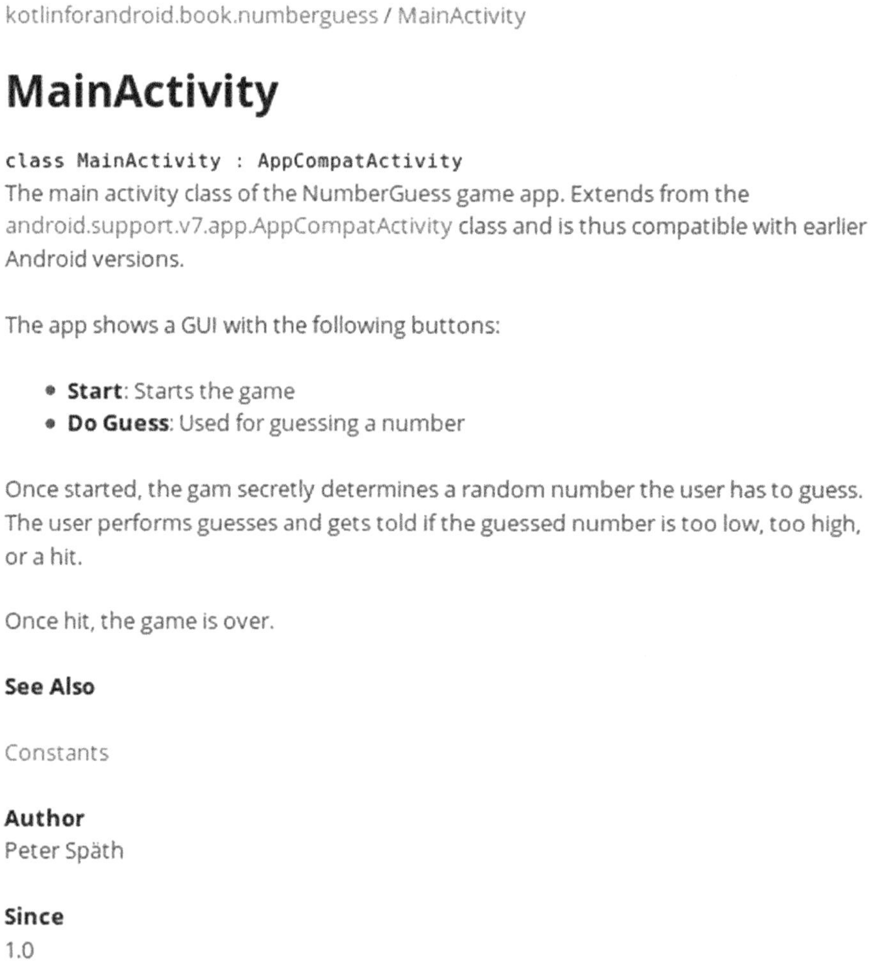

kotlinforandroid.book.numberguess / MainActivity

MainActivity

```
class MainActivity : AppCompatActivity
```
The main activity class of the NumberGuess game app. Extends from the android.support.v7.app.AppCompatActivity class and is thus compatible with earlier Android versions.

The app shows a GUI with the following buttons:

- **Start**: Starts the game
- **Do Guess**: Used for guessing a number

Once started, the gam secretly determines a random number the user has to guess. The user performs guesses and gets told if the guessed number is too low, too high, or a hit.

Once hit, the game is over.

See Also

Constants

Author
Peter Späth

Since
1.0

Figure 6-4. *Documentation for the NumberGuess activity*

Function and Property Comments

For functions and properties, you basically do the same as for classes. Just add /** ... */ in front of any function or property you want to comment. As for class documentation, you start each line with any number of spaces and an asterisk. Inside use Markdown code again. For example:

```
...
class SomeClass {
    /**
    * This describes property prop
    * ...
    */
    val prop:Int = 7

    /**
     * This describes function func
     * ...
     */
    fun func() {
        ...
    }
}
```

As for classes, interfaces, and singleton objects, the first paragraph of such documentation should provide a short summary, as tools might use it for listings.

For properties, there are a couple of additional elements you can use:

- @sample <specifier>: Inserts the specified function's code.

- @see <specifier>: Adds a link to the specified identifier (a class, interface, singleton object, property, or method).

- @author description: Adds authoring information.

- @since description: Adds information about how long the documented element has existed (version info, etc.).

- @suppress: Excludes the property from the documentation.

Function documentation snippets should also describe the function's parameters and return values. In detail, here are all the documentation elements for functions.

- `@param <name> description`: Describes a function parameter.

- `@return description`: Describes what the function returns.

- `@receiver description`: Describes the receiver of an extension function.

- `@throws <specifier>`: Indicates that the function might throw the exception designated by the specifier. We cover exceptions later in the book.

- `@exception <specifier>`: Same as `@throws`.

- `@sample <specifier>`: Inserts the specified function's code.

- `@see <specifier>`: Adds a link to the specified identifier (a class, interface, singleton object, property, or method).

- `@author description`: Adds authoring information.

- `@since description`: Adds information about how long the documented element has existed (version info, etc.).

- `@suppress`: Excludes the property from the documentation.

Exercise 1

Add comments to all packages, classes, and public functions of the `NumberGuess` game app.

Generate Your Own API Documentation

With all elements of a program properly documented, we now need to find a way to extract the documentation for creating, for example, a collection of interlinked HTML documents. The generated documentation should describe all classes, interfaces, and singleton objects, as well as all public methods and properties. Because these elements are enough for a client software to know how to interact with your program, such documentation is commonly referred to as *application programming interface (API) documentation.*

Dokka is a tool Kotlin can use to create exactly this kind of API documentation. To install Dokka, open Android Studio. Inside the Gradle Scripts drawer (you might need to switch back to the Android view type), there are two files named `build.gradle`, one labeled Project NumberGuess and one labeled Module: app (see Figure 6-5). Those two build files are responsible for describing how the app is to be built to run correctly. This includes declaring libraries that need to be made available to your program.

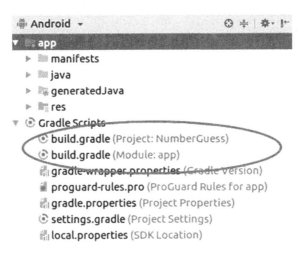

Figure 6-5. *Build scripts*

Note   The term *library* commonly refers to programs built by others, from which parts get used by your app to perform certain tasks. You'll very often add libraries to your projects so you can benefit from the work others have made available to the public.

Open the Project `build.gradle` and add the following line right under `buildscript {`:

```
ext.dokka_version = '0.9.17'
```

In the same file, inside the `dependencies` block also add (one line):

```
classpath "org.jetbrains.dokka:
        dokka-android-gradle-plugin:${dokka_version}"
```

This ensures the Dokka library gets added to the project.

Now open the Module `build.gradle` and underneath all the other apply plugin lines, add

```
apply plugin: 'org.jetbrains.dokka-android'
```

Inside the same file, add this at the bottom:

```
task myDokka(type: org.jetbrains.dokka.gradle.
   DokkaAndroidTask) {
    outputFormat = 'html'
    outputDirectory = "dokka"
    includes = ['packages.md']
    doFirst {
        // build the packages.md file
        def pckg = new File(projectDir.absolutePath +
            File.separator + "packages.md")
        pckg.text = ""
        def s = ""
        projectDir.eachFileRecurse(
              groovy.io.FileType.FILES) { f ->
            if(f.name == 'package-info.md') {
                s += "\n" + f.text
            }
        }
        pckg.text = s
    }
}
```

This configures Dokka and adds a preparation step.

Note   Dokka by default doesn't know how to handle our `package-info.md` files. It instead expects a single file `packages.md`. The preparation step gathers all `package- info.md` files and builds a `packages.md` file. By the way, this little script is written in Groovy, the language on which the Gradle build system relies.

Now to actually perform the documentation generation, open the Gradle tab at the very right edge of the window, then navigate to NumberGuess: ➤ NumberGuess ➤ Tasks ➤ Documentation. Double-click myDokka (see Figure 6-6).

Figure 6-6. *Dokka build task*

You'll now find the API documentation as a collection of interlinked HTML files inside the folder dokka (switch to the Project Files view type to see it inside Android Studio).

CHAPTER 7

Structural Constructs

From the very beginning of computer languages, conditional branching of the program flow has been one of the most basic things program code must be able to express. This branching happens inside functions, so it imposes some kind of substructuring inside classes and singleton objects. In this chapter we cover such branching constructs, together with auxiliary classes that help us write corresponding code.

Ifs and Whens

In real life many actions are based on decisions. If some condition is met, an action A happens; otherwise, action B happens. For any programming language we need something similar, and the most basic way of creating such a branching of the program flow is the venerable if-else if-else construct. You check some condition, and if it is met, the if branch gets executed. If not, optionally you check another else if condition, and if this one is met, the corresponding branch is executed. After potentially more else if clauses, a final else block gets executed if none of the if and else if checks yield true.

In Kotlin, of course, we have such an if-else if-else program construct, which reads

```
if( [condition] ) {
    [statements1]
} else if( [condition2] ) {
    [statements2]
} else if( [condition3] ) {
    [statements3]
... more "else ifs"
} else {
    [statementsElse]
}
```

© Peter Späth 2019
P. Späth, *Learn Kotlin for Android Development*, https://doi.org/10.1007/978-1-4842-4467-8_7

where all the else if and else clauses are optional and each condition must evaluate to a boolean value. How you calculate this value is up to you: It could be a constant, a variable, or a complex expression. As an example, consider a check to determine whether some variable v equals a particular constant, and if so, call some function abc1(). If not, call function abc2() instead. The code reads:

```
if( v == 7 ) {
    abc1()
} else {
    abc2()
}
```

Where blocks contain only one statement, you can omit the curly brackets and even the line break, so

```
if( v == 7) abc1() else abc2()
```

on one line is valid code.

As a specialty and similar to most other constructs in Kotlin, such a conditional construct can have a value and thus can be used inside expressions. For this to work, the last line of all the *statement* blocks must evaluate to corresponding data.

```
val x = if( [condition] ) {
    [statements1]
    [value1]
} else if( [condition2] ) {
    [statements2]
    [value2]
} else if( [condition3] ) {
    [statements3]
... more "else ifs"
} else {
    [statementsElse]
    [valueElse]
}
```

This time the else clause is not optional; otherwise the result of the complete construct was undefined if there was no else value. Needless to say, all the values at the end of the blocks must have the same desired type for this construct to work.

Similar to the nonexpression variant, if there are no statements in the block the brackets and newlines can be omitted, so this is a valid statement:

```
val x = if( a > 3 ) 27 else 28
```

A large conditional branching construct with lots of else if clauses is rather clumsy. That is why there is another more concise construct, which reads as follows:

```
when( [expression] ) {
    val1 -> { ... }
    val2 -> { ... }
    ...
    else -> { ... }
}
```

where the branches { ... } get executed when [expression] yields the value in front of the ->. This one also can evaluate to a value:

```
val x = when( [expression] ) {
    val1 -> { ... }
    val2 -> { ... }
    ...
    else -> { ... }
}
```

where the last element in each { ... } will be used as a value to return in case the corresponding check matches.

To avoid repetition of code blocks, you can also define evaluation groups as in

```
when( [expression] ) {
    val1      -> { ... }
    val2,val3 -> { ... }
    ...
    else -> { ... }
}
```

This also works for the value-yielding variant.

For the values on the left side of the -> you can use arbitrary expressions including function calls:

```
val x = when( [expression] ) {
    calc(val1) + 7 -> { ... }
    val2,val3       -> { ... }
    ...
    else            -> { ... }
}
```

In addition, we can use a special in operator or its negation counterpart !in for inclusion checks:

```
val l = listOf(...)
val x = when( [expression] ) {
    in l          -> { ... }
    in 27..53     -> { ... }
    !in 100..110 -> { ... }
    ...
    else          -> { ... }
}
```

which also works for arrays. The 27..53 and 100..110 define *ranges,* which means they represent the given limits and all values in between. We discuss ranges in more detail in the following section.

Another check that comes in handy is a special is operator that performs a type check:

```
val q:Any = ... // any type
val x = when(q) {
    is Int      -> { ... }
    is String   -> { ... }
    ...
    else        -> { ... }
}
```

There is also a negation variant of is: Not surprisingly, it reads !is.

Once again, for one-line blocks the brackets can be omitted, as shown here:

```
val q = ... // some Int
val x = when( q ){ 1 -> "Jean" 2 -> "Sam" else -> "" }
```

If you need the [expression] from inside when(...) for evaluations inside the inner blocks, it is possible to capture it:

```
val x = when(val q = [some value]) {
    1 -> q * 3
    2 -> q * 4
    ...
    else -> 0
}
```

where the capturing variable is valid only inside the when block.

Ranges

Ranges frequently get used for looping needs. We discuss looping in the next section, so consider this section a preparatory step. A range is defined by two bound values and the way values in between get interpolated.

In Kotlin there are three types of ranges for Int, Long, and Char types. Using the constructors, they can be built as follows:

```
val r1 = IntRange(1, 1000)
val r2 = LongRange(1, 10_000_000_000)
val r3 = CharRange('A', 'I')
```

In addition, to achieve the same you can use the range operator .. as follows:

```
val r1 = 1..1000
val r2 = 1L..10_000_000_000L
val r3 = 'A'..'I'
```

Finally, a couple of Kotlin standard library functions return ranges or act on ranges. Any integral type (i.e., Byte, Short, Int, Long, and Char) has a rangeTo() function to create a range from it. A 7..77 can therefore also be built by writing 7.rangeTo(77).

Ranges also have a `step` property that defines how values get interpolated between the range bounds. As a default, the step is +1, but you can adjust it as follows:

```
1..1000 step 5
(1..1000 step 5).reversed()
```

where the `reversed()` from the last line exchanges bounds and negates the step. Note that by language design, explicitly specifying a negative step is not allowed. It is, however, allowable to use the `downTo` operator:

```
1000 downTo 1 step 5
```

Ranges indicate the first and the last value if you use the `first` or `last` property:

```
(1..1000 step 5).first          // -> 1
(1..1000 step 5).last           // -> 996
(1000 downTo 1 step 5).first    // -> 1000
(1000 downTo 1 step 5).last     // -> 5
```

For and While Loops

A loop corresponds to a program part iterated over and over multiple times. One possibility for such a loop is a `for` loop, which reads as follows:

```
for( i in [loop data] ) {
    // do something with i
}
```

where `[loop data]` is a range, a collection, an array, or any other object that has a function `iterator()` returning an object that has a `next():E` and a `hasNext():Boolean` function (E is the loop variable type). In the latter case all three functions, `iterator()`, `next()`, and `hasNext()`, must be marked with `operator`.

Similar to `for` loops are `while` and `do .. while` loops, which continue to loop until some condition yields `false`:

```
while( [condition] ) {
    // do something
}
```

```
do {
    // do something
} while( [condition] )
```

where in the first case the condition is checked at the very beginning, and in the second case at the end of any iteration (including the first).

Both for and while loops can be primordially exited by using break in the inner program flow. Likewise, using a continue statement anywhere inside the loop forces the next iteration, neglecting anything behind the continue:

```
while( [condition] ) {
    ...
    break // -> exit loop
    ...
    continue // -> next iteration
    ...
}
```

or similarly for for and do .. while loops.

Note   For and while loops are now considered quite old school. Using forEach() on collections gives more power over loop preparation actions like transformation and filtering, so prefer forEach() over for and while. We talk a lot about collections and iterating over collection data in a later chapter.

Scoping Functions

A couple of Kotlin's standard library functions are extremely powerful when it comes to expressiveness of your code. Five of them—apply, let, also, run, and with—are called *scoping functions* because they open a new scope inside a function and thus improve program flow structuring. Let's see what they do and how they help us to write better code.

Note   By the way, if you need a mnemonic to memorize them, read "LET us ALSO RUN WITH APPLY."

The apply Function

Let us look at the first one of these scoping functions, apply. You can hang this at any object, as in

```
object.apply {
    ...
}
```

That doesn't look too adventurous, but the magic is what happens to the object instance inside the curly brackets of apply: It gets transported to this. In addition, apply automatically returns the object instance. Therefore if we write this.someProperty or someProperty, or this.someFunction() alias someFunction(), it refers to the object in front of apply, not to the surrounding context. What does that mean? Well, consider this:

```
class A { var x:Int, var y:Int }
val instance = A()
instance.x = 4
instance.y = 5
instance.y *= instance.x
```

If we now write .apply{ ... } right behind the initialized object, we can use this to access the instance and get

```
class A { var x:Int, var y:Int }
val instance = A().apply{
    this.x = 4
    this.y = 5
    this.y *= this.x
}
```

which can be shortened further, as this. can be omitted:

```
class A { var x:Int, var y:Int }
val instance = A().apply{
    x = 4
    y = 5
    y *= x
}
```

Note   Because propertyName and functionName() target the this instance, we can also say that this represents the *receiver* of such simple property and function accesses. Without a scoping function, this refers to the surrounding class instance or singleton object. With this redefined inside apply{ ... } the instance in front of .apply becomes the new receiver.

If a property or function identifier used inside the apply{} construct does not exist in the receiver object, the surrounding context gets used instead:

```
var q = 37
class A { var x:Int, var y:Int }
val instance = A().apply {
    x = 4
    y = 5
    q = 44 // does not exist in A, so the q from
           // outside gets used
}
```

This strong coupling of the object the apply{ ... } gets operated at, and the this scope functions and properties inside the curly brackets being received by the same object, makes the apply{} construct an extremely good candidate for preparing objects right after their instantiation:

```
val x = SomeClass().apply {
    // do things with the SomeClass instance
    // while assigning it to x
}
```

The this from the surrounding context (class or singleton object) is not lost. If you need it inside apply{}, you can get it by adding a qualifier @Class, as in

```
class A {
    fun goA() { ... }
    ...
    val x = SomeClass().apply {
        this.x = ...      // -> SomeClass.x
        x = ...           // -> SomeClass.x
        this@A.goA()      // -> A.goA()
        ...
    }
}
```

The let Function

The let scoping function frequently gets used to transform an object into a different object. Its complete synopsis reads like this:

```
object.let { o ->
    [statements] // do s.th. with 'o'
    [value]
}
```

The last line must contain the expression that let{} is supposed to return. The let{} construct has a function as a parameter, and if you write it as shown here and using an anonymous *lambda* function with o as a parameter, this parameter function gets the object itself as a parameter. You can also omit the o ->, in which case a special variable it automatically gets used instead:

```
object.let {
    [statements] // do s.th. with 'it'
    [value]
}
```

Note   Writing let { } without a x -> inside the curly brackets looks as if the { } was a function block. This is a syntactical coincidence; in fact, it is an anonymous lambda function with the automatic variable it as the parameter.

Functions with other functions as parameters are called *higher order functions.* We cover higher order functions in Chapter 12.

As an easy example, we take a string and use let{} to append a line break "\n" to it:

```
val s = "Hello World"
val s2 = s.let { it + "\n" }
// or    s.let { string -> string + "\n" }
```

The with Function

The with scoping function is the brother of apply{ ... }. The difference is it just gets the object or value to convert to a receiver as a parameter:

```
val o = ... // some value
with(o){
    // o is now "this"
    ...
}
```

The with function is frequently used to avoid repeatedly writing the object to act on, as in

```
with(object){ f1(37)
    f1(12)
    fx("Hello")
}
```

instead of

```
object.f1(37)
object.f1(12)
object.fx("Hello")
```

The also Function

The `also` scoping function is related to the `apply{ ... }` function, but does not redefine `this`. Instead it provides the object or value in front of `also` as a parameter to the lambda function parameter:

```
object.also { obj ->
    // 'obj' is object
    ...
}
```

or

```
object.also {
    // 'it' is object
    ...
}
```

You use `also{ }` for cross-cutting concerns, which means you do not alter the object (this is what `apply{ ... }` is for), but perform actions that are not primarily related to the current program flow. Performing caching, logging, authentication, or registering the object in some registry object are suitable examples.

The run Function

The `run` scoping function is similar to the `apply{ ... }` function. However, it does not return the receiver object, but instead returns the value of the last statement:

```
val s = "Hello"
val x = s.run {
    // 'this' is 's'
    ...
    [value]
}
// x now has [value]
```

You can see run{ ... } as a general-purpose "do something with an object" bracket. One prominent use case, though, consists of acting on an object only if it is not null. Instead of

```
var v:String? = ...
...
if(v != null) {
    ...
}
```

you can write

```
var v:String? = ...
...
v?.run {
    ...
}
```

Remember that a ?. accesses a property or invokes a function only if the object in front of it is not null. The more concise latter variant might be more readable in some cases.

Conditional Execution

A construct that allows us to write a conditional branching as an instance function reads as follows:

```
someInstance.takeIf { [boolean_expression] }?.run {
    // do something
}
```

Here inside the boolean expression you can use it to refer to someInstance. The takeIf() function returns the receiver (here someInstance) if the boolean expression evaluates to true; otherwise it returns null. This works for any object.

Exceptions: If Something Goes Wrong

For very simple programs it is probably easy to make sure all program parts do exactly what they are supposed to. For programs with a higher level of complexity, those built by many developers, or those that use external programs (libraries), the situation is not that clear. Problems will arise, for example, if lists or arrays get addressed out of bounds, some I/O access to files or network data streams fails, or objects end up in an unanticipated or corrupted state.

This is what *exceptions* are for. Exceptions are objects that get created or *thrown* if something unanticipated and possibly malicious happens. Special program parts can then receive such exception objects and act appropriately.

Kotlin and Exceptions

Kotlin has a rather liberal way of treating exceptional states, but Android does not. If you don't care about exceptions in your app and any program part happens to throw an exception, Android will soberly tell you the app crashed. You can prevent that by putting suspicious program parts into a try-catch block:

```
try {
    // ... statements
} catch(e:Exception) {
    // do something
}
```

or

© Peter Späth 2019
P. Späth, *Learn Kotlin for Android Development*, https://doi.org/10.1007/978-1-4842-4467-8_8

```
try {
    // ... statements
} catch(e:Exception) {
    // do something...
} finally {
    // do this by any means: ...
}
```

In both cases, the construct gets called catching an exception. The optional *finally block* gets executed at the end of the construct, regardless of whether or not an exception got caught. You usually use it to clean up any mess the code inside try { } might have caused, including closing any open file or network resources and similar operations.

Note   As a rule of thumb, using many try-catch clauses in your code hardly increases code quality. Don't do that. Having a few of them at central places of your app usually is a good idea, though.

Once an exception occurs inside the try{ } block—and this includes any method calls from there—the program flow immediately branches to the catch{ } block. What exactly should happen there is a question that is difficult to answer, especially in an Android environment. While you develop an app, writing logging entries certainly is a good idea. This is not part of the Kotlin standard library, but Android provides a singleton object android.util.Log you can use to write logs:

```
import android.util.Log
...
try {
    // ... statements
} catch(e:Exception) {
    Log.e("LOG", "Some exception occurred", e)
}
```

where instead of the logging text shown here you could, of course, write some more specific information.

Note   If you look at the `android.util.Log` class, you can see this is a Java class and function `e()` is a *static* function not requiring an instance. Thus it is not a singleton object in the strict sense, but from a Kotlin perspective you treat it as if it were a singleton object.

While developing an app you can see the logging statements on the Logcat tab, provided you are using an emulator or a connected hardware device with debugging switched on. Using the `e()` function from the Log class provides the advantage that you get a *stack trace*, which means line numbers get indicated and the function calls leading to the erroneous program part get listed. Figure 8-1 shows an example.

Figure 8-1. *Exception logging in Android Studio*

For your end users, providing logging this way is not an option, as in the vast majority of cases your users wouldn't know how to inspect logging files. What you can do instead is present a short error message in the form of a `Toast`, as follows:

```
import android.util.Log
...
try {
    // ... statements
} catch(e:Exception) {
    Log.e("LOG", "Some exception occurred", e)
    Toast.makeText(this,"Error Code 36A",
          Toast.LENGTH_LONG).show()
}
```

What exactly you present to your users depends, of course, on the severity of the exception. Maybe you can somehow clean up the erroneous state and continue with the normal program flow. In really severe cases, you can show an error message dialog box or branch to an error-handling activity.

More Exception Types

The `Exception` class we've seen so far is just one kind of exception. If we use `Exception` in a `catch` statement, we formally express a very general kind of exception. Depending on the circumstances, your app might coexist very well with try-catch clauses using only `Exception` for its exception cases. There are, however, many subclasses of `Exception` you can use as well. There is, for example, an `ArrayIndexOutOfBounds` exception, an `IllegalArgumentException`, an `IllegalStateException`, and many more. You can even use several at once by adding more `catch{ }` clauses:

```
try {
    // ... statements
} catch(e:ExceptionType1) {
    // do something...
} catch(e:ExceptionType2) {
    // do something...
... possibly more catch statements
```

```
} finally {
    // do this by any means: ...
}
```

If an exception gets thrown inside `try{ }`, all the `catch` clauses get checked one after another, and if one of the declared exceptions matches, the corresponding `catch` clause gets executed. What you usually do if you want to catch several exceptions is to put the more specific catches at the beginning of the list and the most general at the end. For example, say you have some code that accesses files, handles arrays, and in addition might throw unknown exceptions. Here you'd write

```
try {
    // ... file access
    // ... array access
} catch(e:IOException) {
    // do something...
} catch(e:ArrayIndexOutOfBoundsException) {
    // do something...
} catch(e:Exception) {
    // do something...
} finally {
    // do this by any means: ...
}
```

where the `finally` clause is optional, as usual.

Throwing Exceptions Yourself

To throw exceptions from your code you write

```
throw exceptionInstance
```

where `exceptionInstance` is the instance of an exception class, as for example in

```
val exc = Exception("The exception message")
throw exc
```

or

```
throw Exception("The exception message")
```

Because exceptions are normal classes, except for their usability in catch clauses, you can also define your own exceptions. Just extend the Exception class or any of its subclasses:

```
class MyException(msg:String) : Exception(msg)
...
try {
    ...
    throw MyException("an error occurred")
    ...
} catch(e:MyException) {
    ...
}
```

Exercise 1

In the NumberGuess game app, define a new class GameException as an extension of Exception. Check the numbers the user inputs and if the minimum or maximum guessable numbers are exceeded, throw a GameException. Catch the new exception inside the guess() function and possibly show a Toast message. Hint: Use if (num. text.toString().toInt() < Constants.LOWER_BOUND) throw ... and if (num. text.toString().toInt() > Constants.UPPER_BOUND) throw ... for the checks.

Exceptions in Expressions

One interesting feature of Kotlin is that you can use try-catch blocks and throw statements in expressions. The outcome of a try-catch block is the value of the last line inside the try{ } or the catch(...){ } block, depending on whether the exception got caught or not. You can use this for default values if something goes wrong, for example. In

```
val x = try{ arr[ind] }
      catch(e:ArrayIndexOutOfBoundsException) { -1 }
```

for some IntArray named arr, the variable x will get a default value −1 if the array bound limits get violated.

Caution   Be careful not to abuse try-catch blocks for somewhat exceptional but otherwise expected program flow paths. You should really use exceptions only for unanticipated problems.

A throw someException has a value, too. It is of type Nothing and in the Kotlin type hierarchy is a subclass of everything. It is thus possible to write

```
val v = map[someKey] ?: throw Exception("no such key in the map")
```

Note that the operator ?: (sometimes called the *Elvis operator*) evaluates to the right side only if the left side yields null; otherwise it takes the left side. Here this means that if map[someKey] evaluates to null, equivalent to the map not having this key, the exception is thrown.

Data Containers

Nature and human civilization are about collections. Families collect relatives, cities collect people acting together, houses collect people and their belongings, math set theory uses collections for relation formulas, galaxies collect stars, atoms collect elementary particles, and so on. It is thus no surprise that computer languages, intended to model real-world scenarios, must be able to model collections as well.

In the real world this is not such a big topic, but computers from the very beginning have drawn a sharp distinction between fixed-size collections and variable-size collections. Fixed-size collections are easier to handle and show high performance, whereas variable-size collections are slower, but show greater flexibility and according to the circumstances could exhibit a lower memory footprint. Both options are needed for various collection-related tasks, so a developer has to learn how to handle both worlds. To make the difference clearer, fixed-size collections are called *arrays*, and for variable-size collections the term used is *collection*.

The built-in libraries of Kotlin contain several functions to mediate between arrays and collections, and to make a developer's life a little bit easier Kotlin also tries to unify the handling of arrays and collections, so the switching between the two worlds is easier to achieve. In the following section we first talk about arrays, as they came first in computer language history, and later switch to collections.

Defining and Using Arrays

Arrays are fixed-size containers for elements, which could be objects or primitive data types. We know a lot about objects by now, but we haven't talked much about primitive data types yet. From the Kotlin point of view, it would be preferable to not have this distinction at all, dealing with objects and nothing else.

© Peter Späth 2019
P. Späth, *Learn Kotlin for Android Development*, https://doi.org/10.1007/978-1-4842-4467-8_9

So why is there something like primitive data types, what exactly are they, and why do we need to use them? The answer is that primitive data types have a *direct* representation on the computer hardware. Thus we neither need to perform instantiations of objects before we can put them into the array, nor do we need to use some kind of a reference to connect array elements to instances (see Figure 9-1).

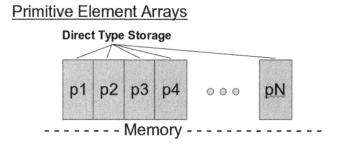

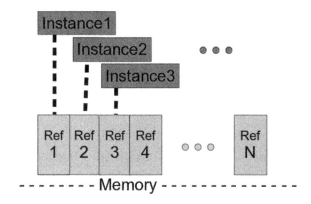

Figure 9-1. *Primitive versus object arrays*

Object arrays get types declared in Kotlin by the string `Array` followed by the element type in angle brackets:

```
Array<ElementType>
```

where ElementType could be any class or interface. Those are then normal types treated as any other type in Kotlin, so you can have vars and vals using them, for example

```kotlin
val someStringArray:Array<String> = ...
var someObjectArray:Array<Any> = ...
```

Note   Any sits on the very top of Kotlin's type hierarchy, and any object implicitly and automatically inherits from it. Therefore any object, no matter how you declared it, automatically also is an instance of Any.

Angle brackets declare a *generic* type. We cover generics later in the book.

Primitive element arrays exist for the following element types: Boolean, Byte, Char, Double, Float, Int, Long, and Short. For the corresponding array types, use any of those and add Array, as in

```kotlin
val byteArr:ByteArray = ...
var intArr:IntArray = ...
...
```

To access array elements, use array[index] where index ranges from 0 to the array length diminished by one. The length itself is given by property size, and the last index by property lastIndex. You can read array elements as in val elem1 = array[0] and write array elements as in array[77] = ... If while accessing array elements you try to address an element that is outside the bounds, your app will crash, so you must take precautions to ensure index limits are not exceeded.

Array Instantiation

Now that we know how to declare arrays, we need to now how to create or instantiate them. This is the right side of val arr:IntArray = ... and alike.

First, we can use the constructors Kotlin provides for the arrays. This is the case for both arrays with object element types, and the specialized primitive element arrays. The first set of constructors allows instantiating primitive element arrays with a specified number of elements (as an example, we give all of them size 7):

```kotlin
val byteArr:ByteArray = ByteArray(7)
val shortArr:ShortArray = ShortArray(7)
val intArr:IntArray = IntArray(7)
val longArr:LongArray = LongArray(7)
val doubleArr:DoubleArray = DoubleArray(7)
val floatArr:FloatArray = FloatArray(7)
val booleanArr:BooleanArray = BooleanArray(7)
```

The elements of these arrays all are initialized with the default values 0 for number types and `false` for the boolean array.

A different set of constructors allows us to set individual array members. All you have to do is add a function as a second parameter to any of the constructors. How can a function be a constructor parameter, though? This is one of the features Kotlin, among other computer languages, has to offer: to treat functions as objects you can pass around in function calls and even let properties point to them. We cover such aspects in detail in Chapter 12. What we need for the moment is a so-called *lambda function* without a function name. Such a lambda function looks like this:

```
{ i ->
    [ program code ]
    [ expression ]
}
```

where `i` is a parameter set to the index inside the array. Using `i` is just an example; you can choose a different name like `ind`, `index`, or whatever you like. The last line `[expression]` must evaluate to a value of the type declared for the array elements. What you do before this last expression statement, though, is up to you. As `[program code]` you can write anything, including using the index parameter. Say, for example, we want to create an `IntArray` of size 10, with the array elements containing the squared index, counting from one: 1, 2, 4, 9, 16, ... We don't need a [program code] here, but the [expression] will be (i + 1) * (i + 1) (remember i as an index will start at 0). The lambda function then reads

```
{ i -> (i+1) * (i+1) }
```

and the complete array declaration and initialization is

```
val arr = IntArray(10, { i -> (i+1) * (i+1) })
```

With the initialization function added we can now also use a constructor for generating object arrays, as in

```
val objArr:Array<SomeType> =
    Array<SomeType>(7, { i -> ... })
```

where for SomeType you substitute an existing class.

Exercise 1

Define and initialize an IntArray with elements 100, 99, 98, ..., 0. Assign it to a val arr.

There is a different way of initializing arrays if we have a known set of initial member values. If, for example, we have five people at hand with ages 26, 56, 12, 17, and 26, and want to put that into an IntArray, there is no elegant way to use a constructor for that aim. Of course, we could write

```
val ages = IntArray(5)
ages[0] = 26
ages[1] = 56
ages[2] = 12
ages[3] = 17
ages[4] = 26
```

but that looks rather lengthy. Kotlin helps us to write that in a shorter form. Inside its *standard library* it contains a couple of functions to create arrays given the element values. For IntArrays this function reads intArrayOf(...) and because it allows for any number of arguments we can write

```
val ages = intArrayOf(26, 56, 12, 17, 26)
```

which looks much more concise. There are accordingly named array initialization functions for all the array types, and you can use them anywhere in your code: `intArrayOf()`, `longArrayOf()`, `doubleArrayOf()`, and so on.

There are also two special array creation functions. The first one creates an array of `null` object references, and you write

```
val size = ...
val arr:Array<ElementType?> = arrayOfNulls(size)
```

to use it (replace `ElementType` with the actual element class you need). The other one creates an empty array of object references:

```
val arr:Array<ElementType?> = emptyArray()
```

Last but not least, collections like sets and lists (we describe them later) can be converted to arrays:

- `coll.toTypedArray(): Array<ElementType>`

  This converts a collection with element type `ElementType` to an array of objects. It never returns a primitive element array.

- `coll.toXXXArray(): XXXArray`

  This converts a collection with element type XXX (one of `Int`, `Long`, `Byte`, `Short`, `Double`, `Float`, `Boolean`, or `Char`) to a corresponding primitive element array.

Exercise 2

Create a `BooleanArray` with values `true`, `false`, `true`.

Array Operations

Apart from accessing elements, arrays allow a couple of operations applied on them (`E` is the element type):

- `first(): E`

  This is the first element of the array.

- `last(): E`

  This is the last element of the array.

- `copyOf(): Array<E>`

  For object arrays, this creates a copy of an array. This is a shallow copy, meaning the copy will contain the same object references as the original array.

- `copyOf(): XXXArray`

  For primitive element type XXX (one of `Int`, `Long`, `Byte`, `Short`, `Double`, `Float`, `Boolean`, or `Char`), creates a copy of the array.

- `fill(element:E>)`

  This sets all array elements to the given `element`.

- `sliceArray(indices:IntRange)`

  This creates a new array from a part of the original array. An `IntRange` could be entered (e.g., `1..100`). Indices are as usual zero-based.

- `contains(element:E): Boolean`

This checks whether the specified element is contained in the array.

- `all(predicate: (E) -> Boolean): Boolean`

  This returns `true` if the predicate is met for all elements. The predicate is a function taking each element and performing a check; for example, `{ element -> ... [boolean expression] }`.

- `any(predicate: (E) -> Boolean): Boolean`

  This returns `true` if the predicate is met for any of the elements. The predicate is a function taking each element and performing a check, for example `{ element -> ... [boolean expression] }`.

This list is not exhaustive. For more functions, refer to the online API documentation.

Note   As of this writing, the API documentation of Kotlin can be found at
`https://kotlinlang.org/api/latest/jvm/stdlib/index.html`. If this
link is out of date, you can easily find the documentation by searching "kotlin stdlib
api documentation" in your favorite search engine.

Android Studio helps a lot in finding object properties and functions. Just enter the
object's name, a dot, and if necessary press Alt+Enter. Android Studio then shows
a list with all properties and functions, which you can scan through using the
cursor up and down keys (see Figure 9-2). You can even go to the sources; place
the cursor over a class name and then press Ctrl+B.

Figure 9-2. *Automatic API documentation*

Sets, Lists, and Maps

Collections get used if you need data containers for many elements and don't know or
don't want to specify the size. We basically have three types of collections:

- *Sets:* Sets are collections of unique elements. They contain any
  number of elements, but duplicates are not allowed. So [1, 27, 3] is a
  set, but [5, 1, 5] is not. Also, sets don't have an order, so [1, 3, 5] is the
  same set as [1, 5, 3].

- *Lists:* A list is an ordered collection of elements in which duplicates
  are allowed. Therefore both [1, 2, 3, 1] and [1, 1, 2, 3] are lists, but they
  are not the same.

- *Maps:* A map is an unordered collection of pairs [A, B] where there is a mapping relation between the pair members: A → B. The idea behind that is, if you have a map A1 → B1, A2 → B2, and A3 → B3, given any A you can determine the corresponding B using map functions or operators. The pair [A, B] is commonly referred to as a *key/value pair*, where A is the key and B is the value. In Kotlin idioms, if m is the map and property a contains a key, both m[a] and m.get(a) can be used to retrieve the corresponding value.

Contrary to arrays, for collections there always exist two variants: The collection can be *mutable* (changeable) or *immutable* (unchangeable). There are not just (immutable) sets, lists, and maps, but also mutable sets, mutable lists, and mutable maps. Speaking of classes, we have the following:

```
Set<MemberType>
List<MemberType>
Map<KeyType, ValueType>

MutableSet<MemberType>
MutableList<MemberType>
MutableMap<KeyType, ValueType>
```

Sets

For creating sets, you can use one of the constructors or library functions:

```
val set1:Set<String> = HashSet()
val set2:MutableSet<String> = HashSet()

val set3 = setOf(4, 7, 55)
val set4 = setOf<Long>(4, 7, 55)
val set5 = mutableSetOf(4, 7, 55)
```

Looking at that code, we need to explain a couple of things.

- Set is not a class, but an interface. For instantiation we need an implementation. The HashSet you see here is a standard implementation that gets used quite often for sets.

- `HashSet` can be used for both mutable and immutable sets. We have to explicitly state the variant in the property declaration. See `set1` and `set2` in the example.

- `setOf()` and `mutableSetOf()` try to infer the element type from their parameters. If it is unclear or you need a conversion to happen, the type must be explicitly declared inside angle brackets, as for `set4` in the example.

Just like the other collection types, the `Set` and `MutableSet` classes contain a vast number of properties and functions. Listing them all here would inflate the size of this book. Instead I present the ones most often used; for all the others, refer to the online API documentation.

Note   As of this writing, the API documentation of Kotlin can be found at `https://kotlinlang.org/api/latest/jvm/stdlib/index.html`. If this link is out of date, you can easily find the documentation by searching "kotlin stdlib api documentation" in your favorite search engine.

As for arrays, you can let Android Studio show you all properties and functions of an object. Enter the object's name, a dot, and if necessary press Alt+Enter (refer back to Figure 9-2). To see the sources, place the cursor over a class name and then press Ctrl+B.

The most often used properties and functions of the `Set` and `MutableSet` interfaces are given here. I start with basic properties and functions.

- `size`

  This indicates the size of the set.

- `add(element:E): Boolean`

  (`MutableSet` only) Add an element. This returns `true` if the element was really added (it didn't exist before).

- `addAll(elements:Collection<E>): Boolean`

  (`MutableSet` only) This adds many elements. A `Collection` is another set or a list. It returns `true` if the set was modified due to that operation.

- `addAll(elements:Array<out E>): Boolean`

  (MutableSet only) This adds all the elements from the specified array. The out inside the array type parameter allows us to add arrays with elements that are also subclasses from the type needed for the set. It returns true if the set was modified due to that operation.

- `intersect(other:Iterable<E>): Set<T>`

  This returns a set of elements contained in both this set and the specified Iterable. Sets and lists are also iterables.

The next group of properties and functions are using in dealing with empty sets.

- `clear()`

  (MutableSet only) This removes all elements.

- `isEmpty(): Boolean`

  This returns true if the set is empty.

- `isNotEmpty(): Boolean`

  This returns true if the set is not empty.

The following properties and functions are used to check.

- `contains(element:E): Boolean`

  This checks whether the specified element is contained in the set.

- `containsAll(elements:Collection<E>): Boolean`

  This checks whether all the specified elements are contained in the set.

For operations on the complete set, use the following properties and functions.

- `toMutableSet(): MutableSet<E>`

  (Non-MutableSet only) This returns a new mutable set based on the elements from the immutable set.

- `map(transform: (E) -> R): List<R>`

  This applies a mapping function on each element of the set and returns a list from that. Given, for example, a set of names, the transform function `{ s -> s + " (${s.length})" }` returns a list of the names with the name lengths appended.

Use the following properties and functions to remove elements.

- `remove(element:E): Boolean`

  (`MutableSet` only) This removes the specified element, if it exists inside the set. It returns `true` if the element existed and was removed.

- `removeAll(elements:Collection<E>): Boolean`

  (`MutableSet` only) This removes all the specified elements, as far as they exist inside the set. A `Collection` is another set or a list. It returns `true` if at least one element was removed.

- `removeAll(elements:Array<E>): Boolean`

  (`MutableSet` only) This removes all the specified elements, as far as they exist inside the set. It returns `true` if at least one element was removed.

- `retainAll(elements:Collection<E>): Boolean`

  (`MutableSet` only) This removes all the elements that are not also inside the specified elements. A `Collection` is another set or a list. It returns `true` if at least one element was removed.

- `retainAll(elements:Array<E>): Boolean`

  (`MutableSet` only) This removes all the elements that are not also inside the specified array. It returns `true` if at least one element was removed.

To check for predicates, use these properties and functions.

- `all(predicate: (E) -> Boolean): Boolean`

  This returns `true` if the predicate is met for all elements. The predicate is a function taking each element and performing a check; for example, `{ element -> ... [boolean expression] }`.

- `any(predicate: (E) -> Boolean): Boolean`

  This returns true if the predicate is met for any of the elements. The predicate is a function taking each element and performing a check; for example, `{ element -> ... [boolean expression] }`.

- `filter(predicate: (E) -> Boolean): List<E>`

  This returns all the elements from the set for which the predicate returns true. The predicate is a function taking each element and performing a check; for example, `{ element -> ... [boolean expression] }`.

This last item is used for looping.

- `forEach(action: (E) -> Unit)`

  This loops through the set. Loops are discussed later in this chapter.

Due to a couple of more extension functions, the + and - operators are supported and can be used to add or remove elements or other collections:

```
setOf(1, 2, 3) + setOf(2, 3, 4) // -> [1, 2, 3, 4]
setOf(1, 2, 3, 4) + 5           // -> [1, 2, 3, 4, 5]
setOf(1, 2, 3) - setOf(3, 4)    // -> [1, 2]
setOf(1, 2, 3) - 2              // -> [1, 3]
```

Exercise 3

Create a mutable set `val fruits` with elements `Apple`, `Banana`, `Grape`, and `Engine` as elements. In a separate statement, add `Cherry` to the set. In another statement, remove `Engine` from the set. Create a new set `val fruits5` from this set, as a result of filtering elements with five characters. Note: You can get a string's length by addressing its `length` property.

Lists

Lists are similar to sets, but they do not require uniqueness, so elements may appear several times. In addition, lists have an order.

To create a list, we again have list implementation constructors and functions from the Kotlin standard library.

```
val list1:List<Int> = ArrayList()
val list2:MutableList<Int> = ArrayList()

val list3 = listOf(4, 7, 55)
val list4 = listOf<Long>(4, 7, 55)
val list5 = mutableListOf(4, 7, 55)
```

What we said for the set examples earlier more or less holds for lists as well:

- `List` is an interface. The implementation we use here, `ArrayList`, is a frequently used choice.

- `ArrayList` can be used for both mutable and immutable lists. We have to explicitly state the variant in the property declaration. See `list1` and `list2` in the example.

- `listOf()` and `mutableListOf()` try to infer the element type from their parameters. If they are unclear or you need a conversion to happen, the type must be explicitly declared inside angle brackets, as for `list4` in the example.

As an additional means, arrays can be easily converted to lists by using the array's `toList()` or `toMutableList()` functions:

```
val array = arrayOf(...)
val list = array.toList()
```

Due to their nature, lists and sets share many properties and methods, so the following list includes methods that were already possible for sets. Again, the list is not exhaustive, so please consult the online documentation for more details.

Note   This commonality is not just a coincidence. In fact, both `Set` and `List` are extending the `Collection` interface. You will see the `Collection` interface used once in a while for certain tasks, but usually the conceptual differences between `Set` and `List` are worth retaining, so set and list interfaces are being used more often.

First, here are some basic properties and functions.

- `size`

  This indicates the size of the list.

- `lastIndex`

  The is the size of the list minus 1.

- `add(element:E): Boolean`

  (MutableList only) This adds an element at the end. It returns `true` if the element was really added. Because this will always happen, the function will always return `true`.

- `addAll(elements:Collection<E>): Boolean`

  (MutableList only) This adds many elements. A `Collection` is another list or a set. It returns `true` if the list was modified due to that operation. Unless the parameter provided belongs to an empty collection, the function will always return `true`.

- `addAll(elements:Array<out E>): Boolean`

  (MutableList only) This adds all the elements from the specified array. The `out` inside the array type parameter allows us to add arrays with elements that are also subclasses from the type needed for the list. It returns `true` if the list was modified due to that operation. Unless the parameter provided belongs to an empty array, the function will always return `true`.

- `get(index:Int): E`

  This retrieves an element from the list. The index is zero based. It maps to the [ ] operator, so you can use `list[index]` to achieve the same result.

- `set(index:Int, element:E): E`

  (MutableList only) This sets an element inside the list. The index is zero based. It maps to the [ ] operator, so you can use `list[index]` = ... to achieve the same result.

The next group of properties and functions are used in dealing with empty lists.

- `clear()`

  (`MutableList` only) This removes all elements.

- `isEmpty(): Boolean`

  This returns `true` if the list is empty.

- `isNotEmpty(): Boolean`

  This returns `true` if the list is not empty.

The following properties and functions are used to check for containment.

- `contains(element:E): Boolean`

  This checks whether the specified element is contained in the list.

- `containsAll(elements:Collection<E>): Boolean`

  This checks whether all the specified elements are contained in the list.

- `indexOf(element:E): Int`

  This retrieves the index of the specified element in the list, or −1 if not found. The index is zero based.

- `lastIndexOf(element:E): Int`

  This retrieves the last index of the specified element in the list, or −1 if not found. The index is zero based.

For operations on the complete list, use the following properties and functions.

- `toMutableList(): MutableList<E>`

  (Non-`MutableList` only) This returns a new mutable list based on the elements from the immutable list.

- `subList(fromIndex:Int, toIndex:Int): List<E>`

  This returns a view of the list starting at index `fromIndex` until (not including) `toIndex`. The view implies that if you change elements in the returned list, the change will also happen in the original list.

- `asReversed(): List<E>`

  This returns a read-only view of the list in reverse order. Any changes in the original list are reflected in the reversed list as well.

- `distinct(): List<E>`

  This returns a new list with duplicates removed.

- `shuffled(): List<E>`

  This returns a new list with the elements from the original list shuffled.

- `map(transform: (E) -> R): List<R>`

  This applies a mapping function on each element of the list and returns a new list from that. Given, for example, a list of names, the transform function `{ s -> s.length }` returns a list of the name lengths from that.

Use the following properties and functions to remove elements.

- `remove(element:E): Boolean`

  (`MutableList` only) This removes the specified element, if it exists inside the list. It returns `true` if the element existed and was removed.

- `removeAt(index:Int): E`

  (`MutableList` only) This removes the element at the specified index (zero based) and returns the removed element.

- `removeAll(elements:Collection<E>): Boolean`

  (`MutableList` only) This removes all the specified elements, as far as they exist inside the list. A `Collection` is another list or a set. It returns `true` if at least one element was removed.

- `removeAll(elements:Array<E>): Boolean`

  (`MutableList` only) This removes all the specified elements, as far as they exist inside the list. It returns `true` if at least one element was removed.

- `retainAll(elements:Collection<E>): Boolean`

  (`MutableList` only) This removes all the elements that are not also inside the specified elements. A `Collection` is another list or a set. It returns `true` if at least one element was removed.

- `retainAll(elements:Array<E>): Boolean`

  (`MutableList` only) This removes all the elements that are not also inside the specified array. It returns `true` if at least one element was removed.

Use the following properties and functions for fetching parts of the list.

- `drop(n:Int): List<E>`

  This returns a new list with n elements removed from the beginning.

- `dropLast(n:Int): List<E>`

  This returns a new list with n elements removed from the end.

- `first(): E`

  This returns the first element.

- `take(n:Int): List<E>`

  This returns a new list with the first n elements of the original list.

- `first(predicate: (E) -> Boolean): E`

  This returns the first element matching the predicate. The predicate is a function taking each element and performing a check; for example, `{ element -> ... [boolean expression] }`.

- `last(): E`

  This returns the last element.

- `takeLast(n:Int): List<E>`

  This returns a new list with the last n elements of the original list.

- `last(predicate: (E) -> Boolean): E`

    This returns the last element matching the predicate. The predicate
    is a function taking each element and performing a check; for
    example, `{ element -> ... [boolean expression] }`.

To check for predicates, use these properties and functions.

- `all(predicate: (E) -> Boolean): Boolean`

    This returns `true` if the predicate is met for all elements. The
    predicate is a function taking each element and performing a
    check; for example, `{ element -> ... [boolean expression] }`.

- `any(predicate: (E) -> Boolean): Boolean`

    This returns `true` if the predicate is met for any of the elements.
    The predicate is a function taking each element and performing a
    check; for example, `{ element -> ... [boolean expression] }`.

- `filter(predicate: (E) -> Boolean): List<E>`

    This returns all the elements from the list for which the predicate
    returns `true`. The predicate is a function taking each element and
    performing a check; for example, `{ element -> ... [boolean
    expression] }`.

These items are used for looping.

- `forEach(action: (E) -> Unit)`

    This method loops through the list.

- `forEachIndexed(action: (index:Int,E) -> Unit)`

    This method also loops through the list.

Due to a couple of additional functions, lists understand the + operator, so you can
add elements or collections (other lists or sets) using +.

```
listOf(1, 2, 3) + listOf(2, 3)     // -> [1, 2, 3, 2, 3]
listOf(1, 2, 3, 4) + 5             // -> [1, 2, 3, 4, 5]
```

Lists can be converted to arrays using `toArray()`, `toIntArray()`, `toDoubleArray()`,
and so on. The conversion to one of the primitive typed arrays will only be successful if
the elements have the correct type.

Maps

Maps are probably the most interesting, but also the most involved part of the collection framework in Kotlin. Maps get used whenever you need a mapping in the mathematical sense, which means unique elements from a set A = {a0, a1, a2, ...} get mapped to (possibly repeated) elements from a collection B = {b0, b1, b2, ...}. As a result, whenever you have an ai you immediately can determine the (one and only) mapped bj from it. In computer languages, the data you map from are usually called the *key*, and the value you map to has the name *value*.

In nature and culture, maps are everywhere: a pair of geographical coordinates on earth map to an altitude, every second of January 23 maps to an air temperature in New York, every Social Security number maps to a name, time maps to Earth's position in its orbit, the temperature maps to the state of aggregation (solid, liquid, gas) of water, the note played by an instrument maps to a frequency, the index of an element in an array maps to some value, and so on.

Similar to sets and lists, we again have the distinction between mutable (changeable) and immutable (unchangeable) maps.

In the following code snippets we will be using the following map: SSN → name (all numbers are made up):

```
152835937 -> Albert Einstein
273495357 -> John Smith
346068589 -> John Smith
484767775 -> Barbra Streisand
```

To declare maps, you use either `Map` or `MutableMap` as the type and add the key and value type in angle brackets after it.

```kotlin
val map1:Map<String,Int> = ...
var map2:Map<Int,Double> = ...
val map3:MutableMap<Int,String> = ...
```

To create maps, we first have the option to use one of the constructors:

```kotlin
val map: MutableMap<Int,String> =
    HashMap<Int,String>().apply {
        this[152835937] = "Albert Einstein"
        this[273495357] = "John Smith"
```

```
        this[346068589] = "John Smith"
        this[484767775] = "Barbra Streisand"
    }
```

where HashMap is one of the implementations used most often. The apply{...} is new. Actually, you can use it for any instance, but here it means this: Take the map we just created and do something with it. The this refers to the instance of the map being created, not the class instance or object we are currently in. We use apply{ ... } at this place to add some key/value pairs.

Next there are Kotlin standard library functions that help us to create and initialize maps:

```
val map = mutableMapOf(
        152835937 to "Albert Einstein",
        273495357 to "John Smith",
        346068589 to "John Smith",
        484767775 to "Barbra Streisand"
    )
val map2 = mapOf(
    152835937 to "Albert Einstein",
    ... )
```

Note   The instances of to in the preceding initializers actually are operators that create an instance of the built-in Pair class. If desired, you could use your own explicit instances of Pair as in val p1 = Pair(152835937, "Albert Einstein") and then mapOf(p1, ...).

Maps are also the result of some operations on lists, sets, and arrays. With any of the latter three, you can use one of these (T is the element type):

- associate(transform: (T) -> Pair<K, V>): Map<K,V>

  This creates a map with key type K and value type V. The transform function is supposed to create a Pair<K,V> given each element of the original set, list, or array. Given, for example, a set of integers (T = Int) such a transform function could read { i -> Pair(i, i*i) }, creating a map mapping integers to their square.

213

- `associateWith(ValueSelector: (K) -> V): Map<K,V>`

  This is much the same as `associate()`, but as a shortcut always takes the original element as the key. The `valueSelector` is supposed to generate the value. Given, for example, a set of integers again, the lambda function `{ i -> i * i }` again maps integers to their square.

- `associateBy(keySelector: (T) -> K): Map<K,V>`

  This is much the same as `associate()`, but as a shortcut always takes the original element as the value. The `keySelector` is supposed to generate the key. Given, for example, a set of doubles, the lambda function `{ d -> Math.floor(d).toInt() }` uses the integer equal to or just below the given double as a key.

- `groupBy(keySelector: (T) -> K): Map<K, List<T>>`

  This gathers elements from the original collection or array and saves them under the generated key in the resulting map. Say, for example, you have several names—John, Adam, Joe, and Gabriel—and apply the `keySelector` `{ s -> s.length }`. The resulting map then maps name lengths to names: 3 → ["Joe"], 4 → ["John", "Adam"], and 7 → ["Gabriel"].

Note that if possible, you should prefer `associateWith()` and `associateBy()` over `associate()`, because the latter implies an object creation, which always takes some time.

Pairs and Triples

Two more types of data containers are pairs and triples. We've already seen the first one, denoted by the `Pair` class and used for mapping purposes. The triple uses class `Triple` and contains only three members. Of course, you can use both for whatever tasks you like. The declaration and initialization are

```
val pair = Pair<FirstType, SecondType>(
    firstVal, secondVal)
```

```
val triple = Triple<FirstType, SecondType, ThirdType>(
    firstVal, secondVal, thirdVal)
```

As usual, the type specification < ... > can be omitted if it can be inferred by the values' types. For example, you can write

```
val pair = Pair("Earth", 12800.0)
```

to get a pair of String and Double.

To fetch the first and second components for pairs, you simply use the properties first and second as in pair.first and pair.second. The components for a triple are accordingly accessible via properties first, second, and third.

Loops over Data Containers

Looping over data containers means visiting each of their members to perform some action on it. This is an important use case for data containers if you want to print it, transform it, or aggregate over it to deduce some container characteristics. Think of summing, concatenating, or averaging.

In the past, computer languages provided some kind of a looping construct circling around some indexing variable, and in fact this is possible with Kotlin as well. We covered this old-fashioned kind of looping earlier in the book, but let me show you here a more elegant and straightforward way to loop over containers in Kotlin.

All collection type data containers like arrays, sets, and lists provide a forEach() function, and you can use it concisely for looping needs. More precisely, write

```
val container = ... // array or set or list
container.forEach { elem ->
    // do something with elem
}
```

Why do we call this a function if it looks like a statement with a block? This is more or less a coincidence; this sample could also be written as container.forEach({ ... }) and the Kotlin compiler allows removal of the superfluous round brackets. In reality the { ... } is not a statement block, but a function literal also called a *lambda function*. The elem is just an identifier; you could also use e or element or whatever you like. In any case, it gets the currently visited element of the array or collection, and automatically has the same type as it. For example, in

```
val container = listOf(1, 2, 3, 4, -1)
container.forEach { elem ->
    Log.d("LOG", elem.toString())
}
```

the elem gets the integers 1, 2, 3, 4, -1, one after the other, and elem automatically has the type Int, because the container is a list of Int elements.

Note   In fact you could add :Int here as in forEach { elem:Int -> ... } if it helps to improve the readability of your code.

If you need the iteration index inside the function you might be tempted to write

```
var index = 0
container.forEach { elem ->
    // ... do s.th. with elem
    index++ // NOT ALLOWED!
}
```

to increment the index variable each iteration. This won't work, however. It is a restriction of *inner* functions to not be allowed to reassign "outside" variables. If you need an index you can use a variant of forEach() that reads forEachIndexed(). This time the inner function receives two arguments, the Int typed index and the element variable:

```
container.forEachIndexed { index, elem ->
    // ... do s.th. with elem
}
```

The index variable gets values 0, 1, 2, ... and always has the type Int. Again, you are free to change the name of the index variable to whatever you like.

Looping through maps happens in a different manner, but it is not complicated either. Maps also have a forEach() function, but with different parameter types.

- If using a single parameter as in map.forEach { me -> ...} this parameter will be of type Map.Entry<K,V> where K is the key type and V is the value type. From me you then get the key via me.key and the value via me.value. You can also write me.toPair() to build a Pair from that.

- (Only for Android API level 24 or greater) If using two parameters they will receive the key and the value during each iteration: `map.forEach { k,v -> ... }`.

Sorting Arrays and Collections

Sorting arrays and collections like lists and sets is a task you frequently need to accomplish before you present data to your app users. Also, sorting must happen before you can start the binary search algorithm we discuss in the section "Searching in Arrays and Collections" later in this chapter.

Sorting can happen in place, which means the array or collection you want to have sorted gets altered, or in a functional style, which means the result of the operation is the sorted array or collection and the original data container stays untouched. Sorting in place will be the faster choice, but bears the risk that other program parts get corrupted if they hold a reference to the original array or collection. Functional sorting can improve program stability, but you can expect some performance penalty, so choose wisely.

For functional style sorting with the original array or collection untouched, you have a couple of options (`T` is the element type).

- `Array.sorted() : List<T>`

  This returns a `List` with the elements from the array sorted according to their *natural* sort order. The type `T` must be a subinterface of `Comparable,` which is the case for all built-in numeric types and strings. As the array, you can use an object array or any of the primitive element type arrays (`IntArray`, `DoubleArray`, etc.).

- `Array.sortedArray() : Array<T>`

  This is the same as `Array.sorted()`, but returns an array instead. Kotlin always returns an object array, never a primitive typed array. Therefore, `arrayOf(1,2,3).sorted()` returns an `Array<Int>`, not an `IntArray`. You can, however, add method `toIntArray()` to convert the `Int` object array to an `IntArray`. The same holds for the other primitive element type objects.

- `Collection.sorted() : List<T>`

  This is the same as `Array.sorted()`, but for collections like sets and lists.

You can add a `Descending` to any of them to reverse the sort order.

A couple of additional methods allow you to explicitly specify the comparison operation for sorting the elements.

- `Array.sortedBy(selector: (T) -> R?) : List<T>`

  This creates a sorted list according to the natural sort order of the value returned by the selector function. Type R must implement the `Comparable` interface. Say, for example, you want to sort an array of `data class Car(val make:Int, val name:String)` by make. You can then write `array.sortedBy({ car -> car.make })`.

- `Collection.sortedBy(selector: (T) -> R?) : List<T>`

  This is the same as `Array.sortedBy()` shown earlier, but for collections like sets and lists.

- `Array.sortedWith(comparator: Comparator<in T>) : List<T>`

  This creates a sorted list according to the comparator provided. You could provide a subclass implementation of `Comparator`, but the Kotlin standard library also provides a couple of `Comparator` generator functions. The `in` in the type specifier indicates it is enough for the comparator to handle a superclass of T as well.

- `Array.sortedArrayWith(comparator: Comparator<in T>) : Array<T>`

  This is the same `Array.sortedWith()` shown earlier, but returns an array.

- `Collection.sortedWith(comparator: Comparator<in T>) : List<T>`

  This is the same as `Array.sortedWith()` shown earlier, but for collections like sets and lists.

You can add a Descending to most of them to reverse the sort order (there is no sortedWithDescending() and no sortedArrayWithDescending()).

For the comparator needed inside any of the sortedWith() functions, Kotlin provides standard library functions you can use to create such a comparator.

- compareBy(vararg selectors: (T) -> Comparable<*>?): Comparator<T>

    and

- compareByDescending(vararg selectors: (T) -> Comparable<*>?): Comparator<T>

    This is an important function you likely want to show up inside sortedWith(). It takes any number of functions evaluating to a Comparable. Those functions get worked through in consecutive order. The first Comparable comparison not resulting in an *equals* will break the chain and continue with the next iteration in the sorting algorithm. As a function element you can write a lambda function as in

    {elem -> elem.someProperty}

    if this property is a Comparable like an Int or a String, but you can also directly refer to property getters by writing T::propertyName. As an example: take a list of

    data class Car(val make:Int, val name:String)

    and consider comparing by the make. Using sortedWith() for sorting then reads

    list.sortWith(compareBy(Car::make)).

- compareBy(comparator: Comparator<in K>, selector: (T) -> K): Comparator<T>

    and

- compareByDescending(comparator: Comparator<in K>, selector: (T) -> K): Comparator<T>

    This creates a comparator that first applies the selector to the incoming data and applies the provided comparator to the result from the selector.

- nullsFirst(): Comparator<T>

  Use this as a first argument to compareBy() to extend the natural-order comparator implicitly used there with the capability to allow null values in the sorted array or collection. Such null values will show up first in the returned list. The nullsFirst() comparator can only be used in a context where Comparable elements get compared, which is automatically the case if you use nullsFirst() as the first parameter in compareBy().

- nullsLast(): Comparator<T>

  This is similar to nullsFirst, but null values will show up last in the list returned.

- reverseOrder(): Comparator<T>

  Use this as a first argument to compareBy() to reverse the order of the natural-order comparator implicitly used there. It is possible to mix with the other comparator extenders, as, for example, in nullsFirst(reverseOrder()).

- then

  Use this as an infix operator to chain comparators. You can, for example, write compareBy(...) then compareBy(...) inside sortWith().

Exercise 4

Using sortWith(), do a sorting of a list val gul = listOf(...) of GameUser instances from the NumberGuess game app, first by the last name, and then by the first name. Assign the result to val sorted.

In-place sorting differs from the sorting functions handled so far in the original array or collection (list or set) being altered to contain the sorted data afterward. For lists and sets, this obviously makes sense only for the mutable variants. The functions for in-place sorting are given here.

- `sort()` and `sortDescending()`

  This sorts the array or mutable collection in place, according to the element's natural sort order. The elements must implement the `Comparable` interface for this to work.

- `sortBy(selector: (T) -> R?)` and `sortByDescending(selector: (T) -> R?)`

  This sorts the array or mutable collection in place, according to the provided selector function, which must return a `Comparable`.

- `sortWith(comparator: Comparator<in T>)`

  This sorts the array or mutable collection in place, according to the provided comparator. The `in` in the comparator type specification means the comparator must handle the elements, but also can handle a superclass of the element type. For the `comparator` parameter, the same Kotlin standard library functions can be used as for the functional style sorting functions described earlier.

Note   You should prefer functional style sorting over in-place sorting, unless performance or resources housekeeping is an important issue.

Exercise 5

Do the same as for Exercise 4, but perform in-place sorting.

Grouping, Folding, Reducing, and Zipping

Grouping, folding, reducing, and zipping are advanced operations on arrays and collections like lists and sets. We discuss each of these in turn.

Grouping

Grouping is about reorganizing your data in such a way that groups of the data are gathered according to some key deduced from the data or imposed on the data. Look at, for example, a set of cars:

```
data class Car(id:Int,make:Int,name:String,vin:String)
val cars = listOf(
    Car(1, 1994, "Sirus",       "WXX 130 007-1J-582943"),
    Car(2, 1997, "Sirus",       "WXX 130 008-1J-582957"),
    Car(3, 2010, "Casto 4.0",   "WXQ 456 088-4K-005614"),
    Car(4, 2010, "Babo MX",     "WYY 518 004-55-171598"),
    Car(5, 1994, "Casto 4.0",   "WXQ 456 005-4K-005658"),
    Car(6, 2011, "Quasto",      "WAO 100 036-00-012378")
)
```

What if we want to find out which cars belong to a certain make year? We can see that we have two cars belonging to 1994, one to 1997, two to 2010, and one to 2011 if looking at the IDs.:

```
1994 -> [ 1, 5 ]
1997 -> [ 2 ]
2010 -> [ 3, 4 ]
2011 -> [ 6 ]
```

This operation is called *grouping*, and in this particular case we group based on the make.

In Kotlin we have a grouping function that helps us to achieve our aim: groupBy(keysSelector: (T) -> K): Map<K, List<T>> where the keySelector is supposed to deduce the grouping key. The type parameter T is the class of the original elements or a superclass of that. Type K is any type you need for the grouping key. The grouping function for the cars example reads:

```
data class Car(id:Int,make:Int,name:String,vin:String)
val cars = listOf( ... )
val groupedByMake = cars.groupBy(Car::make)
...
val group1997:List<Car> = groupedByMake[1997]
```

where we applied the getter function for the make: `Car::make`. Less concisely, but with the same result, we could also use this:

```
val groupedByMake = cars.groupBy { car -> car.make }
```

Exercise 6

With `substring(0,3)` extracting the first three chapters from a string, perform a grouping for the cars list with the first three characters of the `vin` as a key. Call it `val groupedByManufacturer`. Extract the WXX manufacturer from the grouping result.

There are three more grouping functions. The first is `groupBy()` with one more parameter. This one performs a transformation on the values before adding them to the grouping result. Two more functions, `groupByTo()`, save the grouping result into a map provided as a parameter. They are more or less convenience functions. For details, refer to the official Kotlin API documentation.

Folding

Folding is about letting an object scan through all elements of an array or collection (set or list) and update itself each iteration. Think, for example, of a list of invoices and summing up all money amounts. This is nothing spectacular; one could write

```
val someObject = ...
list.forEach { elem ->
    // update someObj using elem
    ...
}
```

However, there is an intrinsic danger that code could initialize the object before the loop starts doing lots of weird things, so there is a function that performs the task using one statement. Actually, it is a set of functions.

- `fold(initial: R, operation: (acc: R, T) -> R)): R`

  The function takes as parameters the object that is going to be updated each loop iteration and a function that performs the updating. This updater takes as parameters the actual version of the gathering object and the current loop element. This returns the gathering object with all data container elements applied. In most practical cases the first parameter is probably a newly constructed object, as in `list.fold(Gatherer(), ...)`.

- `foldRight(initial: R, operation: (T, acc: R) -> R)): R`

  This is similar to `fold()`, but it iterates through the array or collection in reverse order. To express this backward scanning, the parameter order of the inner function gets reversed, too.

- `foldIndexed(initial: R, operation: (index:Int, acc: R, T) -> R)): R`

  This is the same as `fold`, but the inner function gets the loop iteration index as an additional first parameter.

- `foldRightIndexed(initial: R, operation: (index:Int, T, acc: R) -> R)): R`

  This is similar to `foldIndexed()`, but it iterates through the array or collection in reverse order. Again, to express this backward scanning, the parameter order for parameters two and three of the inner function gets reversed, too.

There is also an advanced folding mechanism that includes a grouping operation. If you use `groupingBy()` on an array or a collection (list or set), you will receive a `Grouping` object that you later can apply on an array or a collection like a set or a list. This is kind of a convenience function, as you could do grouping and then folding manually. For details, please consult the Kotlin API documentation.

Reducing

Reducing is the little brother of folding. The gatherer is not specified explicitly and instead the first element of the array or collection (a set or a list) is used. The folding operation or more precisely *reduction* operation then understandably starts with the second element of the data. Reduction functions are listed here.

- `reduce(operation: (acc: S, T) -> S): S`

  This performs the provided reduction operation on the current gatherer value and the current loop element. It then returns the reduction result. The reduction function might return a value of the original data type T or a subclass of it.

- `reduceRight(operation: (T, acc: S) -> S): S`

  This is similar to `reduce()`, but it scans through the data in reverse order. Note that the order of the parameters of the reduction function is reversed, too.

- `reduceIndexed(operation: (index: Int, T, acc: S) -> S): S`

  This is the same as `reduce()`, but the reduction function receives the current looping index as an additional first parameter.

- `reduceRightIndexed(operation: (T, acc: S) -> S): S`

  This is similar to `reduceRight()`, but it scans through the data in reverse order. Note that the order of parameters two and three of the reduction function is reversed, too.

Exercise 7

Create a list $[1, 2, 3, 4, \ldots, 100]$. Then, using `reduce`, calculate the number $1 * 2 * 3 * \ldots * 100$ from it. Hint: You can convert a range ($from..to$) to a list via function `toList()`.

Zipping

Looping, sorting, folding, and reducing already provide a quite versatile tool set for handling arrays and collections (sets and lists). We don't have a tool yet, though, to combine two arrays or collections element-wise. In Kotlin there is a set of functions dealing with exactly this kind of task.

The main functions that help us here are called `zip()` and `unzip()`. The first of them, `zip()`, has the following signature: `zip(other: Array<out R>): List<Pair<T, R>>` or `zip(other: Iterable<R>): List<Pair<T, R>>`. Both of them are defined as infix functions, so you can write

```
array.zip(otherArray)
    -or- array zip otherArray
array.zip(list)
    -or- array zip list
collection.zip(array)
    -or- collection zip array
collection.zip(otherCollection)
    -or- collection zip otherCollection
```

All of them return a list of Pair instances, as shown in Figure 9-3. Note that Iterable is an interface that arrays, collections, and ranges implement, so you could use ranges here as well.

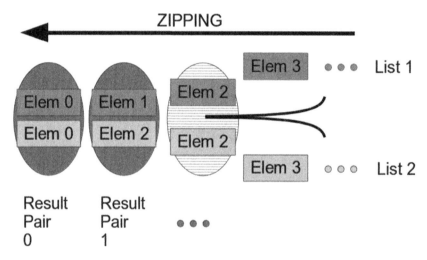

Figure 9-3. *Zipping*

As an example, say we have two lists [Bananas, Apples, Oranges] and corresponding prices [1.69, 2.19, 2.79]. To build a list of pairs [Bananas, 1.69], [Apples, 2.19], and [Oranges, 2.79], all you have to do is write

```
val fruits = listOf("Bananas", "Apples", "Oranges")
val prices = listOf(1.69, 2.19, 2.79)
val fruitsAndPrices = fruits zip prices
// or fruits.zip(prices)
...
```

```
fruitsAndPrices.forEach { p ->
    // p = Pair("Bananas", 1.69) aso.
}
```

If you try to zip arrays or collections of unequal lengths, the bigger one gets clipped at the end and the resulting list will have the size of the smaller one.

The unzip() function performs the inverse operation: It takes a list of pairs and extracts two lists of single elements from it, packed in a pair: unzip(): Pair<List<T>, List<R>>, where types T and R are the types of the first and second element of each pair in the original list.

For zipping there is an alternative function to having a second parameter added. This is a transform function doing something with the paired elements before outputting them to the zip result; for example, list1.zip(list2, a,b -> ... where a and b are the elements of lists 1 and 2 at the same index. This is a way to avoid creating pairs in case you don't need them. The same process works for arrays, too.

Exercise 8

With two lists val fruits = listOf("Bananas", "Apples", "Oranges") and val prices = listOf(1.69, 2.19, 2.79), and a data class Fruit(val name:String, val price:Double), perform a zipping with the resulting list containing Fruit elements.

Searching in Arrays and Collections

We've already seen that by using indexOf() we can find the index of a particular element in an array or a list. For very large arrays or collections (e.g., 1 million entries), that might not be the fastest way to find an element. Internally indexOf() must iterate through the whole array or list and must check for the equality of each data value until a hit occurs.

For sorted arrays or lists there is a better choice: a binary search. In such a binary search, the N elements of an array or list get split into two equal parts of approximate size $N/2$. Then the part that contains the search element is chosen. With the smaller range, we again perform a split in the middle, do another check, and so on. Using this algorithm to search for an element in an array or list of 1 million entries, we don't need more than about 20 checks to find it.

The function signatures for such a binary search (E is the element type) are given here.

- `binarySearch(element:E, fromIndex:Int = 0, toIndex:Int = size)`

  This finds the element in an array or a list using its natural ordering. The element type must have the `Comparable` interface, which is automatically the case for all number types and strings. If the element does not exist in the array or in the list, the appropriate insertion index gets returned. In [1, 2, 4, 5] searching for a 3 thus returns 2, because this is the index of 3 in [1, 2, 3, 4, 5]. Because `fromIndex` and `toIndex` have adequate default values, you can omit them if you want to search the whole list.

- `binarySearch(element:E, comparator: Comparator<in E> fromIndex:Int = 0, toIndex:Int = size)`

  This finds the element in an array or a list using the provided comparator. The list or array must have been presorted according to the comparator provided. If the element does not exist in the array or in the list, the appropriate insertion index gets returned. Because `fromIndex` and `toIndex` have adequate default values, you can omit them if you want to search the whole list. The `in` in the type parameter indicates that the comparator used also can deal with superclasses of E.

Note that in all cases sorting the array or list in ascending order is mandatory. Otherwise the result is undefined.

The Spread Operator

For any function with a `vararg` parameter, you can use an array to pass values to the function:

```
function xyz(a:Int, vararg x:String) {
    ...
}
val arr = arrayOf("1", "2", "3", "4", "5")
xyz(42, *arr)
```

The * in front of the parameter is called a *spread operator*. Note that this works only for arrays, but for lists or sets you can perform an appropriate conversion via `.toArray()`, `.toIntArray()`, `.toDoubleArray()`, and so on.

Queues and Stacks: Deques

Sets and lists are not the only collection types you can use. Kotlin does not explicitly handle collection types other than sets and lists, but it sits on top of the *Java virtual machine (JVM)* and includes a significant subset of the Java standard libraries, including all Java collection types. We do not cover all of them, because some are rather specialized and show features you don't normally need. One interesting type is worth a more thorough investigation, though: *deques*.

Deques are collections that are very similar to lists, but in addition they allow adding elements at the head, and furthermore provide functions for removing elements from both sides of the collection. Before we discuss the functions deques provide, we first clarify a couple of terms:

- *Head:* The head of a list is the element first added to a list. It is thus the element with index 0. For deques you explicitly state that you want to do something with the head by using one of the functions containing `First` in its name.

- *Tail:* The tail of a list is where elements get added via the `add()` function. For deques you explicitly state that you want to do something with the tail by using one of the functions containing `Last` in its name.

Because `Deque` is an interface, we need an implementation. There are several, with `java.util.ArrayDeque` probably the one used most often. Class `ArrayDeque` has three constructors (`E` is the element type).

- `ArrayDeque<E>()`

  This constructs a deque with an initial capacity of 16 elements of type E. From a client-side perspective, you don't have to think about capacities unless performance or resources housekeeping is a problem. If you expect many elements, you could specify a higher initial capacity size using the constructor shown later.

- `ArrayDeque<E>(numElements:Int)`

  This constructs a deque with the given initial capacity.

- `ArrayDeque<E>(c:Collection<out E>)`

  This constructs a deque initialized with the given elements. The `out` in the type specification means subclasses of E are allowed for the parameter.

For example, to create a deque holding `Int` elements, you writ: `val dq = ArrayDeque<Int>()`. Note that the `ArrayDeque` class will let its internal data container grow as necessary; the initial capacity thus is a mere hint.

The following is a nonexhaustive list of functions deques provide in addition to properties and functions a list offers.

- `addFirst(element:E)`

  This adds an element to the HEAD of a deque.

- `addLast(element:E)`

  This adds an element to the TAIL of a deque. It corresponds to `add()` for a list.

- `removeFirst(): E`

  This gets and removes the element at the HEAD of the deque. It throws an exception if the deque is empty.

- `removeLast(): E`

  This gets and removes the element at the TAIL of the deque. It throws an exception if the deque is empty.

- `getFirst(): E`

  This retrieves but does not remove the element at the HEAD of the queue. It throws an exception if the deque is empty.

- `getLast(): E`

  This retrieves but does not remove the element at the TAIL of the queue. It throws an exception if the deque is empty.

In addition, you can use one of the following functions that do not throw an exception if the deque is empty, but instead return null.

- peekFirst():E?

  This gets but does not remove the HEAD of a deque. If the deque is empty, it returns null instead.

- peekLast():E?

  This gets but does not remove the TAIL of a deque. If the deque is empty, it returns null instead.

- pollFirst():E?

  This gets and removes the HEAD of a deque. If the deque is empty, it returns null instead.

- pollLast():E?

  This gets and removes the TAIL of a deque. If the deque is empty, it returns null instead.

Deques can be used to mimic first-in, first-out (FIFO) queues if you use addLast() and removeFirst(). Likewise, last-in, first-out (LIFO) stacks can be simulated by using addLast() and removeLast().

A Statistics Class for the NumberGuess App

Our NumberGuess game app to this point doesn't contain any list-like structures, which is why we didn't mention it for a while. This can be changed readily and the extension we add for that aim is a dedicated statistics activity that counts attempts and hits for us.

Adding an Action Bar to The App

The first thing we do is add an action bar to the NumberGuess app:

1. Update the AndroidManifest.xml file. Add as an XML attribute inside the <activity> tag: android:theme = "@style/AppTheme. NoActionBar" (right after the android:name= ... entry in a new line)

```
<activity
        android:name=...
        android:theme="@style/AppTheme.NoActionBar">
```

2. Update the res/values/styles.xml file. Inside the <resources>
    tag add:

```
<resources>
    ...
    <style name="AppTheme.NoActionBar">
        <item name="windowActionBar">false</item>
        <item name="windowNoTitle">true</item>
    </style>
    <style name="AppTheme.AppBarOverlay"
        parent="ThemeOverlay.AppCompat.Dark.ActionBar"/>
    <style name="AppTheme.PopupOverlay"
        parent="ThemeOverlay.AppCompat.Light"/>
</resources>
```

3. Update the res/layout/activity_main.xml file:

```
<?xml version="1.0" encoding="utf-8"?>
<android.support.design.widget.CoordinatorLayout
    xmlns:android=
            "http://schemas.android.com/apk/res/android"
    xmlns:app="http://schemas.android.com/apk/res-auto"
    xmlns:tools="http://schemas.android.com/tools"
    android:layout_width="match_parent"
    android:layout_height="match_parent"
    tools:context=".MainActivity">

    <android.support.design.widget.AppBarLayout
        android:layout_height="wrap_content"
        android:layout_width="match_parent"
        android:theme="@style/AppTheme.AppBarOverlay">
      <android.support.v7.widget.Toolbar
          android:id="@+id/toolbar"
          android:layout_width="match_parent"
```

```
        android:layout_height="?attr/actionBarSize"
        android:background="?attr/colorPrimary"
        app:popupTheme="@style/AppTheme.PopupOverlay"
    />
  </android.support.design.widget.AppBarLayout>

  <include layout="@layout/content_main"/>
</android.support.design.widget.CoordinatorLayout>
```

4. Create a new file res/layout/content_main.xml:

```
<?xml version="1.0" encoding="utf-8"?>
<android.support.constraint.ConstraintLayout
        xmlns:android=
            "http://schemas.android.com/apk/res/android"
        xmlns:app=
            "http://schemas.android.com/apk/res-auto"
        xmlns:tools=
            "http://schemas.android.com/tools"
        android:layout_width=
            "match_parent"
        android:layout_height=
            "match_parent"
        app:layout_behavior=
            "@string/appbar_scrolling_view_behavior"
        tools:showIn=
            "@layout/activity_main"
        tools:context=
            ".MainActivity">

<LinearLayout
    android:orientation="vertical"
    android:layout_width="match_parent"
    android:layout_height="match_parent"
    android:padding="30dp"
    tools:showIn="@layout/activity_main"
    tools:context=".MainActivity">
```

```xml
<TextView
    android:layout_width="wrap_content"
    android:layout_height="wrap_content"
    android:text="@string/title.numberguess"
    android:textSize="30sp"/>

<Button
    android:id="@+id/startBtn"
    android:onClick="start"
    android:layout_width="match_parent"
    android:layout_height="wrap_content"
    android:text="@string/btn.start"/>

<Space android:layout_width="match_parent"
    android:layout_height="5dp"/>

<LinearLayout
    android:orientation="horizontal"
    android:layout_width="wrap_content"
    android:layout_height="wrap_content">
    <TextView
        android:text="@string/label.guess"
        android:layout_width="wrap_content"
        android:layout_height="wrap_content"/>
    <EditText
        android:id="@+id/num"
        android:hint="@string/edit.number"
        android:layout_width="80sp"
        android:layout_height="wrap_content"
        android:inputType="number"
        tools:ignore="Autofill"/>
    <Button
        android:id="@+id/doGuess"
        android:onClick="guess"
        android:text="@string/btn.do.guess"
        android:layout_width="wrap_content"
```

```
                    android:layout_height="wrap_content"/>
        </LinearLayout>

        <Space android:layout_width="match_parent"
            android:layout_height="5dp"/>

        <TextView
                android:id="@+id/status"
                android:text="@string/status.start.info"
                android:textColor="#FF000000"
                android:textSize="20sp"
                android:layout_width="wrap_content"
                android:layout_height="wrap_content"/>

        <Space android:layout_width="match_parent"
            android:layout_height="5dp"/>

        <TextView android:text="@string/label.log"
                android:textStyle="bold"
                android:layout_width="wrap_content"
                android:layout_height="wrap_content"/>
        <kotlinforandroid.book.numberguess.gui.Console
                android:id="@+id/console"
                android:layout_height="100sp"
                android:layout_width="match_parent"/>

</LinearLayout>
</android.support.constraint.ConstraintLayout>
```

5. Make sure the MainActivity.kt file contains as imports:

```
import kotlinx.android.synthetic.main.activity_main.*
import kotlinx.android.synthetic.main.content_main.*
```

6. Also inside class MainActivity, let function onCreate() read:

```
override fun onCreate(savedInstanceState: Bundle?) {
    super.onCreate(savedInstanceState)
    setContentView(R.layout.activity_main)
    setSupportActionBar(toolbar) // NEW
```

235

```
    fetchSavedInstanceData(savedInstanceState)
    doGuess.setEnabled(started)
}
```

7. Create a menu resource folder. For that aim, right-click the res folder, then select New ➤ Android Resource Directory. As the directory name, enter menu, and from the resource types, select Menu.

8. Create a menu resource: Right-click the res/menu folder, then select New ➤ Menu resource file. As the file name, enter menu_ options. With the file opened, switch to Text view by pressing on the tab at the bottom of the editor view. As contents, write

```
<?xml version="1.0" encoding="utf-8"?>
<menu xmlns:android=
        "http://schemas.android.com/apk/res/android"
      xmlns:app=
        "http://schemas.android.com/apk/res-auto">
    <item android:id="@+id/statistics"
          android:icon=
            "@android:drawable/ic_menu_info_details"
          android:title=
            "@string/statistics.menu_title"
          app:showAsAction="ifRoom"/>
</menu>
```

9. Create a string resource: Open res/values/strings and add

```
<string name="statistics.menu_title">
    Statistics</string>
```

10. In the MainActivity class, add

```
override
fun onCreateOptionsMenu(menu: Menu): Boolean {
    val inflater: MenuInflater = menuInflater
    inflater.inflate(R.menu.menu_options, menu)
    return true
}
```

```kotlin
private fun openStatistics() {
    val intent: Intent = Intent(this,
            StatisticsActivity::class.java)
    startActivity(intent)
}
```

The activity class will now show an error, because the StatisticsActivity does not exist yet. We create it in the following section.

The Statistics Activity

We now create a new activity for the statistics.

1. Right-click app, then select New ➤ Activity ➤ Empty Activity. As the activity's name, enter StatisticsActivity. Make sure Generate Layout file is selected, and use kotlinforandroid. book.numberguess as a package name. As source language select Kotlin and set main as the target source. Click Finish.

2. Open the file res/layout/activity_statistics.xml, switch to the Text view type, and replace its contents with this:

```xml
<?xml version="1.0" encoding="utf-8"?>
<LinearLayout
  xmlns:android=
      "http://schemas.android.com/apk/res/android"
  xmlns:tools=
      "http://schemas.android.com/tools"
  xmlns:app=
      "http://schemas.android.com/apk/res-auto"
  android:id="@+id/statisticsContainer"
  android:layout_width="match_parent"
  android:orientation="vertical"
  android:layout_height="match_parent"
  tools:context=".StatisticsActivity">
</LinearLayout>
```

3. Open the new activity class StatisticsActivity and replace its
   contents with this:

```
package kotlinforandroid.book.numberguess

import android.support.v7.app.AppCompatActivity
import android.os.Bundle
import android.view.ViewGroup
import android.widget.TextView
import kotlinforandroid.book.numberguess.
      statistics.Statistics

class StatisticsActivity : AppCompatActivity() {

    override
    fun onCreate(savedInstanceState: Bundle?) {
        super.onCreate(savedInstanceState)
        setContentView(R.layout.activity_statistics)
        showData(Statistics.getStatistics())
    }

    fun showData(s:List<String>) {
        val container = findViewById<ViewGroup>(
            R.id.statisticsContainer)
        container.removeAllViews()
        s.forEach {line ->
            container.addView(TextView(this).apply {
                text = line
            })
        }
    }
}
```

The last import must be entered in a single line, not like shown
here. The editor will show errors for the class, but we correct them
soon.

4. Create a new package kotlinforandroid.book.numberguess.
   statistics and inside a new object Statistics.

5. For now let the Statistics read:

```
package kotlinforandroid.book.numberguess.statistics

object Statistics {
    fun getStatistics(): List<String> {
        return emptyList()
    }
}
```

The errors in class StatisticsActivity should now disappear.

Now you should be able to run the app in an emulator or in a connected device. If you click the new (i) button on the taskbar, the new statistics activity should appear. For now, it will display an empty screen, but we change that later and add contents to it (see Figure 9-4).

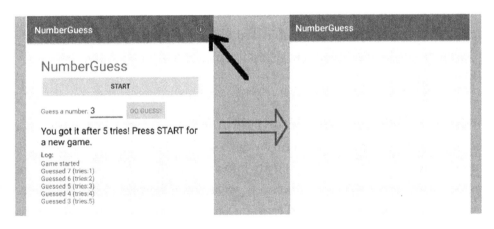

Figure 9-4.   *Empty statistics activity*

State Housekeeping for the Statistics

In the Statistics singleton object we gather the outcome from all game sessions in a list. Because in a session we get two figures—the number to guess and the number of tries needed to guess the number—we define an inner class GameSessionRecord holding one result pair. We therefore update the Statistics object accordingly:

```
package kotlinforandroid.book.numberguess.statistics
```

```
object Statistics {
    data class GameSessionRecord(val numberToGuess:Int,
            val tries:Int) : Serializable
    val data: ArrayList<GameSessionRecord> = ArrayList()

    fun getStatistics(): List<String> {
        return emptyList()
    }
}
```

where the `ArrayList<GameSessionRecord>` means we want a mutable list of exactly such session records. The `: Serializable` is a marker interface that makes sure the objects from this class can be converted into a language-agnostic representation.

Note   Unfortunately we cannot write `val data = mutableListOf()` because this is not marked serializable. We need a language-agnostic representation for the complete list as well, so we have to fall back to the concrete implementation.

This `data` list represents the complete state of the `Statistics` object. We learned from the `MainActivity` that we must find a way to save and restore the state, because Android unexpectedly might put any activity into a suspended state, causing it to lose its properties. We therefore add two functions, `save()` and `restore()`. As parameters they have the `Bundle` instances needed for state saving and restoring as controlled by the activity. We add a function call to `onCreate()`:

```
override
fun onCreate(savedInstanceState: Bundle?) {
    super.onCreate(savedInstanceState)
    setContentView(R.layout.activity_statistics)

    restoreData(savedInstanceState) // new!
    showData(Statistics.getStatistics())
}
```

The two new functions read:

```
fun restoreData(savedInstanceState: Bundle?) {
    savedInstanceState?.run {
        getSerializable("statistics.data")?.run {
            Statistics.data.clear()
            Statistics.data.addAll( this as
                ArrayList<Statistics.GameSessionRecord>)
        }
    }
}

override fun onSaveInstanceState(outState: Bundle?) {
    super.onSaveInstanceState(outState)
    outState?.putSerializable("statistics.data",
        Statistics.data)
}
```

The ?.run{ } constructs make sure the run block gets executed only if the value in front of it is not null. If it gets executed, this contains exactly this value. Therefore the getSerializable() actually translates to this.getSerializable() and thus to the getSerializable() from the savedInstanceState object. The this as ... is needed because the getSerializable() by language design has lost its type information, so we must explicitly state the type.

Communicating Between the Activities

The game itself gets handled by the MainActivity class and the statistics by StatisticsActivity. For those running the same process, we choose the simplest way of communication: using a singleton object for sharing data. We have not yet covered processes; in most cases it is enough to know that a process is a technical bracket around app components, and that singleton objects reside within a process's boundaries.

Note   For more complicated data structures to share between app components, consider using the built-in Android database.

Also, sending a game session's data to the statistics component does not require any user interface actions, so there is no need for any elaborate intra-app communication. We therefore add a simple function to the `Statistics` singleton object for adding records to the list.

```
object Statistics {
    ...
    fun register(numberToGuess:Int, tries:Int) {
        data.add(GameSessionRecord(numberToGuess,
                tries))
    }
}
```

Now, inside the `MainActivity` we invoke this function.

```
fun guess(v:View) {
    ...
    if (g < number) {
        ...
    } else if (g > number) {
        ...
    } else {
        Statistics.register(number, tries)
        ...
    }
    ...
}
```

Note that for this to work the `Statistics` singleton object needs to be imported: `import kotlinforandroid.book.numberguess.statistics.Statistics`.

Implementing Statistical Calculations

With the statistics activity all set up and the data from the game activity communicated, we are now ready for some calculations on the data inside the `Statistics` class. We start with a simple one, the number of game sessions.

```
private fun numberOfSessions() : Int =
    data.size
```

The next calculation is the average number of tries needed to correctly guess the number:

```
private fun averageTriesNeeded() : Double =
    if(data.size > 0) data.map { rec -> rec.tries }
        .sum().toDouble() / data.size ;
    else 0.0
```

Let us investigate this step by step:

1. The `if()` ... `;else` ... checks whether we have data at all. If there is no record, the average cannot be built and we have to avoid dividing by `0.0`. In this case, we return `0.0`.

2. The `map()` applies the provided lambda function to each element of `data` and returns a new list with the number of attempts as elements.

3. The `sum()` is available for any collection with number type elements. Here it obviously sums up all tries.

4. The `toDouble()` is necessary, because otherwise an `Int` by `Int` division will result in an `Int`, not the desired `Double`.

We divide the sum by the number of game sessions to obtain the result.

The next figure we want to calculate is the standard deviation of the tries needed to guess the secret number. In case If you don't know what a standard deviation is, it tells us about the "roughness" of a number, meaning how often and how much the numbers differ from the average we just calculated. The formula for the standard deviation is

$$stddev(tries) = \sqrt{\frac{\sum_i^N \left(tries_i - \overline{tries}\right)^2}{N-1}}$$

where $\overline{tries}$ designates the average. The corresponding Kotlin function reads:

```
private fun triesNeededStdDev() : Double {
    if(data.size < 2) return 0.0
    val avg = averageTriesNeeded()
    return Math.sqrt(
```

```
    data.map {
      rec -> Math.pow(rec.tries - avg, 2.0)
    }.sum() / (data.size - 1))
}
```

and has the following characteristics:

- Because we need the average inside a loop, we introduce a val variable holding the average. It is thus not possible here to use the fun functName() = ... notation. We cannot put it into a single expression. Well, we could, but not without significant performance penalties.

- For the standard deviation we need at least two records. If we have fewer, we prematurely exit the function and return 0.0.

- The Math.sqrt() calculates the square root needed for the calculation: $\sqrt{x}$.

- The Math.pow(x, 2.0) calculates the square: x^2.

- Similar to the average calculation, the map() extracts $\left(tries - \overline{tries} \right)^2$ where $\overline{tries}$ designates the average.

- We again take the sum from the result list by applying sum().

- The division by $size - 1$ is part of the formula.

The next function we write calculates a histogram of the tries. For each possible k tries needed we figure out how often k shows up in the statistics data. This is a typical case for a map Int → Int mapping the ks to their frequencies. The Kotlin function that does this for our Statistics class reads:

```
private fun neededTriesDistrib() : Map<Int, Int> =
    data.groupBy({rec -> rec.tries}).
    mapValues { me -> me.value.size }
```

It performs in this manner:

- We see a practical implementation of groupBy(). You will see groupBy() often when it comes to counting things based on some criterion. Here we count record objects based on the number of tries. This is exactly what the function parameter of groupBy() here does.

- The result of the groupBy() function is a map Int →
  List<GameSessionRecord>. We don't need the list per tries figure,
  though, only the number of records. This is what the mapValues() is
  used for; it converts the value of each mapped to item from the map
  and replaces the list that it happens to be, in this case by the list size.
  The me in the parameter of mapValues() is of type Map.Entry. This is
  something mapValues() prescribes. Map.Entry has two properties:
  the .key and the .value. The key is the tries figure, and the value
  is the list. We take the value and from it the size. The result is the
  desired map.

A last interesting function tries to determine whether the number of tries needed to
guess a number depends on the number itself. We count the tries based on the criterion
numberToGuess and take the average. The code for that reads:

```
private
fun triesByNumberToGuess() : Map<Int, Double> =
    data.groupBy({rec -> rec.numberToGuess})
        .mapValues { me ->
            me.value.map{it.tries}.sum().toDouble()
            / me.value.size }
```

Let us investigate the parts:

- We again use the groupBy() function. This time, however, we need
  to calculate figures for the numberToGuess member and accordingly
  extract this property as the groupBy -key.

- We get a map with a list of GameSessionRecord elements as values.
  We take each list and calculate the average of tries needed. For this
  aim we map the list to a new list containing only the tries figures, take
  the sum, convert it to a double, and divide it by the list size.

All that is left now is adapting the getStatistics() function to include the statistics
figures from the new calculation functions. It could read, for example:

```
fun getStatistics(): List<String> {
    val twoDigits = DecimalFormat().
        apply{ maximumFractionDigits = 2 }
```

```
    val triesDistrib = neededTriesDistrib().
        toSortedMap().toString()
    val triesByNumber = triesByNumberToGuess().
        toSortedMap().mapValues {
            me -> twoDigits.format(me.value) }
        .toString()
  return listOf(
      "Sessions: ${numberOfSessions()}",
      "Average Tries: ${averageTriesNeeded()}",
      "Tries Standard Dev: ${triesNeededStdDev()}",
      "Tries Distrib: ${triesDistrib}",
      "Tries by Number: ${triesByNumber}"
  )
}
```

For this to work, the import `import java.text.DecimalFormat` needs to be added to the imports list. The `NumberFormat` used here is new; we need it to avoid doubles being printed out with too many fraction digits. The `.toSortedMap()` makes sure the maps get sorted according to their keys.

After starting the app and playing the game a couple of times, then launching the statistics activity, the output might look like the display in Figure 9-5.

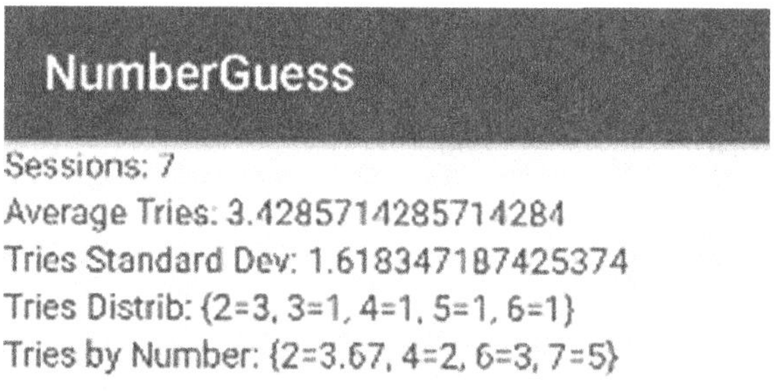

NumberGuess

Sessions: 7
Average Tries: 3.42857142857142841
Tries Standard Dev: 1.618347187425374
Tries Distrib: {2=3, 3=1, 4=1, 5=1, 6=1}
Tries by Number: {2=3.67, 4=2, 6=3, 7=5}

Figure 9-5. *NumberGuess statistics*

True, False, and Undecided: Nullability

At school you learned about the dichotomy of true versus false, and you probably heard that there is nothing else. Reading this book, thus far, you have learned that in Kotlin there exists a boolean type Boolean with exactly those possible values: true and false. Period. Really?

If you think about real life, experience suggests something else. Ask someone: Is it going to rain tomorrow? Maybe the answer is yes, and maybe it is no. Honestly, though, no one knows with 100 percent certainty. We therefore have *true, false,* and *undecided* (or *unknown*). This trichotomy gets called *three-valued logic* (also *trinary, trivalent,* or *ternary* logic). Why are we talking about this here? This is not a philosophy book, is it? For classes and objects, we already pointed out that computer programs need to model real-world scenarios; therefore we need to have something that is neither true nor false in a computer language.

What NULL Is

Even with computer language developers not really being sound philosophers or perhaps just being unaware of this trichotomy, *undecided* has been around from the very beginning of computer language history. It just didn't get called that. Say, for example, you need a variable that represents the size of some list. Depending on circumstances, a list of size zero might make sense, and for coding reasons we might need to express that a list is not yet defined. What can we do? Well, sizes are from the range 0, 1, 2, 3, . . . , so we just take a number that usually makes no sense and *define* this to represent a *not yet defined*. Can you guess what number this could be? A possible answer is −1.

© Peter Späth 2019
P. Späth, *Learn Kotlin for Android Development*, https://doi.org/10.1007/978-1-4842-4467-8_10

With arrays the story is even more diverse. Usually arrays get defined by some *pointer* variable that points to the first element of the array in a computer's memory. If we need to say the array is not yet defined, we use a pointer value that doesn't make sense. This could be −1, but more practical is the value 0. For technical reasons it is impossible that at memory address 0 actually starts an array, so 0 for *undecided* is a valid choice. To clarify the difference between a real memory address and an undecided, the 0 expressing the latter just gets a new name: null. For even more fun, with object orientation we also have pointers to class instances, and those can be null as well as express *undecided* or *not yet defined.*

In addition to a third pseudo-boolean undecided next to true and false, we have another undecided for arrays and objects. How do they relate? Look at the following code snippet:

```
val b:Boolean = ... // some condition
if(b) {
    ... // do something
} else {
    ... // do something else
}
```

Here we branch on whether some condition is met or not. With objects that could be null to express them being not yet defined, in many situations you will have an extended version of this:

```
val instance = ... // some object
val b:Boolean = ... // some condition
if(instance == null) {
    ... // do something
} else if(b) {
    ... // do something else
} else {
    ... // do something else
}
```

Here we make a decision based on whether something is true or false, and also if something is undefined. Now if we had a third boolean value undecided in a fictive computer language, this could read

```
val b:Boolean = ... // some three-valued condition
ifundecided(b) {
    ... // do something
} if(b) {
    ... // do something else
} else {
    ... // do something else
}
```

These two constructs, a fictive three-valued boolean and a null object reference, express the same code. This is where the two undecideds meet. Because in neither Kotlin, nor in any other language I'm aware of, a third boolean value exists, we must continue to use null for that purpose.

There is a serious problem with null: Do you remember what the dereferencing operator . does? It takes the object from the left side of the . and uses the right side to aim at a property or function. Quite naturally for objects that are undecided or null, this dereferencing makes no sense. Unfortunately, many computer languages are not very nice here and crash if we try to dereference on null, or at least break the program flow and indicate an invalid program flow activity. This nullability annoyed generations of developers by introducing instability into programs. The benefits outweighed the problems, though, so just avoiding nullability was never considered a real alternative.

How Nullability Gets Handled Inside Kotlin

Kotlin introduces a couple of new ideas about nullability, allowing its use but avoiding most of the associated pitfalls. First, we notice that by default Kotlin does not allow null values to sneak around in your app. Something like this

```
var p:SomeType = ...
...
p = null
```

just is not allowed for any type of property. The same holds for constructors and function invocation:

```
class A(var p:SomeType) ...
A(null) // does not compile
```

```
fun f(p:SomeType) { ... }
f(null) // does not compile
```

With such non-nullable properties, a dereferencing via . will always succeed. If, on the other hand, we want a property, constructor parameter, or function parameter to be nullable, we have to add a question mark (?) to the type:

```
var p:SomeType? = ...
p = null // OK
```

```
class A(var p:SomeType?) ...
A(null) // OK
```

```
fun f(p:SomeType?) { ... }
f(null) // OK
```

Note   Because you have to add something to allow for nullability, Kotlin slightly favors non-nullability. In fact, in many cases you can avoid null values, and if this is the case, chances are good you have a good app design.

For such nullable types Kotlin knows that a dereferencing via .property or .function() might fail and prohibits using them:

```
var p:SomeType? = ...
...
p.property    // does not compile
p.function()  // does not compile
```

This is even then prohibited if the value happens to be not null.

How can we use such nullable properties then? The answer is that we have to use one of the null-safe operators Kotlin provides. So for the dereferencing . there is a null-safe variant ?. that you can use for nullable properties:

```
var p:SomeType? = ...
...
p?.property    // OK
p?.function()  // OK
```

The difference is that if p is null the p?.property evaluates to null itself, the function in p?.function() will not be invoked, and the call evaluates to null, too.

```
var p:SomeType? = null

val res:TypeOfProperty? = p?.property          // -> null

val res2:TypeOfFunct? = p?.function()          // -> null
// ... and function() not invoked
```

Another operator that by design is null-safe is the *Elvis* operator ?:. We already know this one; it evaluates to its left side if that one is not null, and otherwise to its right side.

```
var p:String? = "Hello"
var s1 = p?:"default" // -> "Hello"
p = null
var s2 = p?:"default" // -> "default"
```

Kotlin cannot always know whether a property is nullable or not. In such cases it might help to use the !! operator, which also gets called the *not null assertion operator*. It takes its left side, and no matter whether or not it might evaluate to null, presumes that it cannot be null. You might use it once in a while if your app needs programs written by others. This is especially true for libraries that are written in other languages and don't apply Kotlin's null-checking mechanism. Of course if you then try to dereference it by using. and the value accidentally is null, your app will crash. By all means try to avoid that, or know what to do.

Caution   Using !! you essentially bypass Kotlin's null-checking mechanism, so try to avoid it.

```
var p:String? = ...
// for whatever reason we know that p cannot be null

val len = p!!.length
// valid, because the !! indicates it cannot be null
// If it accidentally _is_ null, we'll crash here.
```

By the way, Kotlin is quite clever if you apply !!. In subsequent statements of the same function it remembers that we applied this assertion and continues assuming that the value cannot be null. You can write

```
var p:String? = ...
```

```
val len = p!!.length
val intVal = p.toInt()
```

Here the last statement only compiles because of the !! somewhere before this line.

CHAPTER 11

Handling Equality

There is a strong distinction between *identity* and *equality*. Two things are identical if they actually are the same. If you bought a white candle this morning, let's call it A, the white candle in your shopping bag and the white candle that this afternoon is placed in your candleholder are the same and thus identical (presume this is the only candle you own). Now assume you bought a second candle, B, of the same type from the same manufacturer. Apart from some linguistic mistakes you sometimes hear, those two candles are *not* the same. Candles A and B are not the same, but they are *equal*. This is because they have the same characteristics: the same color, the same weight, the same diameter, and the same length. Hold on, though: This is not necessarily true. The manufacturer says such a candle weights 300 g, but a high-precision balance tells us candle A weighs 300.00245 g, and candle B weighs 299.99734 g. If you take a kitchen scale, though, the weights of candles A and B are the same. Therefore you can see that equality depends on strictness and it is *relative*.

This comparison between identity and equality teaches us an important lesson: Identity is the case for things that are the same, whereas equality is relative and depends on some definition.

Identity in Kotlin

In Kotlin there is an identity operator === and its opposite !==. In Kotlin, identity stands for *referential identity,* which means if two variables point to the same object, or *refer* to the same object, they are considered identical:

```
data class A(val x:Double)
val a = A(7.0)
val b = A(7.0)
val c = a
val aIdenticalToC = a === c // -> true
val aIdenticalToB = a === b // -> false
```

© Peter Späth 2019
P. Späth, *Learn Kotlin for Android Development*, https://doi.org/10.1007/978-1-4842-4467-8_11

In reality, you might not use identity very often. Having different variables pointing to the same object in most cases is not considered good coding style anyway, and in addition identity is something that does not differ a lot with different program flows. Finally, the comparison of any two objects evaluating to false despite all properties having the same value in the two objects is confusing and thwarts the readability of your code. The practical use of checking for identity, therefore, is limited.

Note   There is another *identity* notion that is revealed in a database environment. There you often have a numerical ID field for data records. This field gets used as a surrogate for the corresponding object's identity, instead of the language's referential === identity. In this chapter we are not talking about this database kind of identity.

Equality in Kotlin

For equality Kotlin provides the comparison operator ==, and its opposite !=. Other than identity, an object must tell whether it is equal to some other object. If you don't do this explicitly, the base implementation of an equality check is used, which falls back to the identity check.

Equality checks on numbers, booleans, chars, and strings do the obvious thing: Strings are equal if they contain exactly the same characters, characters are equal if they contain the same letter, and numbers and booleans are equal if they have the same value.

Equals and Hash Code

The way a class handles equality checks is governed by two functions: `fun equals(otherObject:Any?): Boolean` and `fun hashCode(): Int`. If your classes need equality checks, you must implement both. It might seem strange that we need two functions for equality checks. Why does it not suffice to have just `equals()` for equality checks? The reason lies in performance, and the precise idea is described later.

First, though, we state that if we write a1 == a2 for some a1 and a2 as instances of class A, the function equals() gets called on class A, and only if it returns true, the result of the comparison is true as well. For == equality checks, then, the equals() function actually does suffice.

For maps, the story is different. If we have a map mapping instances of some class A to whatever, for example

```
class A(val v:Int) {

    override fun hashCode():Int {
        return ...
    }
    override fun equals(other:Any?):Boolean {
        return ...
    }
}
```

```
val m = mapOf(A(7) to 8, A(8) to 9)
```

and then perform a lookup like

```
val searchKey:A = ...
m[searchKey]
```

what actually happens is this:

- The hash code of searchKey gets calculated by invoking hashCode() on it.

- The [] operator (or the get() function) applies a very fast algorithm to find an entry based on the integer *hash* key.

- For entries found during the hash key lookup, a call of equals() happens for all possible entries. If equals() found the precise entry, the [] operator returns the corresponding value for that entry.

- If a hash key lookup failed or all the subsequent equals() checks failed, the [] operator fails as well and returns null.

We observe two things:

1. The equals() gets invoked only if the hash code lookup succeeded.

2. For the process to make sense, for the hashCode() function the following must be true: (1) If a == b, we also need a.hashCode() == b.hashCode(). (2) If a != b, in most cases we also should have a.hashCode() != b.hashCode(). If (1) wasn't true, the map lookup function would fail, and if (2) wasn't true, we'd too often have to call equals().

As an example, consider the class

```kotlin
class Person(val lastName:String,
    val firstName:String,
    val birthday:String,
    val gender:Char)
```

We implement an equals() function based on all properties:

```kotlin
class Person(val lastName:String,
        val firstName:String,
        val birthday:String,
        val gender:Char) {
    override fun equals(other:Any?):Boolean {
        if(other == null) return false
        if(other !is Person) return false
        if(lastName != other.lastName) return false
        if(firstName != other.firstName) return false
        if(birthday != other.birthday) return false
        if(gender != other.gender) return false
        return true
    }
}
```

The first two lines in fun equals() return null if the object other provided for comparison is null or not an instance of Person. You will find similar lines in almost any equals() implementation, although it would be overstating to say you'll find them absolutely everywhere; for some strange reason we might accept comparisons with null or other types.

Because we are already finished if other is not of type Person, starting with the third line Kotlin knows that other is an instance of Person. This automatic type detection sometimes gets called *smart cast*. What comes is a step-by-step comparison of all properties, and only if they all match we return true.

For a hashCode() function you might think of a lot of algorithms, and on the Web you'll also find several ideas about it. Fortunately we don't have to spend too much brain power on that; the object Objects from package java.util provides a convenience function for that and we can write:

```
class Person(val lastName:String,
     val firstName:String,
     val birthday:String,
     val gender:Char) {
   override fun equals(other:Any?):Boolean {
       if(other == null) return false
       if(other !is Person) return false
       if(lastName != other.lastName) return false
       if(firstName != other.firstName) return false
       if(birthday != other.birthday) return false
       if(gender != other.gender) return false
       return true
   }

   override fun hashCode(): Int {
       return Objects.hash(super.hashCode(),
           lastName, firstName, birthday, gender)
   }
}
```

For such obvious cases where equality depends on all properties checked for equality, Kotlin has a shortcut. We already talked about it: *data classes*. They implement an equals() and a hashCode() function exactly based on all properties. For the Person class we can thus remove the explicit equals() and hashCode() functions and simply write

```
data class Person(val lastName:String,
      val firstName:String,
      val birthday:String,
      val gender:Char)
```

Exercise 1

If two variables a and b are identical, which of the following are true?

1. a and b refer to the same object.

2. a == b necessarily yields true.

3. a !== b necessarily yields false.

Exercise 2

If two variables a and b are equal, a == b, which of the following are true?

1. a.equals(b) must be true.

2. a != b necessarily yields false.

3. a.hashCode() == b.hashCode() must be true.

Back to Math: Functional Programming

If you look at the examples and exercises presented so far in this book you can see that we fluctuate between two styles of programming:

```
[statement1] // do something
[statement2] // do something
[statement3] // do something
...
```

and

```
object.
    doSomething1().
    doSomething2().
    doSomething3().
    ...
```

The first style is about a sequence of imperatively telling what a program has to do, whereas the second is about sequentially applying functions on objects in a function invocation chain. Because of this, the first style also gets called *imperative programming*, and the second is known as *functional programming*. Functional programming frequently also implies using functions as arguments to other functions, which then get called *higher order functions*. In addition, functional programming favors handling immutable objects.

© Peter Späth 2019
P. Späth, *Learn Kotlin for Android Development*, https://doi.org/10.1007/978-1-4842-4467-8_12

When using an imperative programming style, the following observations become clear:

- We have a sequence of statements, including if/else, when constructs and loops. Obviously, the order of the statements is important.

- With each statement performing an identifiable program activity, imperative programming at first glance leads to programs that are easy to understand.

- The various statements can handle various different objects.

- Each statement might or might not alter the state of the object in which it is embedded, and also the states of more objects involved. Obviously with various structural constructs like loops and conditional branchings there is no real limit to the complexity of the states and state transitions for all objects involved.

- Statements include function calls that do unexpected things apart from their main responsibilities. Such subsidiary activities frequently get called *side effects*. These side effects can thus be both anticipated and unanticipated, with possibly erroneous program activities.

In contrast functional programming has the following characteristics:

- Functional constructs primarily refer to single objects or a single collection of objects. By virtue of function parameters, other objects or collections might enter the function invocation chain, though.

- Functional programming includes handling functions as function parameters. It thus allows for a higher abstraction compared to imperative programming.

- Functional program parts, by virtue of passing around function invocation results as parameters or input to other functions, allow for a stateless programming style, avoiding complex state transitions.

With functions not referring and not altering object states, we also return to a more math-like function notion. Remember that in math functions have an input and produce an output from that, ignoring any "state" that might influence the calculation.

Object orientation uses a slightly altered function notion where the state of objects plays an important role for the outcome of a function invocation. Functional programming thus moves the function notion to more math-like semantics. Figure 12-1 shows a comparison of imperative and functional programming.

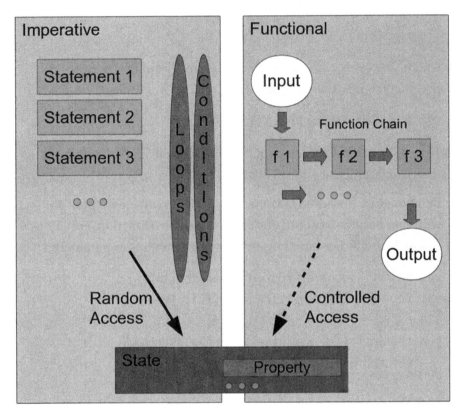

Figure 12-1.   *Functional versus imperative programming*

To this point we didn't favor either of the two programming paradigms over the other, and looking at the characteristics of each programming style you can see that both have their advantages and disadvantages. We continue with that attitude, but point out that according to the circumstances, functional constructs could lead to more elegant and more stable programs. Kotlin allows for both styles, and for each task it is up to you to decide which paradigm best suits your needs.

In the rest of this chapter we deepen our knowledge of functional constructs, so you have an improved tool set at hand for writing good software.

Kotlin and Functional Programming

Kotlin, although a full-fledged imperative language, also allows for a functional programming style by virtue of these features:

- Kotlin has a function type declaration:

  ```
  ([parameters]) -> [result-type]
  ```

  where [parameters] is a comma-separated list of function parameter types. For example,

  ```
  val f : (Int,String) -> String = ...
  ```

  The -> [result-type] cannot be omitted, so if a function doesn't return anything you write -> Unit.

- Functions are first-class citizens: Any variable can have a built-in type, can be an instance of any class, or can be a function. Functions can be higher order functions by allowing functions as parameters.

  ```
  val f1 = { -> Log.d("LOG", "Hello Kotlin") }
  val f2 = { i:Int, s:String -> "${i}: ${s}" }
  ...
  fun ff(fun1: (Int,String) -> String):String {
      return fun1(7, "Hello")
  }
  ff(f2)
  ff( { i:Int,s:String -> "${i}- ${s}" } )
  ```

- Kotlin has anonymous lambda functions; these are function literals that can be used as function invocation parameters. For example:

  ```
  val f = { i:Int, s:String ->
          i.toString() + ": " + s }
  fun fun1(p: (Int,String) -> String) {
      p(42, "Hello")
  }
  fun1 { i:Int, s:String -> i.toString() + ": " + s }
  ```

Here Kotlin infers that f must be of type `(Int, String) -> String`

- Kotlin's standard library has a lot of higher order functions for objects, arrays, and collections.

- A function call `function({ [lambda-function] })` can be abbreviated:

  `function { [lambda-function] }`

- A function call `function(par1, par2, ..., { [lambda-function] })` can be abbreviated: `function(par1, par2, ...) { [lambda-function] }`

- In a function type `([parameters]) -> [result-type]` a parameter usually is of the form `ParType`. A special *receiver type* notation reads `A.(ParType)`. In this case type A is the receiver type and the function called inside an instance of class A means inside the function specification `this` refers to the instance. A dedicated section of this chapter talks about such a receiver type notation.

- Kotlin variables can be immutable: `val s = ....` Immutable variables help to avoid state handling and reduce unanticipated side effects.

- Functions from singleton objects can be addressed as objects themselves by prepending two colons (`::`). If, for example, you want to use the function `add()` from `object X { fun add(a:Int,b:Int):Int = a+b }` you write

```
object X {
    fun add(a:Int, b:Int): Int = a + b
}
...
val f : (Int,Int) -> Int = X::add
```

- Functions from classes can be addressed as objects with receiver type by prepending two colons (::). For example:

```
class X {
   fun add(a:Int, b:Int): Int = a + b
}
...
val f : X.(Int,Int) -> Int = X::add
```

- Functions from instances can be addressed as objects by prepending two colons (::). For example:

```
class X {
   fun add(a:Int, b:Int): Int = a + b
}
...
val x1 = X()
val f : (Int,Int) -> Int = x1::add
```

Functions Without Names: Lambda Functions

We know that normal functions look like

```
fun functionName([parameters]): ReturnType {
   ...
}
```

or

```
fun functionName([parameters]): ReturnType = ...
```

if the function can be reduced to an expression. Functions declared that way get identified by functionName. The question is this: How can it be possible to have functions without identifying the function name? For the answer, we look at variables containing data; here we write

```
val varName = 37
```

The value on the right side of the = doesn't have an identifying name either. All we need is the variable name to handle the data. If we look at functions that get assigned to variables,

```
val f = { i:Int, s:String -> i.toString() + ": " + s }
```

We can see that the { ... } construct doesn't have an identifying name either; the function gets used by the variable to which it got assigned. Such functions thus are anonymous and commonly get referred to as lambda functions.

Note   Expressions with such anonymous functions also sometimes are called *lambda calculus.*

The same holds for functions that have been passed to other functions as parameters:

```
ff( { i:Int,s:String -> "${i}- ${s}" } )
```

Here again we have a function without a name or a lambda function.

To invoke a lambda function, you write one of these:

```
[lambda_function].invoke([parameters])
[lambda_function]([parameters])
```

Lambda functions can have a result. Contrary to a normal function, where you return values via some return statement, the result of a lambda function is whatever the last line evaluated to. The preceding example

```
val f = { i:Int, s:String -> i.toString() + ": " + s }
```

thus returns the string representation of the Int parameter, plus a :, plus the String parameter, all by virtue of the last line of the lambda function.

In a lambda function with a single parameter, for brevity the parameter declaration can be omitted and the special identifier it can be used instead to refer to the parameter. The following two statements are therefore equivalent:

```
{ par ->
    ... // do something with 'par' }
{
    ... // do something with 'it' }
```

Exercise 1

Write as a lambda function: a function that takes an `s:String` and a `num:Int` and outputs a string with `num` copies of `s` concatenated.

Exercise 2

Rewrite

```
val f : (String) -> String = { s:String -> s + "!" }
```

to use `it` instead.

If a lambda function has one or more parameters you don't need in a definition, you can use an underscore wildcard (_) as a parameter name:

```
val f : (String, Int) -> String = { s:String, _ ->
    // the Int parameter is not used
    s + "!"
}
```

Loops Once Again

In Chapter 9 we learned that we can iterate over the elements of an array or collection (set, list) by writing `data.forEach(...)` or `data.forEachIndexed(...)`:

```
val arr = arrayOf("Joe", "Isabel", "John" }
arr.forEach { name ->
    Log.d("A name: ${name}")
}
arr.forEachIndexed { i,s ->
    Log.d("Name #${i}: ${name}")
}
```

Here the `Log` comes from package `android.util`, so you have to import it:

```
import android.util.Log
```

Although at first glance the { } behind forEach or forEachIndexed looks like a statement block, we can see by looking at the -> that in fact both forEach and forEachIndexed are actually functions with a lambda function as a parameter. It is also possible, then, to write arr.forEach({ ... }) or arr.forEachIndexed({ ... }); the parentheses can be left out, as is always the case in Kotlin, if they just enclose curly brackets.

Inside Android Studio for any function invocation we can also look at the sources. For this aim, place the cursor, for example, over forEach and then press Ctrl+B. Android Studio then opens the sources for this function and shows us this:

```
public inline fun <T> Array<out T>.forEach(
        action: (T) -> Unit): Unit {
    for (element in this) action(element)
}
```

Here again we see that what comes after the forEach is a function as a function parameter.

Note   Pressing Ctrl+B is a good way to learn what is going on behind the scenes in Kotlin. Use it extensively to understand Kotlin constructs and functions.

Because forEach and forEachIndexed are functions and not language constructs, they can be intuitively applied to any objects that look like they contain something that can be iterated over. This includes arrays and collections that are the result of applying other functions over arrays and collections. We could therefore include filters and mappings in the function chain that ends up in a loop, as in

```
originalCollection.
    filter([filter_function]).
    map([mapping_function]).
    take(37).
    forEach { elem ->
        ...
    }
```

where we first apply a filter, then a mapping, then a reduction to the first 37 elements before we start the loop. We can see that by virtue of functions being allowed as function parameters, we can achieve a function chain and avoid intermediate variables as data holders.

Functions with Receivers

Functions that are considered function objects and are embedded in a context, as, for example, functions inside a class, are called *functions with receiver types*. You declare them as follows:

```
val f : ReceiverType.([parameters]) = ...
```

Such a function then acts as if it was a member function of class ReceiverType, and inside the function implementation you can use this, which points to the instance. For example, in

```
class A {
    var d:Double = 0.0
    fun plus(x:Double) = d + x
}
val f : A.(Double) -> Double =
        { x:Double -> this.d - x }
fun A.minus(x:Double) = f
```

function f is such a function with receiver type. We use it to extend class A with a minus() function, and the this.d inside the implementation of f points to property d inside the receiver type, A in this case.

In the previous section we already noticed that a direct reference to a function inside a class automatically is such a function with receiver type, because it only works inside the environment of its class:

```
class X {
  fun add(a:Int, b:Int): Int = a + b
}
...
val f : X.(Int,Int) -> Int = X::add
```

Inline Functions

Look at this code snippet:

```kotlin
class A {
  fun function1(i:Int, f:(Int) -> String): String {
    return f(i)
  }
  fun function2() {
    val a = 7

    val s = function1(8) {
      i -> "8 + a = " + (i+a) }
  }
}
```

Inside the invocation of function1() we pass a function object in the form of a lambda function i -> .... This function object must be created during runtime, and in addition the compiler must allow for the local property a to be passed into that object. This introduces a significant performance penalty. More precisely, the Kotlin compiler produces something like this:

```java
public class A {
    public String function1(int i,
          Function1<? super Integer, String> f) {
        return f.invoke(i);
    }

    public void function2() {
        int a = 7;
        String s2 = this.function1(8,
              new Function1<Integer, String>(a){
            final int $a;
            public String invoke(int i) {
                return "8 + a = " + (i + this.$a);
            }
```

```
            {
                this.$a = n;
                super(1);
            }
        });
    }
}
```

This is Java language code, but without going into detail we see that via new Function1(...) a function object must be instantiated, and inside it a copy of property a will be created.

If this performance penalty poses a problem, the function1() can be *inlined*:

```
class A {
  inline fun function1(i:Int, f:(Int) -> String): String
  {
      return f(i)
  }
  fun function2() {
      val a = 7
      val s = function1(8) {
          i -> "8 + a = " + (i+a) }
  }
}
```

What does that mean? It basically says that whenever the inlined function gets used, no actual function invocation happens, but the function code gets copied in place to the point where the function gets used. Again, looking at the compiler output, this time we get

```
public class A {
  public String function1(int i,
        Function1<? super Integer, String> f) {
      return f.invoke(i);
  }
```

```
  public void function2() {
      int a = 7;
      int i$iv;
      int i = i$iv = 8;
      String s2 = "8 + a = " + (i + a);
  }
}
```

You can see that from inside `function2()` the inlined function `function1` is not getting invoked; instead the snippet

```
int i$iv;
int i = i$iv = 8;
String s2 = "8 + a = " + (i + a);
```

replaces the function invocation. No object instantiation happens and this code thus runs much faster compared to the variant that is not inlined.

Using an inlined function yields a couple of nontrivial peculiarities. For example, `return` statements behave differently from inside inlined functions. Also, it is possible to only inline dedicated lambda function parameters and leave others creating function objects. Also, inline functions support a special kind of type parameters, called *reified type parameters,* which allow access to the type of parameters at runtime. We don't go into detail here; if you are interested please consult the online Kotlin documentation for functions.

Filters

If you have a list of some objects, such as instances of a `data class Employee(val firstName:String, val lastName:String, val ssn:String, val yearHired:Int)`, in algorithms you frequently need to extract list members based on some criterion. Using an imperative programming style this often leads to code snippets like this:

```
data class Employee(val firstName:String,
      val lastName:String,
      val ssn:String,
      val yearHired:Int)
```

```
val employees = listOf(
    Employee("John", "Smith", "123-12-0001", 1987),
    Employee("Linda", "Thundergaard", "123-12-0002", 1987),
    Employee("Lewis", "Black", "123-12-0003", 1977),
    Employee("Evans", "Brightsmith", "123-12-0004", 1991)
)
val before1990 = mutableListOf<Employee>()
for(empl in employees) {
    if(empl.yearHired < 1990) before1990.add(empl)
}
... // do something with before1990
```

This code seems very easy to understand and seems to solve the filtering task adequately, but there are a couple of problems if we look closer at it.

- Before we start the loop we need to create the receiving list in a separate statement. The result list creation is decoupled from the loop; the code does not prevent us from adding more statements between the list creation and the loop, for example, because of future requirements. This decoupling might introduce complicated state transitions, which destabilizes the program.

- Inside the loop the result list is nothing but a local variable; the loop exists for the sole purpose of populating the result list, but the code does not prevent us from doing other things there, eventually decreasing code readability.

- If the list gets very lengthy we might be tempted to parallelize the code inside the loop; that is, let several processes do the filtering at the same time. This very easily will lead to concurrency problems, since the `before1990` variable is just a normal local property. Letting several processes concurrently access the same collection frequently leads to data consistency failures.

- With more complicated filtering criteria, we might end up in a complicated stacking of various `if-else/when` branchings inside the loop.

A remedy for almost all these problems consists of switching to functional code:

```
data class Employee(val firstName:String,
     val lastName:String,
     val ssn:String,
     val yearHired:Int)
val employees = listOf(
    Employee("John", "Smith", "123-12-0001", 1987),
    Employee("Linda", "Thundergaard", "123-12-0002", 1987),
    Employee("Lewis", "Black", "123-12-0003", 1977),
    Employee("Evans", "Brightsmith", "123-12-0004", 1991)
)
val before1990 = employees.filter {
    it.yearHired < 1990 }.toList()
... // do something with before1990
```

Here we could avoid writing emp -> ... inside the argument of filter(), as there is only one function parameter and we use the automatic it variable. After the filter() we could insert more filters, or a mapping function as we saw in Chapter 9.

Exercise 3

Create another list startsWithL by applying a filter that only lets employees pass whose first name starts with L. Note: String has a startsWith() function we can use for that purpose.

CHAPTER 13

About Type Safety: Generics

Generics is a term used for denoting a set of language features that allow us to add type parameters to types. Consider, for example, a simple class with a function for adding elements in the form of Int objects:

```kotlin
class AdderInt {
    fun add(i:Int) {
        ...
    }
}
```

and another one for String objects:

```kotlin
class AdderString {
    fun add(s:String) {
        ...
    }
}
```

Apart from what happens inside the add() function, these classes look suspiciously similar, so we could think of a language feature that abstracts the type for the element to add. Such a language feature exists in Kotlin, and it is called *generics*. A corresponding construct reads as follows:

```kotlin
class Adder<T> {
    fun add(toAdd:T) {
        ...
    }
}
```

275

© Peter Späth 2019
P. Späth, *Learn Kotlin for Android Development*, https://doi.org/10.1007/978-1-4842-4467-8_13

where T is the *type parameter*. Here instead of T any other name could be used for the type parameter, but in many projects you will often find T, R, S, U, A, or B as type parameter names.

For instantiating such classes, the type must be known to the compiler. Either you have to explicitly specify the type, as in

```
class Adder<T> {
    fun add(toAdd:T) {
        ...
    }
}
val intAdder = Adder<Int>()
val stringAdder = Adder<String>()
```

or the compiler must be able to infer the type, as in

```
class Adder<T> {
    fun add(toAdd:T) {
        ...
    }
}
val intAdder:Adder<Int> = Adder()
val stringAdder:Adder<String> = Adder()
```

Note   Generics are compile-time constructs. In the code the compiler generates, no generics information appears. This effect is commonly referred to as *type erasure.*

We've already used such a generic type a couple of times in the book. You might remember as a holder for two data elements we talked about the Pair type, which is parameterized:

```
val p1 = Pair<String, String>("A", "B")
val p2 = Pair<Int,String>(1, "A")
```

Of course, we also talked about various collection types, for example:

```
val l1: List<String> = listOf("A","B","C")
val l2: MutableList<Int> = mutableListOf(1, 2, 3)
```

Until now we just took generics as they are, without further explaining them. After all, writing List<String>, the deduction that we are talking about a list of strings is apparent.

The story gets interesting once we start more thoroughly looking at collections. The question is this: If we have a MutableList<Any> and a MutableList<String>, how do they relate? Can we write val l:MutableList<Any> = mutableListOf<String>("A", "B")? Or in other words, is MutableList<-String> a subclass of MutableList<Any>? It isn't, and in the rest of this chapter we talk about generics in depth and try to understand type relationships.

Simple Generics

First, let's address the basics. To type-parameterize a class or an interface, you add a comma-separated list of formal type parameters inside angle brackets after the type name:

```
class TheClass<[type-list]> {
    [class-body]
}
interface TheInterface<[type-list]> {
    [interface-body]
}
```

Inside the class or interface, including any constructor and init{} block, you can then use the type parameters like any other type. For example:

```
class TheClass<A, B>(val p1: A, val p2: B?) {
    constructor(p1:A) : this(p1, null)
    init {
        var x:A = p1
        ...
    }
    fun function(p: A) : B? = p2
}
```

277

Exercise 1

Similar to the Pair class, create a class Quadruple that can hold four data elements. Create an instance with sample Int, Int, Double, and String type elements.

Declaration-Side Variance

If we talk about generics, the term *variance* denotes the ability to use more specific or less specific types in assignments. Knowing that Any is less specific compared to String, variance shows up in the question of whether one of the following is possible:

```
class A<T> { ... }
var a = A<String>()
var b = A<Any>()

a = b // variance?
... or ...
b = a // variance?
```

Why is that important for us? The answer to that question becomes clear if we look at type safety. Consider the following code snippet:

```
class A<T> {
    fun add(p:T) { ... }
}
var a = A<String>()
var b = A<Any>()

b = a // variance?
b.add(37)
```

Adding 37 to a A<Any> does not pose a problem, because any type is a subclass of Any. However, because b by virtue of b = a now points to an instance of A<String>, we'll get a runtime error, because 37 is not a string. The Kotlin compiler recognizes this problem and doesn't allow the b = a assignment.

Likewise, assigning a = b also poses a problem. This one is even more obvious, because a only is for String elements and cannot handle an Int typed value, as b does.

```
class A<T> {
    fun extract(): T = ...
}
var a = A<String>()
var b = A<Any>()

a = b // variance?
val extracted:String = a.extract()
```

The a.extract() in the last statement could evaluate to both an Any and a String type, because b and now a may, for example, contain an Int object, but a is not allowed to contain an Int object, because it can handle String elements only. Hence Kotlin does not allow a = b either.

What can we do? To not allow any variance could be an option, but this would be too harsh. Again, looking at the first sample with the b = a assignment we can see that writing to b causes the error. How about reading? Consider this:

```
class A<T> {
    fun extract(): T = ...
}
var a = A<String>()
var b = A<Any>()

b = a // variance?
val extracted:String = b.extract()
```

The last operation now is safe as types are concerned, so we actually should not have a problem here.

The exact opposite case, taking the a = b sample and applying a writing instead of a reading operation, as in

```
class A<T> {
    fun add(p:T) { ... }
}
```

```
var a = A<String>()
var b = A<Any>()

a = b // variance?
a.add("World")
```

should not pose a problem either. To both a and b we can add strings.

To make this kind of variance possible, Kotlin allows us to add a *variance annotation* to a generic parameter. The first example with b = a does compile if we add the out annotation to the type parameter:

```
class A<out T> {
    fun extract(): T = ...
}
var a = A<String>()
var b = A<Any>()

b = a // variance? YES!
val extracted:String = b.extract()
// OK, because we are reading!
```

The second example with a = b compiles if we add the in annotation to the type parameter:

```
class A<in T> {
    fun add(p:T) { ... }
}
var a = A<String>()
var b = A<Any>()

a = b // variance? YES!.add("World")
// OK, because we are writing!
```

So with the in or out variance annotation added to the type parameters, and confining class operations to allow for either only an input of the generic type or only an output of the generic type, variance is possible in Kotlin! If you need both, you can use a different construct, as covered in the section "Type Projections" later in this chapter.

> **Note**   The out variance for classes also gets called *covariance*, and the in
> variance is called *contravariance*.

> The name declaration-side variance stems from declaring the in or out variance
> in the *declaration* of the class. Other languages, such as Java, use a different type
> of variance that takes effect while *using* the class and hence gets called use-side
> variance.

Variance for Immutable Collections

Because immutable collections cannot be written to, Kotlin automatically makes them
covariant. If you prefer, you can think of Kotlin implicitly adding the out variance
annotation to immutable collections.

Due to this fact, a List<SomeClass> can be assigned to a List<SomeClassSuper>
where SomeClassSuper is a superclass of SomeClass. For example:

```
val coll1 = listOf("A", "B") // immutable
val coll2:List<Any> = coll1  // allowed!
```

Type Projections

In the previous section we saw that for the out style variance the corresponding class is not
allowed to have functions with the generic type as a function parameter, and that for the in
style variance we accordingly cannot have a function returning the generic type. This is, of
course, unsatisfactory if we need both kinds of functions in a class. Kotlin also has an answer
for this type of requirement. It is called *type projection* and because it aims at variance while
using different functions of a class, it is the Kotlin equivalent of use-side variance.

The idea goes as follows: We still use the in and out variance annotations, but
instead of declaring them for the whole class we add them to function parameters.
We slightly rewrite the example from the previous section and add in and out variance
annotations:

```
class Producer<T> {
    fun getData(): Iterable<T>? = null
}
```

```
class Consumer<T> {
    fun setData(p:Iterable<T>) { }
}

class A<T> {
    fun add(p:Producer<out T>) { }
    fun extractTo(p:Consumer<in T>) { }
}
```

The out in the add() functions says that we need an object that produces T objects, and the in in the extractTo() function designates an object that consumes T objects. Let us look at some client code:

```
var a = A<String>()
var b = A<Any>()

var inputStrings = Producer<String>()
var inputAny = Producer<Any>()
a.add(inputStrings)
a.add(inputAny)            // FAILS!
b.add(inputStrings)        // only because o "out"
b.add(inputAny)

var outputAny = Consumer<Any>()
var outputStrings = Consumer<String>()
a.extractTo(outputAny)     // only because of "in"
a.extractTo(outputStrings)
b.extractTo(outputAny)
b.extractTo(outputStrings) // FAILS!
```

You can see that a.add(inputAny) fails because inputAny produces all kinds of objects but a can only take String objects. Similarly, b.extractTo(outputStrings) fails because b contains any kind of object but outputStrings can only receive String objects. This so far has nothing to do with variance. The story gets interesting for b.add(inputStrings). The behavior to allow for strings to be added to A<Any> certainly makes sense, but it only works because we added the out projection to the function parameter. Similarly, a.extractTo(outputAny), although certainly desirable, only works because of the in projection.

Star Projections

If you have a class or an interface with in or out variance annotations, you can use the special wildcard *, which means the following:

- For the out variance annotation, * means out Any?.

- For the in variance annotation, * means in Nothing.

Remember that Any is the superclass of any class, and Nothing is the subclass of any class.

For example:

```
interface Interf<in A, out B> {
    ...
}

val x:Interf<*, Int> = ...
    // ... same as Interf<in Nothing, Int>

val y:Interf<Int, *> = ...
    // ... same as Interf<Int, out Any?>
```

You use the star wildcard in cases where you know nothing about the type, but still want to satisfy variance semantics prescribed by class or interface declarations.

Generic Functions

Functions in Kotlin can also be generic, which means their parameters or some of their parameters can have a generic type. In such cases, the generic type designators must be added as a comma-separated list in angle brackets after the function keyword. The generic types can also show up in the function's return type. Here is an example.

```
fun <A> fun1(par1:A, par2:Int) {
    ...
}
```

```
fun <A, B> fun2(par1:A, par2:B) {
    ...
}

fun <A> fun3(par1:String) : A {
    ...
}

fun <A> fun4(par1:String) : List<A> {
    ...
}
```

To call such a function, the concrete type principally must be specified after the function's name in angle brackets:

```
fun1<String>("Hello", 37)

fun2<Int, String>(37, "World")

val s:String = fun3<String>("A")
```

However, as is often the case in Kotlin, the type arguments can be omitted if Kotlin can infer the type.

Generic Constraints

Until now there was no restriction to the type a generic type identifier could be mapped to during instantiation. Therefore in class TheClass<T> the T generic type could be anything, a TheClass<Int>, TheClass<String>, TheClass<Any>, or whatever. It is, however, possible to restrict the type to a certain class or interface or one of its subtypes. For that aim you write

```
<T : SpecificType>
```

as in

```
class <T : Number> { ... }
```

which confines T to a Number or any of its subclasses, like Int or Double.

This is very useful. Consider, for example, a class that allows us to add something to a Double property.

```kotlin
class Adder<T> {
    var v:Double = 0.0
    fun add(value:T) {
        v += value.toDouble()
    }
}
```

Do you see why this code is illegal? We say that value is of type T, but it is not known to the class what T happens to be during instantiation, so it is not clear whether or not a T.toDouble() function actually exists. Because we know that after compilation all types are erased, the compiler has no chance to check whether there is a toDouble() and it hence marks the code as illegal. If you look at the API documentation you will find out that Int, Long, Short, Byte, Float, and Double all are subclasses of kotlin.Number and they all have a toDouble() function. If we had a way to say that T is a Number or a subclass thereof, we could thus make the code legal.

Kotlin does have a way to confine generic types that way, and it reads <T : SpecificType>. Because T then is confined to SpecificType or any subtype of it lower in the type hierarchy, this is also said to be an upper type bound. To make our Adder class legal all we have to do is write

```kotlin
class Adder<T : Number> {
    var v:Double = 0.0
    fun add(value:T) {
        // T is a Number, so it _has_ a toDouble()
        v += value.toDouble()
    }
}
```

Such type constraints can also be added to generic functions, so we actually could rewrite the Adder class to:

```
class Adder {
    var v:Double = 0.0
    fun <T:Number> add(value:T) {
        v += value.toDouble()
    }
}
```

This has the particular advantage that the generic type does not need to be resolved during instantiation.

```
val adder = Adder()
adder.add(37)
adder.add(3.14)
adder.add(1.0f)
```

Note that unlike class inheritance, type bounds can be multiply declared. This just can't happen inside the angle brackets, but there is a special construct for handling such cases.

```
class TheClass<T> where T : UpperBound1,
                   T : UpperBound2, ...
{
    ...
}
```

or

```
fun <T> functionName(...) where T : UpperBound1,
                   T : UpperBound2, ...
{
    ...
}
```

for generic functions.

Something that you might have to get used to but that helps for generic constraints having generic parameters themselves, is that generic classes might show up on both sides of the colon (:) It is thus completely acceptable to write

```
class TheClass <T : Comparable<T>> {
    ...
}
```

to express that T must be a subclass of Comparable.

Exercise 2

Write a generic class Sorter with a type parameter T and suitable type bound, which has a property val list:MutableList<T> and a function fun add(value:T). With each function invocation, the parameter must be added to the list and the list property must be sorted according to its natural sorting order.

CHAPTER 14

Adding Hints: Annotations

Annotations are for adding meta-information to your code. What does that mean?
Consider the following classes:

```kotlin
class Adder {
    fun add(a:Double, b:Double) = a + b
}
class Subtractor {
    fun subtract(a:Double, b:Double) = a - b
}
```

If we have a larger arithmetic calculation project where the various operations get
handled by classes like `Adder` and `Subtractor` here, we could have something like

```kotlin
val eng = CalculationEngine()
...
eng.registerAdder(Adder::class, "add") eng.registerSubtractor(Subtractor::class, "subtract")
...
```

for registering the particular low-level operations.

We could, however, follow a different approach where the operators somehow
announce their abilities to the framework. They could do this by special documentation
tags, as in

```kotlin
/**
 * @Operator: ADDING
 * @Function: add
 */
```

© Peter Späth 2019
P. Späth, *Learn Kotlin for Android Development*, https://doi.org/10.1007/978-1-4842-4467-8_14

```
class Adder {
    fun add(a:Double, b:Double) = a + b
}
/**
 * @Operator: SUBTRACTING
 * @Function: subtract
 */
class Subtractor {
    fun subtract(a:Double, b:Double) = a - b
}
```

Some parser could then look into the source code to find out which classes and functions are needed for the various operators.

Note   A *framework* is a collection of classes, interfaces, and singleton objects that provide a scaffolding structure to software. A framework is not an executable program itself, but a software project uses the framework to establish a standardized structure. Different projects using a particular framework thus exhibit a similar structure and if a developer knows one project embedded into a particular framework it will be easier to understand other projects using the same framework.

This method of letting classes announce themselves to a program frequently gets used in a server environment where the program needs to be able to communicate with clients over a network.

There is, however, a problem with this approach. Because the meta-information gets presented from inside the documentation, there is no possibility for the compiler to check the correctness of the tags. Concerning the compiler, the contents of the documentation are completely unimportant, and should be unimportant, because this is what the language specification says.

Annotations in Kotlin

This is where annotations enter the game. They exist exactly for this kind of task: not interfering with the class's primary responsibilities, but providing meta-information to the program or framework for maintenance or registration purposes. An annotation looks like this:

```
@AnnotationName
```

or

```
@AnnotationName(...)
```

if there are parameters. A lot of language elements can be marked with such annotations: files, classes, interfaces, singleton objects, functions, properties, lambdas, statements, and even other annotations. The operator classes for the preceding calculation engine example could read

```
@Operator(ADDING)
class Adder {
    @OperatorFunction
    fun add(a:Double, b:Double) = a + b
}

@Operator(SUBTRACTING)
class Subtractor {
    @OperatorFunction
    fun subtract(a:Double, b:Double) = a - b
}
```

Now the compiler is in a better situation. Because annotations are part of the language the compiler can check whether they exist, are spelled correctly, and have the correct parameters provided.

In the following sections we first discuss annotation characteristics, then annotations that Kotlin provides. We then cover how to build and use our own annotations.

Annotation Characteristics

Annotations get declared by annotation classes as follows:

```
annotation class AnnotationName
```

We cover building our own annotations in a later section. For now we mention the declaration because annotations have their characteristics described by their own annotations, which then are meta-annotations:

```
@Target(...)
@Retention(...)
@Repeatable
@MustBeDocumented
annotation class AnnotationName
```

You can use any combination of them in any order, and they have default values if unspecified. We describe them, including possible parameters, here.

- @Target(...)

  Here you specify the possible element types to which the annotation can be applied. The parameter is a comma-separated list of any of the following (all of them are fields of the enumeration `kotlin.annotation.AnnotationTarget`):

  - CLASS: All classes, interfaces, singleton objects and annotation classes.

  - ANNOTATION_CLASS: Only annotation classes.

  - PROPERTY: Properties.

  - FIELD: A field that is the data holder for a property. Note that a property by virtue of getters and setters does not necessarily need a field. However, if there is a field, this annotation target points to that field. You put it in front of a property declaration, together with the PROPERTY target.

  - LOCAL_VARIABLE: Any local variable (val or var inside a function).

  - VALUE_PARAMETER: A function or constructor parameter.

– CONSTRUCTOR: Primary or secondary constructor. If you want to annotate a primary constructor, you must use the notation with the `constructor` keyword added; for example, `class Xyz @MyAnnot constructor (val p1:Int, ...)`.

– FUNCTION: Functions (not including constructors).

– PROPERTY_GETTER: Property getters.

– PROPERTY_SETTER: Property setters.

– TYPE: Annotations for types, as in `val x: @MyAnnot Int = ...`

– EXPRESSION: Statements (must contain an expression).

– FILE: File annotation. You must specify this before the `package` declaration and in addition add a `file:` between the @ and the annotation name, as in `@file:AnnotationName`.

– TYPE_ALIAS: We didn't talk about type aliases yet. They are just new names for types, as in `typealias ABC = SomeClass<Int>`. This annotation type is for such `typealias` declarations.

If unspecified, targets are `CLASS, PROPERTY, LOCAL_VARIABLE, VALUE_PARAMETER, CONSTRUCTOR, FUNCTION, PROPERTY_GETTER`, and `PROPERTY_SETTER`.

- `@Retention(...)`

   This specifies where the annotation information goes during compilation and whether it is visible using one of the following (all are fields from the enumeration class `kotlin.annotation.AnnotationRetention`):

   – SOURCE: Annotation exists only in the sources; the compiler removes it.

   – BINARY: Annotation exists in the compiled classes, interfaces, or singleton objects. It is not possible to query annotations at runtime using reflection.

   – RUNTIME: Annotation exists in the compiled classes, interfaces, or singleton objects, and it is not possible to query annotations at runtime using reflection.

The default is RUNTIME.

- @Repeatable

  Add this if you want to allow the annotation to appear more often than just once.

- @MustBeDocumented

  Add this if you want the annotation to show up in the public API documentation.

You can see that for classes, interfaces, singleton objects, properties, and local properties, you don't have to specify special characteristics if you want the annotations to show up visibly in the compiled files.

Applying Annotations

In general, annotations get written in front of the element to which the annotation is to apply. The story gets a little bit complicated because it is not always clear what is meant by element. Consider this example:

```
class Xyz {
    @MyAnnot var d1:Double = 1.0
}
```

Here we have four elements to which the annotation could be applied: the property, the property getter, the property setter, and the data field. For this reason, Kotlin introduced *use-site targets* in the form of a `qualifier:` written between the @ and the annotation name. The following use-site targets are available:

- file

  We know that a Kotlin file can contain properties and functions outside classes, interfaces, and singleton objects. For an annotation applying to such a file, you write `@file:AnnotationName` in front of the package declaration. For example:

  ```
  @file:JvmName("Foo")
  package com.xyz.project
  ...
  ```

to give the internally created class the name Foo.

- property

  The annotation gets associated with the property. Note that if you use Java to access your Kotlin classes, this annotation is not visible to Java.

- field

  The annotation gets associated with the data field behind a property.

- get

  The annotation gets associated with the property getter.

- set

  The annotation gets associated with the property setter.

- receiver

  The annotation gets associated with the receiver parameter of an extension function or property.

- param

  The annotation gets associated with a constructor parameter.

- setparam

  The annotation gets associated with a property setter parameter.

- delegate

  The annotation gets associated with the field storing the delegate instance.

If you don't specify a use-site target, the @Target meta-annotation is used to find the element to annotate. If there are several possibilities, the ranking is param > property > field.

The following code shows various annotation application examples (for simplicity, all annotations are without parameters and are presumed to have the correct @Target specified):

```
// An annotation applying to a file (the implicit
// internal class generated)
@file:Annot
package com.xyz.project
...

// An annotation applying to a class, a singleton
// object, or an interface
@Annot class TheName ...
@Annot object TheName ...
@Annot interface TheName ...

// An annotation applying to a function
@Annot fun theName() { ... }

// An annotation applying to a property
@property:Annot val theName = ...
@Annot var theName = ...
class SomeClass(@property:Annot var param:Type, ...) ...

// An annotation applying to a function parameter
f(@Annot p:Int, ...) { ... }

// An annotation applying to a constructor
class TheName @annot constructor(...) ...

// An annotation applying to a constructor parameter
class SomeClass(@param:Annot val param:Type, ...) ...

// An annotation applying to a lambda function
val f = @annot { par:Int -> ... }

// An annotation applying to the data field
// behind a property
@field:Annot val theName = ...
class SomeClass(@field:Annot val param:Type, ...) ...
```

```
// An annotation applying to a property setter
@set:Annot var theName = ...
var theName = 37 @Annot set(...) { ... }
class SomeClass(@set:Annot var param:Type, ...) ...

// An annotation applying to a property getter
@get:Annot var theName = ...
var theName = 37 @Annot get() = ...
class SomeClass(@get:Annot var param:Type, ...) ...

// An annotation applying to a property setter
// parameter
var theName:Int = 37
    set(@setparam:Annot p:String) { })

// An annotation applying to a receiver
@receiver:Annot fun String.xyz() { }

// An annotation applying to a delegate
class Derived(@delegate:Annot b: Base) : Base by b
```

To use annotations as annotation parameters, you don't add a @ prefix:

```
@Annot(AnotherAnnot)
```

Annotations with Array Parameter

Using arrays as an annotation constructor parameter is easy: Just use the vararg qualifier in the annotation declaration, and in the annotation instantiation use a comma-separated parameter list:

```
annotation class Annot(vararg val params:String)
...
@Annot("A", "B", "C", ...) val prop:Int = ...
```

If you need to use an annotation with a single array parameter from a Java library you included in your project, the parameter gets automatically converted to a vararg parameter, so you basically do the same:

```
@field:JavaAnnot("A", "B", "C", ...) val prop:Int = ...
```

297

If annotations have several named parameters with one or several of them being an array, you use the special array literal notation:

```
@Annot(param1 = 37, arrParam = [37, 42, 6], ...)
```

Reading Annotations

For reading annotations with retention type SOURCE you need a special annotation processor. Remember that for SOURCE type annotation the Kotlin compiler removes the annotation during the compilation step, so in this case we must have some software looking at the sources before the compiler does its work. Most source type annotation processing happens inside bigger server framework projects; here the annotations get used to produce some synthetic Kotlin or Java code that glues together classes to model complex database structures. There is a special plug-in to be used for such purposes, KAPT, which allows for the inclusion of such source type annotation preprocessors.

You can find more information about KAPT usage in the online Kotlin documentation. For the rest of this section we talk about RUNTIME retention type annotation processing.

For reading annotations that have been compiled by the Kotlin compiler and ended up in the bytecode that gets executed by the runtime engine, the *reflection API* gets used. We discuss the reflection API later in this book; here we mention only annotation processing aspects.

Note   To use reflection, the `kotlin-reflect.jar` must be in the class path. This means you have to add `implementation "org.jetbrains.kotlin:kotlin-reflect:$kotlin_version"` inside the dependencies section of your module's `build.gradle` file.

To get the annotations for the most basic elements, see Table 14-1, which describes how to get an annotation or a list of annotations.

Table 14-1. *Annotations by Element*

Element	Reading Annotations

Classes, singleton objects, and interfaces	Use
	
	`TheName::class.annotations`
	
	to get a list of `kotlin.Annotation` objects you can further investigate. You can, for example, use the property `.annotationClass` to get the class of each annotation. If you have a property and first need to get the corresponding class, use
	
	`property::class.annotations`
	
	To read a certain annotation, use
	
	`val annot = TheName::class.findAnnotation<AnnotationType>()`
	
	where for AnnotationType you substitute the annotation's class name. From here you can, for example, read an annotation's parameter via `annot?.paramName`.

Properties	Use
	
	`val prop = ClassName::propertyName`
	`val annots = prop.annotations`
	`val annot = prop.findAnnotation<AnnotationType>()`
	
	to fetch a property by name and from there get a list of annotations or search for a certain annotation.

Fields	To access a field's annotations use `val prop = ClassName::propertyNameval field = prop.javaFieldval annotations = field?.annotations`

(continued)

Table 14-1. (*continued*)

Element	Reading Annotations
Functions	To access a nonoverloaded function by name write TheClass::functionName. In case you have several functions using the same name but with different parameters you can write

```
val funName = "functionName"
    // <- choose your own
val pars = listOf(Int::class)
    // <- choose your own
val function =
   TheClass::class.
   declaredFunctions.filter {
       it.name == funName }
   ?.find { f ->
     val types = f.valueParameters.map{
         it.type.jvmErasure}
     types == pars
}
```

Once you have the function, you can use .annotations for a list of annotations, or .findAnnotation<AnnotationType>() to search for a certain annotation.

Built-in Annotations

Kotlin provides a couple of annotations from the start. Table 14-2 shows some general-purpose annotations.

Table 14-2. *Built-in Annotations: General*

Annotation Name	Package	Targets	Description
Deprecated	kotlin	class, annotation class, function, property, constructor, property setter, property getter, type alias	Takes three parameters: `message:String`, `replaceWith:ReplaceWith` `= ReplaceWith("")` and `level:DeprecationLevel =` `DeprecationLevel.WARNING` Mark the element as deprecated. `DeprecationLevel` is an enumeration with fields: `WARNING`, `ERROR`, `HIDDEN`
ReplaceWith	kotlin	—	Takes two parameters: `expression:String` and `vararg imports:String`. Use this to specify a replacement code snippet inside @ `Deprecated`.
Suppress	kotlin	class, annotation class, function, property, field, local variable, value parameter, constructor, property setter, property getter, type, type alias, expression, file	Takes one vararg parameter: `names:String`. Retention type is SOURCE. Use this to suppress compiler warnings. The `names` parameter is a comma-separated list of warning message identifiers. Unfortunately finding an exhaustive list of compiler warning identifiers is not that easy, but Android Studio helps: Once a compiler warning appears, the corresponding construct gets highlighted and pressing Alt+Enter with the cursor over it allows us to generate a corresponding suppress annotation. See Figure 14-1 (use arrow keys to navigate in the menu).

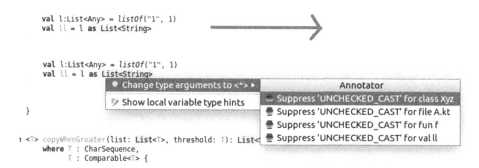

Figure 14-1. *Suppress annotation in Android Studio*

Custom Annotations

To define your own simple annotations, you write

```
@Target(...)
@Retention(...)
@Repeatable
@MustBeDocumented
annotation class AnnotationName
```

For the annotations for the annotation (i.e., the meta-annotations), note that they are all optional and the order is free. For their meanings, see the section "Annotation Characteristics" earlier in this chapter.

If you need annotations with parameters, you add a primary constructor to the declaration:

```
[possibly meta-annotations]
annotation class AnnotationName(val p1:Type1, val p2:Type2, ...)
```

where the following parameter types are allowed: types that correspond to primitive types (i.e., Byte, Short, Int, Long, Char, Float, Double), strings, classes, enums, other annotations, and arrays of those. You can add vararg for a variable number of arguments. Note that for annotations used as parameters for other annotations, the @ for the parameter annotations gets omitted.

As an example, we start a calculation engine in the form of a class `Calculator`. We introduce an annotation to avoid division by 0.0. The annotation reads:

```
@Target(AnnotationTarget.VALUE_PARAMETER)
@Retention(AnnotationRetention.RUNTIME)
annotation class NotZero()
```

For the class and two operators `divide` and `multiply` we write:

```
class Calculator {
  enum class Operator(val oper:String) {
      MULTIPLY("multiply"),
      DIVIDE("divide")
  }

  fun operator(oper:Operator,
               vararg params:Double): Double {
      val f = Calculator::class.declaredFunctions.
          find { it.name == oper.oper }
      f?.valueParameters?.forEachIndexed { ind, p ->
          p.findAnnotation<NotZero>()?.run {
              if (params[ind] == 0.0)
                  throw RuntimeException(
                  "Parameter ${ind} not unequal 0.0")
          }
      }
      val ps = arrayOf(this@Calculator,
          *(params).toList().toTypedArray<Any>())
      return (f?.call(*ps) as Double?) ?: 0.0
  }

  fun multiply(p1:Double, p2:Double) : Double {
      return p1 * p2
  }

  fun divide(p1:Double, @NotZero p2:Double) : Double {
      return p1 / p2
  }
}
```

The `operator()` function acts as follows:

- It finds the function corresponding to the first parameter. The `Calculator::class.declaredFunctions` lists all the directly declared functions of the `Calculator` class. This means it does not also look into superclasses. The `find` selects `divide()` or `multiply()`.

- From the function, we loop though the parameters via `.valueParameters`. For each parameter, we see whether it has annotation `NotZero` associated with it. If it does, we check the actual parameter, and if it is `0.0`, we throw an exception.

- If no exception was thrown, we invoke the function. The `arrayOf()` expression concatenates the receiver object and the function parameters into a single `Array<Any>`.

The `@NotZero` annotation makes sure the parameter gets checked when `Calculator.operator()` is called. To use the calculator, you write something like this:

```
Calculator().
    operator(Calculator.Operator.DIVIDE,
            1.0, 1.0)
```

To see whether the annotation works, try another invocation with `0.0` as the second parameter.

Exercise 1

To the `Calculator` example, add a new annotation `@NotNegative` and a new operation `sqrt()` for the square root. Make sure a negative parameter for this operator is not allowed. Note: The actual square root gets calculated via `java.lang.Math.sqrt()`.

CHAPTER 15

Using the Java and Kotlin APIs

Kotlin has a language kernel that handles classes, objects, properties, functions, structural constructs, and all that stuff. We've been talking about these a lot to this point. Once in a while we have mentioned and used the term *Kotlin standard library* without explicitly stating what that actually is. In real life a library is a place where extensive information is available. Whenever you need to know something you can go there and try to find a book that can show you what things are or how they work, or what you have to do to achieve something. For a computer language, a *library* is something similar: a repository with lots of classes and functions that you can use for certain tasks. We already talked about collections, which are governed by library classes and functions.

APIs go hand in hand with libraries. An API focuses more on the external *face* of a library; that is, how a library gets used from outside without having to know about the internal functioning.

There are many examples of libraries you can think of; for example, math, chemistry, physics, biology, sociology, encryption standards, web services, user interfacing, sound processing, and graphics, to name just a few, and writing a single book about all of them is just not possible. It makes sense, though, to distinguish between basic libraries that get shipped with Kotlin and external libraries that you can add on demand. Just looking the built-in libraries is a much more feasible task, and in this chapter we look at the libraries that get shipped with Kotlin.

Note that it is neither possible nor desirable in a book like this to list all classes and functions a library has to offer. There are just too many in any but very simple libraries. We can, however, try to describe the libraries, show how to use them, and list the most important classes and functions. This happens in subsequent chapters.

© Peter Späth 2019
P. Späth, *Learn Kotlin for Android Development*, https://doi.org/10.1007/978-1-4842-4467-8_15

Kotlin and Java Libraries

Before we start looking at the different APIs, we need to talk about where the Kotlin libraries come from. Kotlin sits on top of the JVM, and the Kotlin developers did a good job to allow for easy interoperation between Kotlin and Java. This includes the ability to use Java APIs and libraries. With Java around for more than 20 years, it is not hard to imagine that there are some extremely well-tailored Java libraries out there, and there is no need for Kotlin to redo everything. What Kotlin instead does is include some of the libraries that were already included with a Java distribution, and then extends or redefines them at a couple of places using its class extension mechanisms.

Using the Online Resources

For any of the APIs included in Kotlin, having the official API documentation at hand always is a good idea. The place to go is `https://kotlinlang.org/`. There you will find a LEARN link that gets you to the language and standard library reference manual. If this link is out of date, search "kotlin programming language" in your favorite search engine to find it.

As already pointed out, Kotlin has a strong relation to Java; it is especially easy to incorporate Java standard modules into Kotlin. The Android platform includes various Java APIs, and you don't have to do anything to use them if you use Android Studio for development. The API level 28 we have been using throughout this book has the following Java APIs from Java 8:

- java.beans
- java.io
- java.lang
- java.math
- java.net
- java.nio
- java.security
- java.sql
- java.text

- java.time

- java.util

- javax.crypto

- javax.microedition.khronos

- javax.net

- javax.security

- javax.sql

- javax.xml

On the Oracle web site you will find the API documentation for the Java libraries. The link more precisely reads `https://docs.oracle.com/javase/8/docs/api/`, but if this link is out of date, an online search for "java 8 api" will readily lead you to these pages.

For the APIs we describe in the following chapters, we remove the burden of thinking about whether they come from Kotlin or Java. If you are interested, it is usually easy to see where the classes and interfaces come from by looking at the `import` statements. If they start with `java.` or `javax.`, the classes and interfaces come from Java, otherwise they are from Kotlin.

Making a Local Copy of the Documentation

Inside Android Studio, once you press Ctrl+B over any class or interface name, you will be taken to the Java or Kotlin sources. If you do this for the first time, Android Studio might need to download the sources from the Internet, but afterward you will have the sources locally stored inside your Android Studio installation.

If you want to have a local copy of the API documentation on your PC, for Java the corresponding links on the Oracle downloads web site are easy to find. For Kotlin, go to `https://github.com/JetBrains/kotlin/releases`, choose a release, and then download the source code as a compressed archive.

You can also fetch the sources from your Android Studio. Make sure the sources were downloaded by pressing Ctrl+B over any Kotlin standard library class, then go to `STUDIO-INST/plugins/Kotlin/kotlinc/lib`. There you'll find a file `kotlin-stdlib-sources.jar`. This is a ZIP archive. You can extract all files from the archive and save them anywhere on your PC.

CHAPTER 16

The Collections API

We already talked about collections in Chapter 9, namely lists, sets, and maps. The collections API, however, is extensive and contains more classes and interfaces than we described in Chapter 9. For Java the API even gets called the *collections framework*. Without claiming to be exhaustive in this chapter, we revise what we already know and also talk about a couple of more interesting collection interfaces, classes, and functions.

Unfortunately there is nothing like a `java.collections` package. Concerning Java, the collections API is scattered with its main part lying inside the `java.util` package.

Note We'll exhibit a way to designate generic type parameters in this chapter. Where obvious, for brevity they are not shown. In all cases we use E as the element type of a list or a set, and K and V for the keys and values of maps.

Interfaces

Although Java already has interfaces for sets, lists, and maps, Kotlin has its own interfaces for them. This mainly stems from Kotlin's need to distinguish between mutable and immutable collections and maps. For most use cases you can just use the Kotlin versions, and the compiler even might warn you if you instead try to use the Java variants. It is not forbidden, though, to use the Java variants as well, and there might be reasons to do so. Table 16-1 provides an overview.

© Peter Späth 2019
P. Späth, *Learn Kotlin for Android Development*, https://doi.org/10.1007/978-1-4842-4467-8_16

Table 16-1. *Collection Interfaces*

Interface	Description
kotlin.collections.Iterable	An iterable, or something that can be iterated through in a loop. Any iterable can be used in a `for( x in a )` loop, so if you provide your own classes implementing this interface, you can use it in loops. All collections (i.e., lists and sets) are iterables.
kotlin.collections. MutableIterable	Same as `Iterable`, but in addition supports removal of the currently iterated over element.
java.lang.Iterable	The Java variant of an iterable; don't use it unless you have good reasons to do so.
kotlin.collections.Collection	A general immutable collection interface. This is a subinterface of `Iterable`.
kotlin.collections. MutableCollection	A general mutable collection interface. This is a subinterface of `MutableIterable`.
java.util.Collection	The Java variant of a collection interface; don't use it unless you have good reasons to do so.

(continued)

Table 16-1. (*continued*)

Interface	Description
java.util.Deque	A two-ended queue. Use this to implement or use queues or stacks. You can put elements at the beginning and at the end, and you can read and withdraw elements on both sides. The number of functions available for deques is a little bit overwhelming; usually you can be happy with the following set: • size(): Int to get the size. • addFirst(element:E) to add an element to the HEAD of a deque. • addLast(element:E) to add an element to the TAIL of a deque. • removeFirst(): E to get and remove the element at the HEAD of the deque (throws an exception if the deque is empty). • removeLast(): E to get and remove the element at the TAIL of the deque (throws an exception if the deque is empty). • getFirst(): E to retrieve, but not to remove, the element at the HEAD of the queue (throws an exception if the deque is empty). • getLast(): E to retrieve, but not to remove the element at the TAIL of the queue (throws an exception if the deque is empty). There is no Kotlin variant for this; deques are always mutable.
java.util.Queue	A one-ended queue. Normally you can use a two-ended deque instead. There is no Kotlin variant for this; queues are always mutable.
kotlin.collections.List	An immutable list.
kotlin.collections.MutableList	A mutable list.

(*continued*)

Table 16-1. (*continued*)

Interface	Description
java.util.List	The Java variant of a list; don't use it unless you have good reasons to do so.
kotlin.collections.Set	An immutable set.
kotlin.collections.MutableSet	A mutable set.
java.util.Set	The Java variant of a set; don't use it unless you have good reasons to do so.
java.util.SortedSet	A set with its elements sorted in their natural sorting order.
java.util.NavigableSet	A SortedSet that can additionally be iterated through in both directions.
kotlin.collections.Map	An immutable map.
kotlin.collections.MutableMap	A mutable map.
java.util.Map	The Java variant of a map; don't use it unless you have good reasons to do so.
java.util.SortedMap	A map with its keys sorted in their natural sorting order.
java.util.NavigableMap	A SortedMap that can additionally be iterated through in both directions.

Note that all those interfaces have generic types that must be specified between angle brackets, unless the Kotlin compiler can infer the types. For maps we need two type parameters; all the others require one.

Looking a little bit closer at the table, you might notice two somewhat strange constructs: a sorted set in the form of SortedSet and a sorted map in the form of SortedMap. These are language constructs that help under circumstances, but have no direct counterparts in math. In math both sets and maps are unordered! In your code perhaps it is best if you don't use them where it can be avoided. If you do use them, the algorithm should not strongly depend on the order of elements. This is, of course, a matter of personal preference; take it as a hint or advice.

Classes

Table 16-2 lists the classes that implement the collection and map interfaces.

Table 16-2. *Collection Classes*

Class	Description
kotlin.collections.ArrayList	A list implementation for both mutable and immutable lists.
java.util.ArrayList	The Java variant of an ArrayList; don't use it unless you have good reasons to do so.
kotlin.collections.HashSet	A set implementation for both mutable and immutable sets.
java.util.HashSet	The Java variant of a HashSet; don't use it unless you have good reasons to do so.
kotlin.collections. LinkedHashSet	A set implementation for both mutable and immutable sets. Because the set elements are linked to each other, the iteration order is the same as the insertion order.
java.util.LinkedHashSet	The Java variant of a LinkedHashSet; don't use it unless you have good reasons to do so.
kotlin.collections.HashMap	A map implementation for both mutable and immutable maps.
java.util.HashMap	The Java variant of a HashMap; don't use it unless you have good reasons to do so.
kotlin.collections. LinkedHashMap	A map implementation for both mutable and immutable maps. Because the map elements are linked to each other, the iteration order is the same as the insertion order.
java.util.LinkedHashMap	The Java variant of a LinkedHashMap; don't use it unless you have good reasons to do so.
java.util.ArrayDeque	A Deque implementation.
java.util.EnumSet	A specialized java.util.Set implementation for enumeration elements.
java.util.LinkedList	A java.util.List implementation with linked list elements.

(continued)

Table 16-2. (*continued*)

Class	Description
java.util.PriorityQueue	A java.util.Queue implementation with elements inserted at a position according to their natural ordering or according to an ordering defined by the comparator passed in during construction.
java.util.Stack	A last-in, first-out (LIFO) implementation of a java.util.List.
java.util.TreeSet	A java.util.Set implementation with the elements sorted according to their natural ordering, or sorted by the comparator passed in during construction.
java.util.concurrent.ArrayBlockingQueue	A queue (first-in, first-out list) with a fixed size. Blocks both if trying to add an element when the queue is full or trying to remove an element when the queue is empty.
java.util.concurrent.ConcurrentLinkedDeque	A deque implementation allowing concurrent access to the elements.
java.util.concurrent.ConcurrentLinkedQueue	A queue implementation allowing concurrent access to the elements.
java.util.concurrent.ConcurrentSkipListSet	A NavigableSet implementation allowing concurrent access to the elements.
java.util.concurrent.CopyOnWriteArrayList	A java.util.List implementation allowing concurrent access to the elements. Each write operation leads to a fresh copy of the complete list.
java.util.concurrent.CopyOnWriteArraySet	A java.util.Set implementation allowing concurrent access to the elements. Each write operation leads to a fresh copy of the complete set.
java.util.concurrent.DelayQueue	A java.util.Queue implementation where elements must be subclasses of java.util.concurrent.Delayed. Allows removal of elements only when the delay has expired.

(*continued*)

Table 16-2. (*continued*)

Class	Description
java.util.concurrent. LinkedBlockingQueue	A queue (first-in, first-out list) optionally with a fixed size. Blocks both if trying to add an element when the queue is full or trying to remove an element when the queue is empty.
java.util.concurrent. PriorityBlockingQueue	A java.util.Queue implementation with elements inserted at a position according to their natural ordering or according to an ordering defined by the comparator passed in during construction. Potentially blocks retrieval operations until elements are available.
java.util.concurrent. SynchronousQueue	A java.util.Queue implementation where insert operations are only possible if the element is concurrently asked for. Otherwise the insert operation blocks and waits.

Note that in properties declarations it is generally desirable to use an interface for the property type, but to use a class only for the instantiation. This way we express what the property does, not how it does it.

```
var l:MutableList<String> = ArrayList()
// ... = ArrayList<String>() is unnecessary, because
// Kotlin can infer the type.
```

Generator Functions

Kotlin provides hundreds of functions inside its own collection classes, adds extension functions to Java's collection classes, and in addition serves us with many top-level functions. Without being exhaustive, this section and those that follow list perhaps the most important collection functions of both Kotlin and Java.

Table 16-3 shows top-level generator functions you can use to create collections. Unless otherwise noted, the returned collections and maps are instances of classes from inside package kotlin.collections only.

Table 16-3. *Collection Generators*

Function	Description
emptyList<E>()	Creates an immutable empty list of the given element type.
listOf<E>(...)	Creates an immutable list of the elements given as parameters; for example, listOf(1, 2, 3)
mutableListOf<E>(...)	Creates a mutable list of the elements given as parameters; for example, mutableListOf(1, 2, 3)
listOfNotNull<E>(...)	Creates an immutable list of the elements given as parameters, but filters out null valued parameters; for example, listOfNotNull(1, 2, null, 3)
List<E>(size: Int, init: (index: Int) -> E)	Creates an immutable list calculated by the lambda function given as the second parameter. Note that despite the name starting with an uppercase letter, this is a function.
MutableList<E>(size: Int, init: (index: Int) -> E)	Creates a mutable list calculated by the lambda function given as the second parameter. Note that despite the name starting with an uppercase letter, this is a function.
emptySet<E>()	Creates an immutable empty set.
setOf<E>(...)	Creates an immutable set of the elements given as parameters; for example, setOf(1, 2, 3)
mutableSetOf<E>(...)	Creates a mutable set of the elements given as parameters; for example, mutableSetOf(1, 2, 3)
emptyMap<K,V>()	Creates an immutable empty map.
mapOf<K,V>()	Creates an immutable map of the Pair elements given as parameters; for example, mapOf(1 to "A", 2 to "B")
mutableMapOf<K,V>(...)	Creates a mutable map of the Pair elements given as parameters; for example, mutableMapOf(1 to "A", 2 to "B")

As is usually the case for Kotlin, the type parameters can be omitted if Kotlin can infer the types. So you can write

listOf(1, 5, 7, 9)

and Kotlin knows that this is a List<Int>.

Collection and Map Setters and Removers

Table 16-4 shows you how to add elements to mutable collections or maps, and also how to remove them.

Table 16-4. *Collection Mutators*

For	Function	Description
Lists, sets	add(element:E)	Add an element at the TAIL of a list, or add an element to a set.
Lists	set(index:Int, element:E)	Overwrites element at the given index. The element to overwrite must exist.
Lists	list[index] = value	Same as set()
Lists, sets	addAll(elements: Collection<E>) addAll(elements: Array<out E>)	Adds all elements from the array or collection provided as the parameter to the TAIL of a list, or add elements to a set.
Maps	put(key:K, value:V)	Puts a key/value pair into a map. If the key already exists, the value gets overwritten.
Maps	map[key:K] = value:V	Same as put().
Maps	putIfAbsent(key:K, value:V)	Puts a key/value pair into a map, but only if the key didn't exist before.
Maps	set(key:K, value:V)	Same as put().
Maps	putAll(from: Map<out K,V>)	Performs a put() for all the elements from the map that gets provided as the function parameter.

(*continued*)

Table 16-4. (*continued*)

For	Function	Description
Lists, sets	`remove(element:E)`	Remove the given element from the set or list.
Lists, sets	`removeIf { (E) -> Boolean }`	Remove all elements for which the lambda function provided returns `true`. Returns `true` if at least one element was removed.

Lists, sets	`removeAll(`
	`elements:Collection<E>)`
	`removeAll(elements:Array<out T>)`
		Remove all elements from the list or set that is also included in the collection or array parameter provided.

Lists, sets	`removeAll { (E) -> Boolean }`	Same as `removeIf()`.
Maps	`remove(key:K)`	Removes the element at the given key, if it exists. Returns the previous value, or `null` if it didn't exist.
Maps	`remove(key:K, value:V)`	Removes the element at the given key, if it exists and has the given value. Returns `true` if the element was removed.
Lists, sets	`retainAll(` `elements:Collection<E>)`	Changes the given set or list and makes it retain only those elements that are also inside the parameter collection given.
Maps, lists, sets	`clear()`	Removes all elements.

Deterministic Getters

Deterministic getters to retrieve elements from collections and maps are listed in Table 16-5.

Table 16-5. *Getters*

For	Function	Description
Lists	get(index:Int)	Retrieves the element at the specified index.
Lists	getOrNull(index:Int)	Retrieves the element at the specified index, or null if the index is out of bounds.
Lists	list[index:Int]	Same as get().
Lists	first()	Returns the first element.
List	firstOrNull()	Returns the first element, or null if the list is empty.
Lists	last()	Returns the last element.
Lists	lastOrNull()	Returns the last element, or null if the list is empty.
Lists, sets	random()	Returns a random element from the list or set.
Maps	get(key:K)	Returns the value for the given key, or if it does not exist null.
Maps	map[key:K]	Same as get().
Maps	getOrDefault(key:K, defaultValue:V)	Returns the value for the given key, or if it does not exist the defaultValue.
Maps	getOrElse(key:K, defaultValue: (K) -> V)	Returns the value for the given key, or if it does not exist the result from the lambda function provided as the second parameter.
Maps	getOrPut(key:K, defaultValue: () -> V)	Returns the value for key key. However, if the key does not exist yet, call the lambda function and put the result as the value for that key into the map. In the latter case, return the new value.
Lists, sets	single()	Retrieves the single element if there is just one element inside. Otherwise throws an exception.
Lists, sets	singleOrNull()	Retrieves the single element if there is just one element inside. Otherwise returns null.
Lists	drop(n:Int)	Returns an immutable list with the elements from the original list with the first n elements dropped.

(continued)

Table 16-5. (*continued*)

For	Function	Description
Lists	dropLast(n:Int)	Returns an immutable list with the elements from the original list with n elements dropped from the end.
Lists	slice(indices:IntRange)	Returns an immutable list containing the elements at the indices given by the range parameter.
Lists	take(n:Int)	Returns an immutable list with the first n elements from the original list.
Lists	takeLast(n:Int)	Returns an immutable list with the last n elements from the original list.

Collection and Map Characteristics

For collection and map characteristics, see Table 16-6.

Table 16-6. *Characteristics*

Receivers	Function	Description
Maps, lists, sets	Size	The size of the collection or map.
Maps, lists, sets	count()	Same as size.
Maps, lists, sets	isEmpty()	Returns true if empty.
Maps, lists, sets	isNotEmpty()	Returns true if not empty.
Lists, sets	count((E) -> Boolean)	Counts the elements that for the given predicate lambda function return true.
Maps	count((K,V) -> Boolean)	Counts the elements that for the given predicate lambda function return true.
Lists, sets	indices	Valid indices as an IntRange.
Lists	lastIndex	The last valid index.

Traversing Collections and Maps

For traversing collections and maps, you can use one of the constructs shown in Table 16-7.

Table 16-7. *Traversing*

For	Construct	Description
List, sets, implements Iterable	`for( i in x ) { ... }`	A language construct, i is the loop variable and receives the elements.
Maps	`for( me in x ) { ... }`	A language construct, me is the loop variable and receives `Map.Element<K,V>` elements. You can fetch the key via me.key and the value via me.value
Maps	`for( (k,v) in x ) { ... }`	A language construct, k and v are the loop variables and receive key and value for each map element.
List, sets, implements Iterable	`x.forEach { i -> ... }`	Iterates through all elements of x, i receives each element.
List, sets, implements Iterable	`x.onEach { i -> ... }`	Same as `forEach()`, but afterward returns the iterated-over list, set, or iterable.
List, sets, implements Iterable	`x.forEachIndexed { ind, i -> ... }`	Iterates through all elements of x, i receives each element. Ind is the index variable (0, 1, 2, ...).
Maps	`x.forEach { me -> ... }`	Iterates through all elements of map x, me has type `Map.Element<K,V>`. You can fetch the key via me.key and the value via me.value
Maps	`x.forEach { k,v -> ... }`	Iterates through all elements of map x, k is the key and v the value of each element.

Transformations

The possibilities to transform a collection or map into another collection or map are potentially endless. Table 16-8 shows functions to extract the keys and the values from a map.

Table 16-8. *Extraction Keys and Values*

Construct	Returns	Description
map.keys	MutableSet<K>	Get the keys from a map as a set.
map.values	MutableCollection<V>	Get the values from a map as a collection.

Throughout this section we use list, set, map, coll, and iter for variables of type List, Set, Map, Collection, and Iterable, respectively. Remember that a list or set is a collection and that any collection is an iterable.

Table 16-9 shows various functions to transform collection or map elements on an element-by-element basis.

Table 16-9. *Transforming: Mapping*

Construct	Returns	Description
iter.map(transform: (E) -> R)	List<R>	Transform all the collection's or any other iterable's entries according to the lambda function given. Returns an immutable list.
iter.mapIndexed(transform: (Int, E) -> R)	List<R>	Transforms all the collection's or any other iterable's entries according to the lambda function given. The lambda function gets the index (0, 1, 2, ...) as its first parameter. Returns an immutable list.
map.map(transform: (Map. Entry<K,V>) -> R)	List<R>	Creates a new immutable list from the results of the lambda function provided to each map element.

(continued)

Table 16-9. (*continued*)

Construct	Returns	Description
`map.mapKeys( transform:` `(Map.Entry<K,V>) -> R))`	`Map<R,V>`	Creates a new immutable map with the keys derived from the lambda function provided.
`map.mapValues( transform:` `(Map.Entry<K, V>) -> R))`	`Map<K,R>`	Creates a new immutable map with the values derived from the lambda function provided.

For a description of functions for changing the sort order of lists or transforming a list or set to a sorted list, see Table 16-10.

Table 16-10. *Transforming: Reordering*

Construct	Returns	Description
`list.asReversed()`	`List<E>` or `MutableList<E>`	Reverses a list's iteration order without changing the list. Maintains mutability of the original list. Note that changes to the resulting list get reflected in the original list.
`list.reverse()`	`Unit`	Reverses a mutable list in place. The original list gets changed.
`iter.reversed()`	`List<E>`	Returns a new immutable list with the sort order of the elements from the original collection or iterable reversed.
`iter.distinct()`	`List<E>`	Returns a new immutable list containing only the distinct elements from the original collection or iterable.
`iter.distinctBy(` `selector: (E) -> K)`	`List<E>`	Returns a new immutable list containing only the distinct elements from the original collection. For the equality check the results from the lambda function provided get used.

(*continued*)

Table 16-10. (*continued*)

Construct	Returns	Description
list.shuffle()	Unit	Randomly shuffles the elements from a mutable list in place.
iter.shuffled()	List<E>	Returns an immutable list with the elements from the original collection or iterable randomly shuffled.
list.sort()	Unit	Sorts a mutable list in place according to the natural sort order. The elements must implement the Comparable interface. The sortDescending() function sorts in reverse order.
list.sortBy (selector: (E) -> R?)	Unit	Sorts a mutable list in place according to the natural sort order of the selector result. The selector result must implement the Comparator interface. The sortDescending() function sorts in reverse order.
iter.sorted()	List<E>	Returns a new immutable list with the elements sorted in the natural sort order. The elements must implement the Comparable interface. The sortedDescending() function sorts in reverse order.
iter.sortedBy(selector: (E) -> R?)	List<E>	Returns a new immutable list with the elements sorted in the natural sort order of the selector result. The selector result must implement the Comparable interface. The sortedByDescending() function sorts in reverse order.

(*continued*)

Table 16-10. (*continued*)

Construct	Returns	Description
list.sortWith(comparator: Comparator<in E>	Unit	Sorts a mutable list in place according to the comparator given as a parameter. The selector result must implement the Comparator interface. The sortDescending() function sorts in reverse order.
iter.sortedWith(comparator: Comparator<in E>	List<E>	Returns a new immutable list with the elements sorted according to the comparator given as a parameter.

A couple of functions can be used to gather the elements of sublists or submaps; that is, lists and maps as elements of lists or maps (see Table 16-11).

Table 16-11. *Transforming: Flattening*

Construct	Returns	Description
iter.flatten(...)	List<E>	Here iter is an Iterable<Iterable<E>>, which is, for example, the case for collections containing collections. Returns a new immutable list with all elements concatenated in a single list.
iter.flatMap(transform: (E) -> Iterable<R>)	List<R>	With the transform function applied to all elements in the original collection or iterable, and returning an Iterable like a list or a set, returns a single immutable list with all transformation result elements concatenated.
map.flatMap(transform: (Map.Entry<K,V>) -> Iterable<R>)	List<R>	With the transform function applied to all elements in the original map and returning an Iterable like a list or a set, returns a single immutable list with all transformation result elements concatenated.

Lists and sets can be transformed to maps by associating elements to keys or values of the new map. Table 16-12 shows such association functions.

Table 16-12. *Transforming: Associating*

Construct	Returns	Description
iter.associate (transform: (E) -> Pair<K, V>)	Map<K,V>	Given the input list or set or iterable, the transform lambda function is supposed to return a Pair<K,V> that will be used for a new element in the map returned.
iter.associateBy (keySelector: (E) -> K)	Map<K,E>	Given the input list or set or iterable, the keySelector lambda function gets used to create a key for the new element in the map returned. The value is the original element.
iter.associateBy (keySelector: (E) -> K, valueTransform: (E) -> V)	Map<K,V>	Given the input list or set or iterable, the keySelector lambda function gets used to create a key for the new element in the map returned. The values will be taken from the valueTransform invocation result.
iter.associateWith (valueSelector: (E) -> V)	Map<E,V>	Given the input list or set or iterable, the valueTransform lambda function gets used to create a value for the new element in the map returned. As a key the original element gets used.

Exercise 1

Given a class data class Employee(val lastName:String, val firstName:String, val ssn:String) and a list

```
val l = listOf(
    Employee("Smith", "Eve", "012-12-5678"),
    Employee("Carpenter", "John", "123-06-4901"),
    Employee("Cugar", "Clara", "034-00-1111"),
    Employee("Lionsgate", "Peter", "965-11-4561"),
    Employee("Disney", "Quentin", "888-12-3412")
)
```

get a new immutable list from that sorted by SSN.

Exercise 2

Given the employee list from Exercise 1, create an immutable map mapping SSNs to employees.

Exercise 3

What is the output of

```
listOf(listOf(1, 2), listOf(3, 4)).flatten()
```

Exercise 4

What is the output of

```
listOf(listOf(1, 2), listOf(3, 4)).
    flatMap { it.map { it.toString() }    }
```

Filtering

Strongly related to transformations are filtering functions. They are used to get a new collection or map based on some criterion. Table 16-13 lists the filtering functions.

Throughout this section we use list, set, map, coll, and iter for variables of type List, Set, Map, Collection, and Iterable, respectively. Remember that a list or set is a collection and that any collection is an iterable.

Table 16-13. *Filtering*

Function	Description
iter.filter(predicate: (E) -> Boolean)	Returns a new immutable list containing only those elements that match the given predicate.
iter.filterNot(predicate: (E) -> Boolean)	Returns a new immutable list containing only those elements that do not match the given predicate.

(continued)

Table 16-13. (*continued*)

Function	Description
iter.filterIndexed(predicate: (index:Int, T) -> Boolean)	Returns a new immutable list containing only those elements that match the given predicate. The lambda function retrieves the index (0, 1, 2, …) as a first parameter.
map.filter(predicate: (Map. Entry<K,V>) -> Boolean)	Returns a new immutable map containing only those elements that match the given predicate.
map.filterNot(predicate: (Map. Entry<K,V>) -> Boolean)	Returns a new immutable map containing only those elements that do not match the given predicate.

Exercise 5

Given the employee list from Exercise 1, create a new immutable list containing only SSNs starting with a 0. Hint: String.startsWith(...) checks whether a string starts with certain characters.

Changing the Mutability

You can see in Table 16-14 that transformations of mutable maps and lists often return immutable maps or collections. If you need a mutable map or collection instead, Kotlin helps you.

Table 16-14. *Changing Mode*

Function	Description
list.toMutableList()	Transforms an immutable list to a mutable list.
set.toMutableSet()	Transforms an immutable set to a mutable set.
map.toMutableMap()	Transforms an immutable map to a mutable map.
mutableList.toList()	Transforms a mutable list to an immutable list.
mutableSet.toSet()	Transforms a mutable set to an immutable set.
mutableMap.toMap()	Transforms a mutable map to an immutable map.

Element Checks

To check whether any or all elements of a collection or a map satisfy some criterion, you can use one of the functions depicted in Table 16-15. Throughout this section we use list, set, map, coll, and iter for variables of type List, Set, Map, Collection, and Iterable, respectively. Remember that a list or set is a collection and that any collection is an iterable.

Table 16-15. *Checks*

Function	Description
iter.any(predicate: (E) -> Boolean)	Returns true if any of the elements satisfy the predicate.
iter.all(predicate: (E) -> Boolean)	Returns true if all of the elements satisfy the predicate.
iter.none(predicate: (E) -> Boolean)	Returns true if none of the elements satisfy the predicate.
map.any(predicate: (Map.Entry<K,V>) -> Boolean)	Returns true if any of the elements satisfy the predicate.
map.all(predicate: (Map.Entry<K,V>) -> Boolean)	Returns true if all of the elements satisfy the predicate.
map.none(predicate: (Map.Entry<K,V>) -> Boolean)	Returns true if none of the elements satisfy the predicate.

Exercise 6

Create a check for list listOf(1, 2, 3, 4) to see whether all elements are greater than 0.

Finding Elements

For finding particular elements from a collection or map, you can use one of the functions shown in Table 16-16, to which we have also added containment checks.

Table 16-16. *Finding*

For	Function	Description
Lists, iterables	`indexOf(element:E)`	Determines the index (`Int`) of the element in the list or iterable, or −1 if the element cannot be found.
Lists, iterables	`find(predicate: (e) -> Boolean)`	Returns the first element for which the predicate lambda function returns `true`, or `null` if no element matches.
Lists, iterables	`findLast(predicate: (e) -> Boolean)`	Returns the last element for which the predicate lambda function returns `true`, or `null` if no element matches.
Lists	`binarySearch( element: E?, fromIndex: Int = 0, toIndex: Int = size)`	Performs a fast binary search in a list. The list must be sorted according to the natural ordering of the elements, which must thus implement the `Comparable` interface. Returns the index if the element was found, or - `insertion_point` − 1 where `insertion_ point` is the index where the element would be inserted to maintain the list's sorting order.
Lists	`binarySearch( element: E?, comparator: Comparator<in E>, fromIndex: Int = 0, toIndex: Int = size)`	Same as `binarySearch()`, but uses the comparator provided for comparing elements.
Lists, sets, iterables	`contains(element: E)`	Returns `true` if the list, set, or iterable contains the element specified.
Maps	`contains(key: K)`	Returns `true` if the map contains the key specified.
Maps	`containsKey(key: K)`	Same as `contains()` for maps.
Maps	`containsValue(value: V)`	Returns `true` if the map contains the value specified.

Exercise 7

Given a list l of Ints, find a one-expression way, not using if, to throw an exception if the list contains 42. Hint: Use find() or contains(), possibly takeIf(), and ?.run.

Aggregating, Folding, and Reducing

Aggregators deduce the sum, the maximum, the minimum, or the average from collections. These are listed in Table 16-17.

Throughout this section we use list, set, map, coll, and iter for variables of type List, Set, Map, Collection, and Iterable, respectively. Remember that a list or set is a collection and that any collection is an iterable.

Table 16-17. *Aggregating*

For	Function	Description
A collection of numbers (Byte, Short, Int, Long, Float, Double)	sum()	Sums up the elements. Types Byte and Short yield an Int-valued sum; all others yield the same result type as the elements.
Any collection or iterable	sumBy(selector: (E) -> Int)	Sums up the elements after applying the lambda function to each element. Results in an Int number.
Any collection or iterable	sumByDouble(selector: (E) -> Double)	Sums up the elements after applying the lambda function to each element. Results in a Double number.
A collection of numbers (Byte, Short, Int, Long, Float, Double)	average	Calculates the average of all elements, as a Double.
A collection of elements implementing Comparable	max()	Returns the maximum value.

(continued)

Table 16-17. (*continued*)

For	Function	Description
Any collection or iterable	maxBy(selector: (E) -> R)	Returns the maximum value after applying the selector (must return a Comparable).
Any map	maxBy(selector: (Entry<K, V>) -> R)	Returns the maximum value after applying the selector (must return a Comparable).
Any collection or iterable	maxWith(comparator: Comparator<in E>)	Returns the maximum value according to the comparator provided.
Any map	maxWith(comparator: Comparator<in Map. Entry<K,V>)	Returns the maximum value according to the comparator provided.
A collection of elements implementing Comparable	min()	Returns the minimum value.
Any collection or iterable	minBy(selector: (E) -> R)	Returns the minimum value after applying the selector (must return a Comparable).
Any map	minBy(selector: (Entry<K, V>) -> R)	Returns the minimum value after applying the selector (must return a Comparable).
Any collection or iterable	minWith(comparator: Comparator<in E>)	Returns the minimum value according to the comparator provided.
Any map	minWith(comparator: Comparator<in Map. Entry<K,V>)	Returns the minimum value according to the comparator provided.

A *reduction* takes the first element of a collection or an iterable, stores it in a variable, and then repeatedly applies an operation with all the other elements from the collection or iterable. If, for example, the operation is addition, in the end you get the sum of the collection:

```
start with: (1, 2, 3)
take 1st element:                  (1),      remains (2, 3)
take next element, apply "+":  (1+2),    remains (3)
take next element, apply "+":  (1+2+3),  done.
result is 1+2+3 = 6
```

A reduction from right traverses the collection in reverse order; that is, it first takes the last element, applies the operator to the second-last element, and so on. Reduction functions are shown in Table 16-18.

Table 16-18. *Reducing*

Function	Returns	Description

`<S, E : S> iter<E>.`
`reduce( operation:`
`(acc: S, E) -> S)`
	S	Reduces over a collection or iterable. The operation lambda function receives the current accumulator value and the currently iterated-over element.

`<S, E : S> iter<E>.`
`reduceIndexed(`
`operation: (index:`
`Int, acc: S, E) -> S)`
	S	Same as `reduce()`, but the operation additionally receives the current iteration index (0, 1, 2, ...).

`<S, E : S> list<E>.`
`reduceRight( operation:`
`(E, acc: S) -> S)`
	S	Reduce from right. Note that this does not work for iterables, because there is nothing like a right iteration.

`<S, E : S> list<E>.`
`reduceRight- Indexed(`
`operation: (index: Int,`
`E, acc: S)-> S)`
	S	Same as `reduceRight()`, but the operation additionally receives the current iteration index (0, 1, 2, ...).

Note that although the iteration goes over elements of type E, the operation function is allowed to also evaluate to a supertype of E. This is what the E : S in the type specification stands for. In this case the accumulator and the overall result will have the same type as this supertype.

A *folding* is the big brother of reduction. Whereas the reduction starts with the first element of the collection or iterable, and then uses the rest of the elements to update it, the folding works with a dedicated folding accumulator object that receives step by step all the iterated-over elements and therefore can update its state. Because the accumulator object can have any suitable type, folding is more powerful than reduction. Folding functions are listed in Table 16-19.

Table 16-19. *Folding*

Function	Returns	Description
`iter.fold( initial: R,` `operation: (acc: R, E) -> R)`	R	Folds over a collection or iterable. The first parameter receives the accumulator object. The operation lambda function receives the current accumulator object and the currently iterated-over element.

`iter.foldIndexed( initial: R,`
`operation: (index:Int, acc: R,`
`E) -> R)`
	R	Same as `fold()`, but the operation additionally receives the current iteration index (0, 1, 2, …).

`list.foldRight( initial: R,` `operation: (E, acc: R) -> R)`	R	Folds over a list, starting from the last object and iterating in reverse order. The first parameter receives the accumulator object. The operation lambda function receives the current accumulator object and the currently iterated-over element.

`list.foldRightIndexed(`
`initial: R, operation:`
`(index:Int, E, acc: R) -> R)`
	R	Same as `foldRight()`, but the operation additionally receives the current iteration index (0, 1, 2, …).

Exercise 8

Given a class data class `Parcel(val receiverId:Int, val weight:Double)` and a list

```
val l = listOf( Parcel(1267395, 1.45),
    Parcel(1515670, 0.46),
    Parcel(8345674, 2.50),
    Parcel(3418566, 1.47),
    Parcel(3491245, 3.04)
)
```

calculate the weight sum without using a `for` or `while` loop.

Joining

Sometimes instead of a full-fledged folding operation with an object receiving all the elements from the iteration, all you need is a way to create a string representation of a collection or an iterable, joining the string representations of all elements. Although this is possible via `fold()`, a dedicated joining function provided by Kotlin has a couple of extra features, namely a prefix and a postfix, and a limit and a truncation designator. You use

```
fun <E> Iterable<E>.joinToString(
    separator: CharSequence = ", ",
    prefix: CharSequence = "",
    postfix: CharSequence = "",
    limit: Int = -1,
    truncated: CharSequence = "...",
    transform: (E) -> CharSequence = null
): String
```

on the collection or iterable, with the following characteristics:

- If you specify a separator, this one will be used for separating the items in the output string. Otherwise a **,** will be used.

- If you specify a prefix, it will be used as a prefix for the output string. Otherwise none will be used.

- If you specify a postfix, it will be used as a postfix for the output string. Otherwise none will be used.

- If you specify a limit, the number of elements used for constructing the output string will be limited. Otherwise −1 will be used, which signifies no limit.

- If you specify a truncation string, it will be used to signify a truncation because the limit (if given) was exceeded. Otherwise ... will be used.

- If you specify a transform function, it will be used to create a string from each element. Otherwise null will be used, which means toString() will be applied to each element.

Grouping

Grouping is about splitting a list into sublists based on some criterion. Think of a list of employees with each employee having an employer field, and you want to create a list for each employer. This is not hard to do by writing a few lines of code, but because it is a recurring task, there are standard library functions that can help us. See Table 16-20 for grouping-related functions.

Table 16-20. *Grouping*

Function	Returns	Description
<E, K> iter.groupBy(keySelector: (E) -> K)	Map<K, List<E>>	Groups based on the key calculated by the keySelector function.
<E, K> iter.groupBy(keySelector: (E) -> K, valueTransform: (E) -> V)	Map<K, List<V>>	Groups based on the key calculated by the keySelector function, but also transforms the values by the valueTransform function.
<E, K> iter.groupingBy(keySelector: (E) -> K)	Grouping<E,K>	Prepares a grouping based on the key calculated by the keySelector function. Creates a special Grouping object that can be used for further operations.

(continued)

Table 16-20. (*continued*)

Function	Returns	Description
grouping.aggregate(operation: (key: K, accumulator: R?, element: E, first: Boolean) -> R)	Map<K, R>	Takes the result from groupingBy() and builds a map using the original keys. As for the values, use the operation to accumulate the values for each group (e.g., the accumulator could be a list).
grouping.eachCount()	Map<K, Int>	Returns a map with the element counts per group.
grouping.fold(initialValueSelector: (key: K, element: E) -> R, operation: (key: K, accumulator: R, element: E) -> R)	Map<K, R>	Takes the result from groupingBy() and builds a map using the original keys. As for the values, use the operation to accumulate the values for each group. The initial accumulator per group gets constructed by the initialValueSelector function.

Throughout this section we use list, set, map, coll, and iter for variables of type List, Set, Map, Collection, and Iterable, respectively. Remember that a list or set is a collection and that any collection is an iterable.

Zipping

If you have two related lists and want to bring them together, Kotlin provides a zipping function that can help you. Say, for example, you have a list of employees and another list of yearly salaries for a year that has not yet been registered. Both lists have the same size and each index points to a matching pair of employee and salary. In an imperative programming style, you'd write something like this to get an updated employee list:

```
class Employee {
    ...
    fun setSalary(year:Int, salary:Double) {}
}

val employees = ... // list
val newSalaries = ... // list
val newYear = 2018
val newEmployees = mutableListOf<Employee>()
for(ind in employees.indices) {
    val e = employees[ind]
    val sal = newSalaries[ind]
    e.setSalary(newYear, sal)
    newEmployees.add(e)
}
```

We can rewrite this in a functional style using the zipping function the standard library provides:

```
<E, R> Iterable<E>.zip(
    other: Iterable<R>
): List<Pair<E, R>>
```

which gives us:

```
val employees = ... // list
val newSalaries = ... // list
val newYear = 2018
val newEmployees = employees.zip(newSalaries).
    map{ p ->
      p.first.setSalary(newYear, p.second)
      p.first
    }
```

Here the zip() gives us a list of Pairs each containing an Employee and a salary (e.g., Double). The map() investigates each pair and updates the employee accordingly.

There is also a reverse operation for creating two lists out of one, fittingly called *unzipping*.

```
<E, R> Iterable<Pair<E, R>>.unzip():
      Pair<List<E>, List<R>>
```

More precisely, this is the second part of such an unzipping operation; you would first create a list of Pairs using a mapping function; for example:

```
list.map { item ->
    Pair(item.something, item.somethingElse)
}.unzip()
```

Windowing

For user interface programming you frequently need to split a list into chunks of a given size. Say, for example, the user interface shows chunks of size 10 and provides page forward and page backward buttons to show the next or the previous chunk of a longer list. For this aim the standard library provides a windowing function (see Table 16-21).

Table 16-21. *Windowing*

Function	Returns	Description
`<E> iterable.windowed( size: Int, step: Int = 1, partialWindows: Boolean = false )`	`List<List<E>>`	Creates a windowed view of an iterable or a collection. Each chunk has size `size`, and `step` indicates the index offset for each chunk (usually you set step = size). You must set `partialWindows` to true if you want to allow smaller chunks at the end.
`<E, R> iterable. windowed( size: Int, step: Int = 1, partialWindows: Boolean = false, transform: (List<E>) -> R)`	`List<R>`	Same as `windowed()`, but provides a `transform` function to act on each chunk.

Sequences

Sequences are lazily evaluated collections. By that we mean that other than for collections from the `kotlin.collections` package, no large amounts of data are held in memory. So, if you create a collection of size 1,000,000 there will be 1,000,000 items in the form of object references or primitives allocated in memory. A sequence of size 1,000,000, however, just indicates we have something that can be iterated over 1,000,000 times, without all the values associated with it. Sequence interfaces, classes, and functions have their own package: `kotlin.sequences`.

Sequences expose a lot of functions we already know from collections. You can use `forEach()`, apply filters, perform mappings, use reductions, perform foldings, and more. We don't show them all here; instead we list a few of the more important ones to get you started. For more information, refer to the Kotlin documentation.

To create a sequence given a list of values, you can use the `sequenceOf()` function; for example:

```
sequenceOf(1, 2, 7, 5)
```

Or, you can take any `Iterable` (set or list or range, or any collection) and write

```
iter.asSequence()
```

To create genuine sequences that do not depend on existing collections or arrays, there are several possibilities. The easiest of them perhaps consists of using the function `generateSequence()` as in

```
// Signature:
// fun <T : Any> generateSequence(
//     nextFunction: () -> T?
// ): Sequence<T>

var iterVar = 0
val seq = generateSequence {
    iterVar++
}
```

Here all we have to do is provide a function that generates the next sequence value. The downside of this approach is that we have a state, namely the iteration property `iterVar`, somewhere in the surrounding scope of `generateSequence()`. This is an antipattern thinking of clean code. What comes to the rescue is another variant of generateSequence():

```
fun <T : Any> generateSequence(
  seed: T?,
  nextFunction: (T) -> T?
): Sequence<T>
// or
fun <T : Any> generateSequence(
  seedFunction: () -> T?,
  nextFunction: (T) -> T?
): Sequence<T>
```

Here we can provide a seed, either directly or via a generator function, and the nextFunction() lambda receives the current iterator value and is supposed to return the next iterator value. A very simple sequence (0, 1, 2, ...) thus reads

```
val seq = generateSequence(
  seed = 0,
  nextFunction = { curr -> curr + 1 }
)

// example usage:
seq.take(10).forEach { i ->
  // i will have values 0, 1, 2, ..., 9
  ...
}
```

The iteration variable doesn't have to be an Int, or even a number at all. As an example, consider the Fibonacci sequence 1, 1, 2, 3, 5, 8, ... where each item is the sum of its two predecessors. This can be handled by a Pair and the sequence reads

```
val seqFib = generateSequence(
    seed = Pair(1,1),
    nextFunction = { curr ->
        Pair(curr.second, curr.first + curr.second)
    }
)
```

```
// example usage
seqFib.take(10).map { it.second }.forEach {
    Log.e("LOG", "fib: " + it)
}
```

The nextFunction starts with a pair(1,1), continues with a pair(1,2), pair(2,3), pair(3,5), and so on. The mapping in the example usage snippet extracts the second value of each pair and shows it. Interestingly, for higher numbers the ratio of the second to the first member of each pair approaches the *golden ratio* $0.5 \cdot (1 + \sqrt{5}) = 1.6180339887$:

```
val p = seqFib.take(40).last
val gr = p.second * 1.0 / p.first
// =  1.618033988749895
```

A somewhat more flexible, albeit more involved approach consists of using another sequence generation function: sequence(). Its signature reads

```
fun <T> sequence(
    block: suspend SequenceScope<T>.() -> Unit
): Sequence<T>
```

This function actually instantiates a kotlin.sequences.Sequence object in the following way:

```
Sequence { iterator(block) }
```

where iterator() creates and returns an instance of SequenceBuilderIterator. This SequenceBuilderIterator and the suspend in front of the lambda function make sure the sequence can be used in a parallelized execution environment. We'll talk about concurrence execution later in the book. What we need to know for now is that by virtue of the lambda with receiver specification SequenceScope<T>.() -> Unit we are, as concerns the block lambda function, acting in the environment of the SequenceScope object. To make this construct do something sensible, from inside block you must at least call one of

```
yieldAll([some implementation of Iterable])
// or
yieldAll([some implementation of Iterator])
// or
yieldAll([some implementation of Sequence])
```

As an example consider this:

```
val sequence = sequence {
    // This is an iterable:
    yieldAll(1..10 step 2)
}

// Usage example:
sequence.take(8).forEach {
    Log.e("LOG", it.toString())
}
// -> 1, 3, 5, 7, 9
```

Operators

For iterables, including all collections like sets and lists, and also for maps, there are a couple of operators, shown in Table 16-22, you can use to combine two of them.

Table 16-22. *Operators*

Operand	Operator	Operand	Returns
Iterable (collections, lists, sets)	intersect	Iterable (collections, lists, sets)	Creates a new immutable Set that contains all elements that are included in both operands.
Iterable (collections, lists, sets)	union	Iterable (collections, lists, sets)	Creates a new immutable Set that contains all elements that are included in either or both operands.
Iterable (collections, lists, sets)	+	E	Returns a new immutable List with all the elements from the left operand, appended to the right operand.
Iterable (collections, lists, sets)	+	Iterable, array, sequence	Returns a new immutable List with all the elements from the left operand, appended to all the elements from the right operand.

(continued)

343

Table 16-22. (*continued*)

Operand	Operator	Operand	Returns
Iterable (collections, lists, sets)	-	E	Returns a new immutable List with all the elements from the left operand, minus the right operand if it exists in the left operand.
Iterable (collections, lists, sets)	-	Iterable, array, sequence	Returns a new immutable List with all the elements from the left operand, minus all the elements from the right operand that also existed in the left operand.
Map	+	Pair<K,V>	Returns a new immutable map with all entries from the left operand, plus the right operand. If the key existed before, the entry gets overwritten.
Map	+	Iterable< Pair<K,V>>, Array<out Pair<K, V>>, Sequence< Pair<K,V>>, Map<out K, V>	Returns a new immutable map with all entries from the left operand, plus all the elements from the right operand. If any key from the right operand existed in the left operand as well, the corresponding entry gets overwritten by the right operand.
Map	-	K	Returns a new immutable map with all entries from the left operand, but with the key specified by the right operand removed (if it exists).
Map	-	Iterable<K>, Array<out K>, Sequence<K>	Returns a new immutable map with all entries from the left operand, but with all the keys specified by the right operand removed (only for those that exist in the left operand).

Because a lot of the other operators like *, /, %, and so on are undefined, and as we know we can define them by operator overloading, you can achieve a lot of things designing your own operators for collections and maps. Just make sure you provide good documentation so that others can understand what they do.

CHAPTER 17

More APIs

This chapter gathers a couple of more APIs you can use in your app. First we have the math API that gets used for mathematical calculations. For date and time handling, including transformations between different time representations, and parsing and formatting dates and times, we describe the date and time API. For input and output, which for Android boils down to file handling, we give an overview of the input and output API. For dynamically acquiring class member information the reflection API gets used; this is not a prominent part of object orientation but can help under some circumstances, so we include a treatise on reflection. Regular expressions provide a very powerful means to investigate and manipulate patterns inside strings, so we finish the chapter with a survey of regular expression constructs.

The Math API

Kotlin allows you to import the `Math` package from package `java.lang`

```
import java.lang.Math
```

This can be used like a singleton object and has a lot of mathematical functions like `sin()`, `cos()`, `tan()`, and others. You can look them all up in the Java API documentation. Kotlin provides a copy of some of them inside the `kotlin.math` package, so in most cases you can go without the `java.lang` import. The sine function, for example, is provided as an out-of-class function inside the `kotlin.math` package, so to use it you can write

```
import kotlin.math.sin
...
val x = sin(1.562)
```

The same holds for many other functions. Table 17-1 includes a nonexhaustive list. For a complete list, please see the official Kotlin documentation on the Web.

347

© Peter Späth 2019
P. Späth, *Learn Kotlin for Android Development*, https://doi.org/10.1007/978-1-4842-4467-8_17

Table 17-1.   *Kotlin Math Functions*

Function	Description
sin(), cos(), tan()	The sine, cosine, and tangent functions. Same as Math.sin(), Math.cos(), and Math.tan(), but in addition allow a Float as argument.
asin(), acos(), atan(), atan2()	The arc sine, arc cosine, and arc tangent functions. Function atan2() takes two arguments that correspond to (x, y) coordinates. Same as Math.asin(), Math.acos(), Math.atan(), and Math.atan2(), but in addition allow Floats as arguments.
sinh(), cosh(), tanh()	The hyperbolic sine, cosine, and tangent functions. Same as Math.sinh(), Math.cosh(), and Math.tanh(), but in addition allow a Float as argument.
asinh(), acosh(), atanh()	The inverse hyperbolic sine, cosine, and tangent functions. Same as Math.asinh(), Math.acosh(), and Math.atanh(), but in addition allow a Float as argument.
abs()	The absolute value of a number.
floor(), ceil()	For a Float or a Double the lower or upper next integer value. The type stays intact, so you have to add .toInt() or .toLong() to convert it to an integer type. Same as Math.floor() and Math.ceil(), but in addition allow a Float as argument.
round()	Half-up rounds to the nearest integer. The type stays intact, so you have to add .toInt() or .toLong() to convert it to an integer type. Same as Math.round(), but in addition allows a Float as argument.
exp(), log()	The exponential function and the logarithm. Same as Math.exp() and Math.log(), but in addition allow a Float as argument.
pow()	The power function (two parameters) x^y. Same as Math.pow(), but in addition allows a Float as argument.
sqrt()	The square root. Same as Math.sqrt(), but in addition allows a Float as argument.
min(), max()	The minimum and maximum of two numbers.
sign()	The signum function. Returns −1.0 for negative values, 0.0 for 0.0, and 1.0 for positive numbers. Same as Math.sign(), but in addition allows a Float as argument.

The same package, `kotlin.math`, contains a couple of extension properties. For example, you can write

```
import kotlin.math.absoluteValue
...
val x:Double = -3.5
val y = x.absoluteValue // -> 3.5
```

The complete list of such extensions includes `.absoluteValue` for the absolute value of a number (`Double`, `Float`, `Int`, or `Long`). The constants `E` and `PI` are the base of the natural logarithm and pi (π). The property `.sign` returns the signum for a number (`Double`, `Float`, `Int`, or `Long`), and `.ulp` returns the unit in the last place of a `Float` or `Double` (this is the smallest measurable distance between two numbers).

The Date and Time API, API Level 25 or Less

Kotlin does not have a separate date and time API, which is why you wouldn't find any information on how to handle date and time in the Kotlin documentation. However, you can use the date and time API from Java, which is included in Android and accessible to Kotlin.

Note   The date and time API substantially changed with Java 8. Android API versions up to 25 don't use Java 8, but the later API versions do; this is why we need to describe two date and time APIs. This section is for all Android API levels and therefore refers to the older Java 7 date and time API.

The date and time API borrowed from Java version 7 centers around the following expressions:

```
import java.util.Date
import java.util.GregorianCalendar
import java.text.SimpleDateFormat

val timeMillis:Long = System.currentTimeMillis()
val d = Date()
val cal = GregorianCalendar()
val sdf = SimpleDateFormat("yyyy-MM-dd HH:mm:ss")
```

The first one, `System.currentTimeMillis()`, expresses the idea of an absolute time. More precisely this is the number of milliseconds since January 1, 1970, 00:00:00 UTC. This is low-level information that often gets used as a reliable timestamp for database entries. You'll also see it for a quick and dirty timing of program parts during performance measurement:

```
val t1 = System.currentTimeMillis()
...
Log.d("LOG", "Calculation took " +
      (System.currentTimeMillis() - t1) + "ms")
```

The `Date` class is a thin wrapper around the absolute time. It represents it as an object, and also provides for a simple `toString()` implementation that outputs the time in a human-readable format:

```
import java.util.Date
...
val d = Date() // current time
Log.d("LOG", d.toString())
// -> s.th. like
// Sun Jan 13 10:12:26 GMT+01:00 2019
```

A `Date` instance gives us the number of milliseconds that have passed since 1970-01-01 00:00:00 UTC until its current value. To get that number—it is a `Long` type number—use its `time` property:

```
import java.util.Date
...
val d = Date()  // current time
val tm = d.time // ms since 1970-01-01T00:00:00 UTC
```

The `GregorianCalendar` class gives us tools to fiddle with months, weeks, time zone, time of day, minutes during the hour, seconds during the minute, and all those things.

```
import java.util.Date
import java.util.Calendar
import java.util.GregorianCalendar
import java.util.TimeZone
...
```

```
val cal = GregorianCalendar()
// <- will hold the current time

cal.timeZone = TimeZone.getTimeZone("US/Hawaii")
// Note: TimeZone.getAvailableIDs().forEach {
//     Log.e("LOG","!!! " + it) }
// shows a list

// Set to current time
cal.time = Date()

// Set to 2018-02-01T13:27:44
cal.set(2018, Calendar.FEBRUARY,  1, 13, 27 ,44)

val month = cal.get(Calendar.MONTH)
val hour = cal.get(Calendar.HOUR_OF_DAY)
```

The SimpleDateFormat class helps us in producing human-readable string representations of dates and times, and also allows us to convert such string representations back to Date instances:

```
import java.util.Date
import java.text.SimpleDateFormat
import java.util.Locale
...
val d = Date() // now
val sdf = SimpleDateFormat("yyyy-MM-dd HH:mm")
Log.d("LOG", sdf.format(d)) // -> 2019-01-13 13:41

val loc = Locale("en")
val sdf2 = SimpleDateFormat("yyyy-MMM-dd HH:mm", loc)
Log.d("LOG", sdf2.format(d)) // -> 2019-Jan-13 13:41

val d2:Date = sdf.parse("2018-12-12 17:13")
Log.d("LOG", d2.toString())
// ->  Wed Dec 12 17:13:00 GMT+01:00 2018
```

These examples use the time zone they retrieve by querying the operating system. You could also set a time zone on the SimpleDateFormat object as follows:

```
import java.text.SimpleDateFormat
import java.util.Date
import java.util.TimeZone

...
val sdf = SimpleDateFormat("yyyy-MM-dd HH:mm")
sdf.timeZone = TimeZone.getTimeZone("US/Hawaii")

val d:Date = sdf.parse("2018-12-12 17:13")
Log.d("LOG", d.toString())
// ->   Thu Dec 13 04:13:00 GMT+01:00 2018
```

By the way, Date.toString() implicitly uses the time zone it gets by querying the operating system (Europe/Berlin in my case).

Caution   Both Date and SimpleDateFormat are *not* thread safe; you must not share instances of them between different threads.

For details about all these date and time API interfaces and classes, and also related interfaces and classes, consult Oracle's Java documentation. Make sure you don't use the documentation for a Java version higher than 7. We deal with the Java 8 related date and time API in the next section.

The Date and Time API, API Level 26 or Greater

Note   This section is for Android API levels starting from 26 (Android 8.0), and therefore refers to the Java 8 date and time API.

Starting with Android API level 26 (Android 8.0) a couple of new date and time related interfaces and classes are available. You can continue using the old API described in the previous section, but the new API contains some improvements we outline in this section.

Note   As of the beginning of 2019, the number of devices using API level 26 or greater is not very high. You should consult a distribution survey before you start developing for API levels beyond 25.

The new API can only be used if in your module's `build.gradle` file you set the `minSdkVersion` to 26 or greater:

```
android {
    ...
    defaultConfig {
        ...
        minSdkVersion 26
        ...
    }
    ...
}
```

The new interfaces and classes reside in the package `java.time`. For the rest of this section we usually omit the corresponding imports.

Local Dates and Times

Local dates and times get described from the context of the observer and basically use the following classes from the `java.time` package:

- `LocalDate`

    This class corresponds to a date representation of the format `yyyy-MM-dd` (e.g., 2018-11-27) and disregards the time of day.

- `LocalTime`

    This class corresponds to a time representation of the format `HH:mm:ss` (e.g., 21:27:55) and disregards the date.

- `LocalDateTime`

    A combination of `LocalDate` and `LocalTime`, possibly represented by `yyyy-MM-ddTHH:mm:ss` (the T is a literal).

The format designators yyyy, HH, and so on are described in the API documentation of java.time.DateTimeFormatter.

All three of them include factory methods to generate object instances. This includes taking the current date and time:

```
import java.time.*

// current day in the default time zone
val ld1 : LocalDate = LocalDate.now()

// "Now" corresponds to different days in different
// time zones. The following allows us to specify a
// different time zone
val z2 = ZoneId.of("UTC+01")
val ld2 : LocalDate = LocalDate.now(z2)

val ld3 = LocalDate.of(2018, Month.MARCH, 27)
val ld4 = LocalDate.of(2018, 3, 27) // the same

val lt1 : LocalTime = LocalTime.now()
val lt2 = LocalTime.now(z2) // different time zone
val lt3 = LocalTime.of(23, 27, 55) // 23:27:55

val ldt1 = LocalDateTime.now()
val ldt2 = LocalDateTime.now(z2)
val ldt3 = LocalDateTime.of(2018, Month.APRIL, 23, 23, 44, 12)
// <- 2018-04-23T23:44:12
```

Note that despite the ability to add a time zone specification to further specify to which time "now" corresponds, this information is by no means somehow stored in the date and time object. Local dates and times are by definition time-zone agnostic.

We can parse strings to obtain instances of LocalDate, LocalTime, and LocalDateTime:

```
import java.time.*
import java.time.format.*

// Parse ISO-8601
val ld1 = LocalDate.parse("2019-02-13")
```

```
// Parse other formats. For the format specification,
// see API documentation of class DateTimeFormatter.
val formatter1 = DateTimeFormatter.ofPattern("yyyy MM dd")
val ld2 = LocalDate.parse("2019 02 13", formatter1)

val lt1 = LocalTime.parse("21:17:23")
val lt2 = LocalTime.parse("21:17:23.3734")

val formatter2 = DateTimeFormatter.ofPattern("HH|mm|ss")
val lt3 = LocalTime.parse("21|17|23", formatter2)

val ldt1 = LocalDateTime.parse("2019-02-13T21:17:23")
val ldt2 = LocalDateTime.parse("2019-02-13T21:17:23.3734")

val formatter3 = DateTimeFormatter.ofPattern("yyyy.MM.dd.HH.mm.ss")
val ldt3 = LocalTime.parse("2019.04.23.17.45.23", formatter3)
```

We can tailor our own string representations of LocalDate, LocalTime, and LocalDateTime instances:

```
import android.util.Log
import java.time.*
import java.time.format.*

val s1 = LocalDate.now().format(
    DateTimeFormatter.ofPattern("yyyy|MM|dd"))
Log.d("LOG","s1 = ${s1}") // -> 2019|01|14

val s2 = LocalDate.now().format(
    DateTimeFormatter.ISO_LOCAL_DATE)
Log.d("LOG","s2 = ${s2}") // -> 2019-01-14

val s3 = LocalTime.now().format(
    DateTimeFormatter.ofPattern("HH mm ss"))
Log.d("LOG","s3 = ${s3}") // -> 14 46 20
```

```
val s4 = LocalTime.now().format(
    DateTimeFormatter.ISO_LOCAL_TIME)
Log.d("LOG","s4 = ${s4}") // 14:46:20.503

val s5 = LocalDateTime.now().format(
    DateTimeFormatter.ofPattern(
"yyyy MM dd - HH mm ss"))
Log.d("LOG","s5 = ${s5}") // -> 2019 01 14 - 14 46 20

val s6 = LocalDateTime.now().format(
    DateTimeFormatter.ISO_LOCAL_DATE_TIME)
Log.d("LOG","s6 = ${s6}") // -> 2019-01-14T14:46:20.505
```

You can perform time arithmetics with `LocalDate`, `LocalTime`, and `LocalDateTime` instances:

```
import java.time.*
import java.time.temporal.*

val ld = LocalDate.now()
val lt = LocalTime.now()
val ldt = LocalDateTime.now()

val ld2 = ld.minusDays(7L)
val ld3 = ld.plusWeeks(2L)
val ld4 = ld.with(ChronoField.MONTH_OF_YEAR, 11L)

val lt2 = lt.plus(Duration.of(2L, ChronoUnit.SECONDS))
val lt3 = lt.plusSeconds(2L) // same

val ldt2 = ldt.plusWeeks(2L).minusHours(2L)
```

From `LocalDateTime` we can calculate the number of seconds that have passed since 1970-01-01:00:00:00 UTC, similar to the `System.currentTimeMillis()` function from the old API:

```
import java.time.*

val ldt : LocalDateTime = ...
val secs = ldt.toEpochSecond(ZoneOffset.of("+01:00"))
```

Note that to get the epoch seconds, a better solution is to take a ZonedDateTime. We'll talk about zoned dates and times later.

Instants

An instant is an instantaneous point on the timeline. Use this for cases where you need unique absolute timestamps, for example, to register events in databases and the like. The precise definition is somewhat involved; for an introduction read the API documentation for java.time.Instant.

You can get an Instant by, for example, querying the system clock, specifying the elapsed time since 1970-01-01T00:00:00Z, or parsing a time string, or from other date and time objects:

```
import java.time.*

val inz1 = Instant.now() // default time zone

// Specify time zone
val inz2 = Instant.now(Clock.system(
    ZoneId.of("America/Buenos_Aires")))

val secondsSince1970 : Long = 1_000_000_000L
val nanoAdjustment : Long = 300_000_000 // 300ms
val inz3 = Instant.ofEpochSecond(
    secondsSince1970, nanoAdjustment)

// "Z" is UTC ("Zulu" time)
val inz4 = Instant.parse("2018-01-23T23:33:14.513Z")

// Uniform converter, for the ZonedDateTime class
// see below
val inz5 = Instant.from(ZonedDateTime.parse("2019-02-13T21:17:23+01:00
        [Europe/Paris]"))
```

Offset Dates and Times

Offset dates and times are like Instants with an additional time offset from UTC/ Greenwich. For such offset dates and times, we have two classes, OffsetTime and OffsetDateTime, for which you can get instances as follows:

```
import java.time.*
import java.time.format.DateTimeFormatter

// Get now ----------------------------------------

// System clock, default time zone
val ot1 = OffsetTime.now()
val odt1 = OffsetDateTime.now()

// Use a different clock
val clock:Clock = ...
val ot2 = OffsetTime.now(clock)
val odt2 = OffsetDateTime.now(clock)

// Use a different time zone
val ot3 = OffsetTime.now(
    ZoneId.of("America/Buenos_Aires"))
val odt3 = OffsetDateTime.now(
    ZoneId.of("America/Buenos_Aires"))

// From time details -------------------------------

val ot4 = OffsetTime.of(23, 17, 3, 500_000_000,
    ZoneOffset.of("-02:00"))
val odt4 = OffsetDateTime.of(
    1985, 4, 23,           // 19685-04-23
    23, 17, 3, 500_000_000, // 23:17:03.5
    ZoneOffset.of("+02:00"))

// Parsed ------------------------------------------

val ot5 = OffsetTime.parse("16:15:30+01:00")
val odt5 = OffsetDateTime.parse("2007-12-03T17:15:30-08:00")
```

```
val ot6 = OffsetTime.parse("16 15 +00:00",
      DateTimeFormatter.ofPattern("HH mm XXX"))
val odt6 = OffsetDateTime.parse("20181115 - 231644 +02:00",
      DateTimeFormatter.ofPattern("yyyyMMdd - HHmmss XXX"))

// From other objects -------------------------------

val lt = LocalTime.parse("16:14:27.235")
val ld = LocalDate.parse("2018-05-24")
val inz = Instant.parse("2018-01-23T23:33:14.513Z")
val ot7 = OffsetTime.of(lt, ZoneOffset.of("+02:00"))
val odt7 = OffsetDateTime.of(ld, lt, ZoneOffset.of("+02:00"))
val ot8 = OffsetTime.ofInstant(inz, ZoneId.of("America/Buenos_Aires"))

val odt8 = OffsetDateTime.ofInstant(inz, ZoneId.of("America/Buenos_Aires"))

val zdt = ZonedDateTime.of( // see below
      2018, 2, 27,          // 2018-02-27
      23, 27, 33, 0,        // 23:27:33.0
      ZoneId.of("Pacific/Tahiti"))
val odt9 = zdt.toOffsetDateTime()

// uniform converter
val ot10 = OffsetTime.from(zdt)
val odt10 = OffsetDateTime.from(zdt)
```

With offset dates and times you can do arithmetics and formatting basically the same way as possible for local dates and times. In addition, for conversion operations, we have

```
import java.time.*

val ot = OffsetTime.parse("16:15:30+01:00")
val lt : LocalTime = ot.toLocalTime()
```

```
val odt = OffsetDateTime.parse("2007-12-03T17:15:30-08:00")
val ldt : LocalDateTime = odt.toLocalDateTime()
val lt2 : LocalTime = odt.toLocalTime()
val ld2 : LocalDate = odt.toLocalDate()
val ot2 : OffsetTime = odt.toOffsetTime()

val zdt : ZonedDateTime = odt.toZonedDateTime()
// see below for class ZonedDateTime
```

Zoned Dates and Times

Local dates and times are great if we aren't concerned about user location. If we have different entities, users, computers, or devices all over the world entering dates and times, we need to add the time zone information. This is what the class ZonedDateTime is for.

Note that this is not the same as a date and time with a fixed time offset information, as is the case for OffsetDateTime. A time zone includes things like Daylight Saving Time that need to be taken into account.

Similar to LocalDateTime, the ZonedDateTime has factory methods for getting *now:*

```
import java.time.*

// Get "now" using the system clock and the default
// time zone from your operating system.
val zdt1 = ZonedDateTime.now()

// Get "now" using a time zone. To list all available
// predefined zone IDs, try
//      Log.d("LOG", ZoneId.getAvailableZoneIds().
//                   joinToString { it + "\n" })
val z2 = ZoneId.of("UTC+01")
val zdt2 = ZonedDateTime.now(z2)

// Get "now" using an instance of Clock
val clock3 = Clock.systemUTC()
val zdt3 = ZonedDateTime.now(clock3)
```

We can also get a ZonedDateTime using detailed time information, and parse a string representation of a timestamp to get a ZonedDateTime:

```
import java.time.*

val z4 = ZoneId.of("Pacific/Tahiti")
val zdt4 = ZonedDateTime.of(
    2018, 2, 27,             // 2018-02-27
    23, 27, 33, 0,           // 23:27:33.0
    z4)
// The 7th par is nanoseconds, so for
// 23:27:33.5 you have to enter
// 500_000_000 here

val localDate = LocalDate.parse("2018-02-27")
val localTime = LocalTime.parse("23:44:55")
val zdt5 = ZonedDateTime.of(localDate, localTime,
    ZoneId.of("America/Buenos_Aires"))

val ldt = LocalDateTime.parse("2018-02-27T23:44:55.3")
val zdt6 = ZonedDateTime.of(ldt,
    ZoneId.of("America/Buenos_Aires"))

val inz = Instant.parse("2018-01-23T23:33:14.513Z")
val zdt7 = ZonedDateTime.ofInstant(inz,
    ZoneId.of("America/Buenos_Aires"))

val zdt8 = ZonedDateTime.parse(
    "2018-01-23T23:33:14Z[America/Buenos_Aires]")
```

A ZonedDateTime allows for operations like plusWeeks(weeks:Long) and minusDays(days:Long) to build a new instance with the time given added or subtracted. This works for any of Years, Months, Weeks, Days, Hours, Minutes, Seconds, or Nanos.

There are various getter functions for the different time fractions: getYear(), getMonth(), getMonthValue(), getDayOfMonth(), getHour(), getMinute(), getSecond(), and getNano(), plus a few others. To get the time zone, write getZone().

To parse a date and time string and to convert a ZonedDateTime to a string, write:

```
import java.time.*
import java.time.format.DateTimeFormatter

val zdt1 = ZonedDateTime.parse(
    "2007-12-03T10:15:30+01:00[Europe/Paris]")

val formatter = DateTimeFormatter.ofPattern(
    "HH:mm:ss.SSS")
// See DateTimeFormatter API docs for more options
val str = zdt1.format(formatter)
```

The connection between a ZonedDateTime and a LocalDateTime happens via

```
import java.time.*

val ldt = LocalDateTime.parse("2018-02-27T23:44:55.3")
val zdt = ZonedDateTime.of(ldt,
    ZoneId.of("America/Buenos_Aires"))

val ldt2 = zdt.toLocalTime()
```

Duration and Periods

A duration is the physical time span between two instances. A period is similar, but only handles years, months, and days, and takes the calendar system into account. there are the special Duration and Period classes for handling durations and periods:

```
import java.time.*
import java.time.temporal.ChronoUnit

val ldt1 = LocalDateTime.parse("2018-01-23T17:23:00")
val ldt2 = LocalDateTime.parse("2018-01-24T16:13:10")
val ldt3 = LocalDateTime.parse("2020-01-24T16:13:10")

// Getting a duration: -----------------------------

val d1 = Duration.between(ldt1, ldt2)
// Note: this works also for Instant and ZonedDateTime
// objects
```

```
val d2 = Duration.of(27L, ChronoUnit.HOURS) // 27hours

val d3 = Duration.ZERO.
            plusDays(3L).
            plusHours(4L).
            minusMinutes(78L)

val d4 = Duration.parse("P2DT3H4M")
// <- 2 days, 3 hours, 4 minutes
// For more specifiers, see the API documentation
// of Duration.parse()

// Getting a period: --------------------------------

val ld1 = LocalDate.parse("2018-04-23")
val ld2 = LocalDate.parse("2018-08-16")

val p1 = Period.between(ld1, ld2)
// Note, end date not inclusive

val p2 = Period.of(2, 3, -1)
// <- 2 years + 3 months - 1 day

val p3 = Period.parse("P1Y2M-3D")
// <- 1 year + 2 months - 3 days
// For more specifiers, see the API documentation
// of Period.parse()
```

You can perform arithmetic calculations on instances of the Duration or Period classes:

```
import java.time.*

// Duration operations: -----------------------------

val d = Duration.parse("P2DT3H4M")
// <- 2 days, 3 hours, 4 minutes

val d2 = d.plusDays(3L)
// also:   .minusDays(33L)
```

```
// or      .plusHours(2L)     or  .minusHours(1L)
// or      .plusMinutes(77L) or  .minusMinutes(7L)
// or      .plusSeconds(23L) or  .minusSeconds(5L)
// or      .plusMillis(11L)   or  .minusMillis(55L)
// or      .plusNanos(1000L) or  .minusNanos(5_000_000L)

val d3 = d.abs()           // make positive
val d4 = d.negated()       // swap sign
val d5 = d.multipliedBy(3L)    // three times as long
val d6 = d.dividedBy(2L)       // half as long

// Period operations: --------------------------------

val p = Period.of(2, 3, -1)
// <- 2 years + 3 months - 1 day

val p2 = p.normalized()
// <- possibly adjusts the year to make the month lie
// inside [-11;+11]

val p3 = p.negated()

val p4 = p.minusYears(11L)
// also:  .plusYears(3L)
// or      .minusMonths(4L) or  .plusMonths(2L)
// or      .minusDays(40L)  or  .plusDays(5L)

val p5 = p.multipliedBy(5) // 5 times as long
```

You can use duration and periods to add or subtract time amounts to and from LocalDate, LocalTime, LocalDateTime, ZonedDateTime, and Instant objects.

```
import java.time.*

val d = Duration.parse("P2DT3H4M")

val p = Period.of(2, 3, -1)
// <- 2 years + 3 months - 1 day
```

```
val ld = LocalDate.parse("2018-04-23")
val lt = LocalTime.parse("17:13:12")
val ldt = LocalDateTime.of(ld, lt)
val zdt = ZonedDateTime.parse(
      "2007-12-03T10:15:30+01:00[Europe/Paris]")
val inz = Instant.parse("2018-01-23T23:33:14.513Z")

// ---- Using a LocalDate
val ld2 = ld.plus(p)  // or .minus(p)
// val ld3 = ld.plus(d) // -> exception
// val ld4 = ld.minus(d) // -> exception

// ---- Using a LocalTime
val lt2 = lt.plus(d)  // or .minus(d)
// val lt3 = lt.minus(p) // -> exception
// val lt4 = lt.plus(p) // -> exception

// ---- Using a LocalDateTime
val ldt2 = ldt.plus(d)  // or .minus(d)
val ldt3 = ldt.plus(p)  // or .minus(p)

// ---- Using a ZonedDateTime
val zdt2 = zdt.plus(d)  // or .minus(d)
val zdt3 = zdt.plus(p)  // or .minus(p)

// ---- Using an Instant
val inz2 = inz.plus(d)  // or .minus(d)
// val inz3 = inz.minus(p) // -> exception
// val inz4 = inz.plus(p) // -> exception
```

Note that some of the operations are not allowed and lead to an exception. Those are commented out in the previous listing. The reasons for the exceptions are possible precision losses or mismatches in the time concepts. See the API documentation for details.

Clock

A Clock sits in the depths of the date and time API. For many, if not most applications, you can work well with local dates and times, offset and zoned dates and times, and instants. It might be necessary to tweak the clock usage for getting *now* for testing and special cases:

```
import java.time.*

val clock : Clock = ...
val ldt = LocalDateTime.now(clock)
val zdt = ZonedDateTime.now(clock)
val inz = Instant.now(clock)
```

Apart from overwriting the abstract Clock class, Clock itself provides a couple of functions to tweak clock usage. These two are particularly interesting:

1. Clock.fixed(fixedInstant:Instant, zone:ZoneId): This is always a clock that always returns the same instant.

2. Clock.offset(baseClock:Clock, offsetDuration:Duration): Returns a new clock derived from the base clock with the specified duration added.

If, however, you overwrite the clock, you must implement at least the abstract functions from the Clock base class. Here is an example of a clock that always returns the same instant and doesn't care about zones:

```
import java.time.*

val myClock = object : Clock() {
    override fun withZone(zone: ZoneId?): Clock {
        // Supposed to return a copy of this clock
        // with a different time zone
        return this
    }

    override fun getZone(): ZoneId {
        // Supposed to return the zone ID
        return ZoneId.of("Z")
```

```
    }

    override fun instant(): Instant {
        // This is the engine of the clock. It must
        // provide an Instant
        return Instant.parse("2018-01-23T23:33:14Z")
    }
}

... use myClock
```

Exercise 1

Create a clock `ClockTwiceAsFast` with a constructor fetching the time from the UTC system clock. After that, the clock should run twice as fast. Disregard zone information. To prove that it is running the intended way, use

```
import java.time.*

val myClock = ClockTwiceAsFast()
Log.d("LOG", LocalDateTime.now(myClock).format(
      DateTimeFormatter.ISO_LOCAL_DATE_TIME))
Thread.sleep(1000L)
Log.d("LOG", LocalDateTime.now(myClock).format(
      DateTimeFormatter.ISO_LOCAL_DATE_TIME))
```

Input and Output

In an Android environment you probably won't use input and output very often. The users of your app don't see a console a `println("Hello World")` would print to, and any logging your app produces is not supposed to be seen by end users anyway. In addition, for persisting and reading data of any kind you can use the built-in database.

Having said that and in case you absolutely need it, you still can read from and write to files for doing input and output. In Android it is best to use files that lie in a designated file system space that is accessible to your app. You do so by writing

```
import java.io.File

// We are inside an Activity or other Context!
val dataDir:File = getFilesDir()
```

Despite the class naming `File` in this listing, the `dataDir` corresponds to a directory, not a data file in the narrow sense. The rest of this section assumes you have prepended the snippet `val dataDir = getFilesDir()`.

Kotlin's file handling relies heavily on Java interfaces and classes and adds extensions to some Java classes. There are also a couple of out-of-class functions that get defined in the package `kotlin.io`. You don't have to import `kotlin.io`; it is imported by default and all class extensions from this package thus are enabled by default.

Creating Some Test Files

Just to have some files to get you started experimenting with the I/O API, run the following once:

```
dataDir.resolve("a.txt").takeIf{ !it.exists() }.appendText("Hello World A")
dataDir.resolve("b.txt").takeIf{ !it.exists() }.appendText("Hello World B")
File(dataDir,"dir1").mkdirs()dataDir.resolve("dir1").resolve("a.txt").
    takeIf{ !it.exists() }.appendText("Hello World dir1-A")
```

We discuss those functions later.

File Names

For maximum interoperability you should restrict file names to contain only characters from A–Z, a–z, 0–9, _, -, and . Also, to indicate that a file `file` lies inside a directory `dir`, write `dir/file`. To designate the root directory of the file system, use `/`.

Note   The slash (/) is the file system separator on Android. Other operating systems use different separators. If you want to be really polyglot, you can write `"dir" + File.separator + "file"`. The runtime engine will then pick up the appropriate separator for the operating system in which it works.

To address a file `fileName` inside a given directory you can use

```
val someDir:File = ...
```

```
val file:File = someDir.resolve("fileName")
```

which works for real files and subdirectories.

Listing Directories

To list the files of the app's file storage write

```
dataDir.walk().maxDepth(1).forEach { file ->
    Log.d("LOG", file.toString())
}
```

This shows the immediate contents of the data directory. If you ran the little preparation code from earlier, the logging output will look like this:

```
/data/user/0/multipi.pspaeth.de.multipi/files
/data/user/0/multipi.pspaeth.de.multipi/files/instant-run
/data/user/0/multipi.pspaeth.de.multipi/files/a.txt
/data/user/0/multipi.pspaeth.de.multipi/files/b.txt
/data/user/0/multipi.pspaeth.de.multipi/files/dirs1
/data/user/0/multipi.pspaeth.de.multipi/files/dir1
```

The `multipi.pspaeth.de.multipi` happens to be the sample app where I'm running the code, and in the second line, `instant-run` belongs to a directory Android installed by default. You can, of course, apply `walk()` to any other directory, just make sure you have the appropriate file system access rights. The `maxDepth(1)` confines traversal to the immediate children of the directory only. Omitting it would traverse all contents recursively, including files in directories, files in directories in directories, and so on.

Both walk() and maxDepth() return an instance of class FileTreeWalk. This class is a Sequence and mimics all functions of Iterable, so you could apply filters, mappings, folding, grouping, and the other processes we investigated in Chapter 9. You can also write asIterable() if you need a real Iterable (a Sequence itself does not inherit from Iterable).

Note   The reason the Sequence interface exists is that sequences potentially can be iterated over several times, which is not the case for implementations of Iterable.

For example, to recursively list all real files inside dataDir, omitting directories, you'd apply a filter as follows:

```
dataDir.walk().filter { it.isFile() }.forEach {
    file ->
    Log.d("LOG", file.toString())
}
```

You can use the same filtering procedure to only list files that have a certain ending:

```
dataDir.walk().filter { it.endsWith(".txt") }.
forEach {
    file ->
    Log.d("LOG", file.toString())
}
```

There is also a function startsWith("someString") to see whether a file name starts with a certain string. You can also check the name against a regular expression:

```
dataDir.walk().filter {
    it.name.matches(".*invoice\\d\\d.*\\.txt")
}.forEach {
    file ->
    Log.d("LOG", file.toString())
}
```

This would match any file with a name that contains an invoice with two numbers added, and ends with .txt.

Writing to Files

To write or append text to a file, you can use

```
val file = dataDir.resolve("a.txt")
// or any other file

// Write to the file
file.writeText("In the house, there was no light")

// Append to the file
file.appendText("\nIn the house, there was no light")
```

Note that writeText(text:String) and appendText(text:String) use the UTF-8 character set. If you need a different character set, you can add an instance of java.nio.charset.Charset as a second parameter: writeText("...", Charsets.ISO_8859_1) (Charsets is a Kotlin class: kotlin.text.Charsets).

To get more low level, it is also possible to write the raw bytes from a ByteArray to a file:

```
val file = dataDir.resolve("a.txt")
val bytes = byteArrayOf(27, 34, 13, 47, 50)

// Write to the file
file.writeBytes(bytes)

// Append to the file
file.appendBytes(bytes)
```

Note   If you need really heavy file handling with large files or many fine-grained file operations, Kotlin provides more extensions that can help you, and you can also use the plethora of Java file handling classes and methods. Because on Android you have a built-in fast database for such use cases, I don't think you will use such special file handling very often, but feel free to explore the Kotlin and Java documentation.

Reading from Files

To read from files, you have to decide whether you want to read the complete file into memory, you want to read a text file line by line, or you want to read a file containing binary data block-wise.

To read a moderately sized text file as a whole into a property, write this (again we assume you ran that little preparatory program from the beginning of the chapter):

```
val file = dataDir.resolve("a.txt")
val fileText:String = file.readText()
```

Here the UTF-8 character set gets used. To read a file with a different character set, add a parameter:

```
val file = dataDir.resolve("a.txt")
val fileText:String = file.readText(
    Charsets.ISO_8859_1)
```

If you don't have a text file, but a file with some raw byte data, to read the bytes from a file use this:

```
val file = dataDir.resolve("a.txt")
val fileBytes:ByteArray = file.readBytes()
```

Reading a text file as a whole into a property certainly makes sense for small text files. To handle larger text files, you can also read them line by line:

```
val file = dataDir.resolve("a.txt")

val allLines = file.readLines()
allLines.forEach { ln ->
  // do something with the line (a String)
}
```

The documentation says you shouldn't do this for huge files. Internally the file gets read into a big list containing all lines. Files with up to 100,000 lines do not actually cause a problem, though. If you target Android devices starting from API level 26, there is also a more efficient way for reading lines into a stream:

```
val file = dataDir.resolve("a.txt")

// Only API level > 25
file.bufferedReader.use {
    it.lines().forEach { ln ->
        // do something with the line (a String)
    }
}
```

This time no list gets used; the lambda function receives exactly the currently read line. The use is necessary for the file system resource to get closed properly after usage.

Reading a binary data file chunk-wise helps to handle large binary files:

```
import java.io.File

...

val file = dataDir.resolve("a.txt")

// Buffer size implementation dependent
file.forEachBlock{ buffer:ByteArray, bytesRead:Int ->
    // do something with the buffer
}

// Or, if you want to prescribe the buffer size
file.forEachBlock(512) { buffer, bytesRead ->
    // do something with the buffer
}
```

Deleting Files

To delete a file or a directory you write

```
import java.io.File

...

val file:File = ...
val wasDeleted:Boolean = file.delete()
```

This works both for files and directories; however, the directory must not contain any files. To delete a directory and all its contents, including other directories, you can instead use this:

```
import java.io.File
...

val file:File = ...
val wasDeleted:Boolean = file.deleteRecursively()
```

If anything happens while deleting the contents—for example, a file cannot be deleted because of missing access rights—you'll end up with a partially deleted file structure. It is also possible to work with a file in your app and request an automatic deletion when the app terminates:

```
import java.io.File
...

val file:File = ...
file.deleteOnExit()
```

If you have several deleteOnExit() in your app, the deletion happens in reverse order. Note that as for normal delete() calls, it is possible to do that for directories as well, but they must be empty.

Working with Temporary Files

If you need temporary files it is easier to use

```
import java.io.File
...

val prefix = "tmpFile"
val suffix = ".tmp"
val tmpFile:File = File.createTempFile(prefix, suffix)
tmpFile.deleteOnExit()

... use tmpFile
```

compared to manually making up temporary files.

This will use a directory provided by your operating system especially for temporary files, and it will make sure the file does not exist by adding some random, but unique characters to the file name. For both the prefix and suffix you can use what you want, but the prefix must be at least three characters long. If you use null for the suffix, .tmp gets used by default.

If you want to provide your own directory for temporary files, just add a File denoting the directory as a third argument to createTempFile().

More File Operations

Copying a file using the functions we already know is relatively easy: file2.writeBytes(file1.readBytes()). There is also a library function, however, to make it more expressive and also add some options:

```
import java.io.File

...

val file1:File = ...
val file2:File = ...

f1.copyTo(f2)        // f2 must not exist
f1.copyTo(f2, true) // overwrite if necessary

// To fine-tune performance, you can tweak the
// buffer size
f1.copyTo(f2, bufferSize = 4096)
```

The copyTo() function returns the target file.

The ability to copy a complete directory recursively including all subdirectories and their files is provided by another standard library function:

```
import java.io.File

...

val dir1:File = ...
val dir2:File = ...

f1.copyRecursively(f2)        // f2 must not exist
f1.copyRecursively(f2, true) // overwrite if necessary
```

```
// To fine-tune error handling, you can add a handler.
// Otherwise an IOException gets thrown.
f1.copyRecursively(f2, onError = {
    file:File, ioException:IOException ->
    // do something.

    // What to do now? Just skip this file, or
    // terminate the complete function?
    OnErrorAction.SKIP // or .TERMINATE
})
```

Renaming a file happens via

```
import java.io.File
...

val file1:File = ...
val file2:File = ...

file1.renameTo(file2)
```

The File class has more functions that tell us about the details of a file:

```
import java.io.File
import java.util.Date
...

val file = dataDir.resolve("a.txt")
val log = { msg:String -> Log.d("LOG", msg) }

log("Name: " + file.name)
log("The file exists: " + file.exists())
log("You can read the file: " + file.canRead())
log("You can write to the file: " + file.canWrite())
log("Is a directory: " + file.isDirectory())
log("Is a real file: " + file.isFile())
log("Last modified: " + Date(file.lastModified()))
log("Length: " + file.length())
```

Note   The java.nio package contains more classes and functions that give more information about files, if you need even more details.

Reading URLs

The file API contains very convenient functions to read the contents of an Internet URL. Just write

```
import java.net.URL
import kotlin.concurrent.thread

thread {
    val contents:String =
      URL("http://www.example.com/something.txt").
      readText()

    val isoContents =
      URL("http://www.example.com/something.txt").
      readText(Charsets.ISO_8859_1)

    val img:ByteArray =
      URL("http://www.example.com/somepic.jpg").
      readBytes()
}
```

Note   On Android, you must request Internet access permission for this to work. Add <uses-permission android:name = "android.permission. INTERNET"/> right inside the manifest element in the AndroidManifest. xml file.

On Android, this must be run in a background thread. This is why I wrapped the read operation in a thread{ } construct. This is easy, but in a serious app you should instead use one of Android's genuine background execution features, for example, an IntentService. That one implies considerably more work. Consult the Android documentation for more details.

This is just a very simplistic way of accessing Internet resources. For more options use a dedicated software like, for example, the Apache HttpClient library.

Using Reflection

Reflection is about considering classes as objects. How can that be? We learned that objects are instances of classes. We also learned, though, that objects are identifiable units describing something via properties, and giving methods at hand for doing something with the properties using functions.

The trick is this: Classes are also identifiable units, and if you want to describe them you'd explain the nature of their properties and functions. Reflection is exactly that: Classes are objects describing the properties and functions of the class to which they are referring. In addition, we can also dynamically look up the interfaces a class implements, and possible superclasses.

Note   Kotlin reflection is not part of the standard library. You must add

```
implementation "org.jetbrains.kotlin:kotlin-reflect:$kotlin_
version"
```

(one line) to the dependencies section of your app module's `build.gradle` file.

We start with a simple class extending some base class, implementing some arbitrary interface and furthermore with a constructor, two properties, and a function:

```
import android.util.Log

open class MyBase(val baseProp:Int)
class MyClass(var prop1:Int) :
      java.io.Serializable, MyBase(13) {
   var prop2:String
       get() = "Hi"
       set(value) { /* ignore */ }

   init {
       Log.d("LOG", "Hello from init")
   }
```

```
    fun function(i:Int):Int {
        return prop1 * i
    }
}
```

```
val instance = MyClass(42)
```

We first note that there is a Class class for describing class objects (not class instances). It is from the package java.lang. Kotlin exhibits some peculiarities compared to Java, however, making it necessary for Kotlin to have its own class class. It is called KClass and you can find it in the package kotlin.reflect. They have a strong relation with each other. We fetch the KClass for MyClass:

```
val clazz = MyClass::class
```

```
// We can also get it from instances
val clazz = instance::class
```

From here it is still possible to get the Java class, in case you need it: val javaClass = clazz.java

Once we have a KClass object, we can introspect the class, and that lets us show constructors, properties, and functions:

```
import android.util.Log
import kotlin.reflect.*
import kotlin.reflect.full.*

Log.d("LOG", "**** constructors")
clazz.constructors.forEach { c ->
    Log.d("LOG", c.toString())
}

// show only our own properties
Log.d("LOG", "**** declaredMemberProperties") clazz.
declaredMemberProperties.forEach { p ->
    Log.d("LOG", p.toString())
}

// show also inherited properties
Log.d("LOG", "**** memberProperties")
```

```
clazz.memberProperties.forEach { p ->
    Log.d("LOG", p.toString())
}

// show only our own functions
Log.d("LOG", "**** declaredFunctions")
clazz.declaredFunctions.forEach { f ->
    Log.d("LOG", f.toString())
}

// show also inherited functions
Log.d("LOG", "**** functions")
clazz.functions.forEach { f ->
    Log.d("LOG", f.toString())
}
```

We can obtain a specific property or function if we use a finder filter:

```
val p1: KProperty1<out MyClass, Any?> =
    clazz.declaredMemberProperties.find {
        it.name == "prop1" }!!
val f1: KFunction<*> =
    clazz.declaredFunctions.find {
        it.name == "function" }!!
```

With KProperty1 and KFunction instances you can do several interesting things, like finding out whether it is private or public, whether it is final or open, or whether a property belongs to a cons or is a lateinit. For functions we can determine the parameter types and the return type, and so on. Please consult the API documentation for these classes to see all the details.

We can invoke functions on or get and set properties from actual instances:

```
...
val instance = MyClass(42)

val p1: KProperty1<out MyClass, Any?>? =
    clazz.declaredMemberProperties.find {
        it.name == "prop1" }!!
```

```
val p1Mutable: KMutableProperty1<out MyClass, Any?> =
    p1 as KMutableProperty1

// getting
val prop1Val = p1.getter.call(instance)

// setting
p1Mutable.setter.call(instance, 55)

// invoking
val f1: KFunction<*> =
    clazz.declaredFunctions.find {

        it.name == "function" }!!
val res = f1.call(instance, 44) as Int
```

We can fetch the superclasses and interfaces from which the class inherits:

```
// Only directly declared superclasses and interfaces
clazz.superclasses.forEach { sc ->
    Log.d("LOG", sc.toString())
}

// All superclasses and interfaces
clazz.allSuperclasses.forEach { sc ->
    Log.d("LOG", sc.toString())
}
```

To dynamically create instances, we have to distinguish between no-arg constructors and constructors with parameters:

```
val clazz : KClass = ...


// If we have a no-arg primary constructor
val instance1 = clazz.createInstance()

// Otherwise for the primary constructor
val instance2 = clazz.primaryConstructor?.call(
    [parameters]
)
```

```
// Otherwise
val instance3 = clazz.constructors.
      find { [criterion] }!!.
    call( [parameters] )
```

Caution   Do not make the mistake of taking the improved dynamics of reflection over normal class, property, and function usage as a sign that using reflection for all property and function accesses is the better way of writing programs. Using reflection, you'll get a considerable performance degradation, you'll lose expressiveness and conciseness, and you also develop somewhat "around" object orientation. Use reflection with care.

Regular Expressions

Regular expressions try to give answers to the following questions:

- Does a string contain a certain character pattern? For example, we want to know whether the string invoice 2018-01-01-A4536 contains a substring that starts with A. Or whether the same string contains any date yyyy-MM-dd. We want to be pretty versatile here; patterns should allow us to specify character classes like letters, lowercase letters, uppercase letters, numbers, character enumerations, spaces, repetitions, and more.

- How can we split a string at delimiters in the form of patterns? For example, we have a string A37 | Q8 | 156-WE and we want to split it at | to get a string array ["A37 ", " Q8 ", " 156-WE"]. For the split marker it should also be possible to specify a longer string, or a pattern.

- How can we extract certain substrings from a string given a pattern? For example, we have a string The invoice numbers are X-23725, X-7368 and X-71885 and we want to extract all the invoice numbers X-<some digits> to get an array ["X-23725", "X-7368", "X-71885"].

- How can we replace certain patterns in a string by other strings? For example, we have a string For version v1.7 it is possible, ... another advantage of version v.1.7 is that ... and we want to replace all occurrences of v<digit>.<digit> by LEOPARD.

Patterns

Before we talk about how to achieve regular expression operations, we investigate the patterns that can be used for them. A pattern is a string with regular expression constructs, as shown in Table 17-2. You can enter patterns in a normal string with backslashes (\) escaped: The pattern ^\w{3} (three word characters at the beginning) thus must be entered as ^\\w{3}. You can use *raw* strings to avoid escaping:

```
val patStr = "^\\w{3}$"      // exactly 3 word chars
val patStr2 = """^\w{3}$""" // the same
```

Note Table 17-2 is not exhaustive; it shows the constructs most often used. For a complete reference, consult the Java API documentation for java.util.regex.Pattern.

Table 17-2. *Regular Expression Pattern*

Construct	Matches
x	Any character x
\\	The backslash character \
\X	A literal X, if X otherwise stands for a pattern construct
\n	A newline character
\r	A carriage return character
[abc]	Any of a, b, or c
[^abc]	Anything but a, b, or c
[A-Z]	Anything between A and Z
[0-9a-z]	Anything between 0 and 9 or between a and z
.	Any character

(continued)

383

Table 17-2. (*continued*)

Construct	Matches
\d	Any digit [0–9]
\D	Any nondigit [^0–9]
\s	A whitespace character
\s	A nonwhitespace character
\w	A word character [a–z_A–Z_0–9]
\W	A nonword character [^\w]
^	The beginning of a line
$	The end of a line
\b	A word boundary
\B	A nonword boundary
xy	A x followed by a y
x|y	Either x or y
(p)	Any subpattern p as a group

Quantifiers are for declaring repetitions of pattern constructs. There are three types of quantifiers:

- *Greedy*: During pattern matching, the pattern will consume as much of the string as is possible, not thwarting subsequent pattern parts.

- *Reluctant:* During pattern matching, the pattern will consume only as much of the string as is necessary.

- *Possessive:* During pattern matching, the pattern will consume as much of the string as possible, disregarding subsequent pattern parts.

The greedy and reluctant quantifiers get used most often, and the possessive quantifier is more or less a candidate for corner cases only. To understand the differences, consider the input string 012345abcde and the pattern \d+.*. The * here means zero or more times greedily, and the + means one or more times greedily. If we perform the match, the \d+ will consume as many digits as possible (i.e., all of them, 012345). The .* as a matcher for any characters will match the remaining abcde.

If we instead use a reluctant pattern \d+?.*?, the \d+? will match as many digits as is necessary. Because the \d+? matcher by virtue of the + is happy with one occurrence of a digit, and the .*? matcher is able to match any number of characters, the \d+? will be happy to match the 0, and the .*? matcher will consume the rest 12345abcde.

The functioning of the less important possessive quantifier is best described by an input string 012345abcde and a possessive pattern .*+de. The .*+ matcher here is able to take the string from the beginning all the way to the end. Because it doesn't care about the rest of the pattern, it will consume all characters. However, the de needs the already consumed string part de; it thus has nothing to match and the whole regular expression match will fail. The quantifiers are listed in Table 17-3.

Table 17-3. *Regular Expression Quantifiers*

Construct	Type	Matches
X?	Greedy	X once or not at all.
X*		X zero or more times.
X+		X one or more times.
X{n}		X exactly n times.
X{n,}		X n times or more often.
X{n,m}		X n to m times.
X??	Reluctant	X once or not at all.
X*?		X zero or more times.
X+?		X one or more times.
X{n}?		X exactly n times.
X{n,}?		X n times or more often.
X{n,m}?		X n to m times.
X?+	Possessive	X once or not at all.
X*+		X zero or more times.
X++		X one or more times.
X{n}+		X exactly n times.
X{n,}+		X n times or more often.
X{n,m}+		X n to m times.

Determining Matches

To see whether a string matches a given regular expression, you can use the following function:

```
val re = Regex("^\\w{3}$")      // exactly 3 word chars

val matches1 = "Hello".matches(re) // -> false
val matches2 = "abc".matches(re)   // -> true
```

Exercise 2

Write a string extension function that allows us to write

```
"Hello" % ".*ll.*"
```

instead of

```
"Hello".matches(Regex(".*ll.*"))
```

Hint: The operator % writes as `.rem()`.

The Regex class has constructors that allow specification of one or more options:

```
Regex(pattern:String, option:RegexOption)
Regex(pattern:String, options:Set<RegexOption>)
```

RegexOption is an `enum class` including the following members (see the API documentation for the complete list):

- IGNORE_CASE: Use this to perform case-insensitive matches.

- DOT_MATCHES_ALL: Use this if you want a `.` pattern to also include line breaks.

- MULTILINE: Use this if you want ^ and $ to respect line breaks.

- COMMENTS: Allow comments in regular expression patterns.

If you add the RegexOption.COMMENTS flag, you can add comments to your regular expression patterns. This is invaluable if regular expressions are more complex. As an example, consider this:

```
val re1 = Regex("^A(/|_)\\d{4}$")

// This is the same:
val ENDS = "$"
val re2 = Regex("""
    ^        # begins with
    A        # an "A"
    (/|_)    # a "/" or a "_"
    \d{4}    # 4 digits
    $ENDS    # ends here
""", RegexOption.COMMENTS)
```

(Ignore the multiple spaces warning.) We had to add the clumsy val ENDS = "$"
here to avoid a $-induced string interpolation. You can see the spaces get ignored (use \s
if you need to include spaces in the pattern) and a # starts a line comment.

Splitting Strings

To split a string around a regular expression as a delimiter you write

```
val re = Regex("\\|")
// <- use "\" escape to get a "|" as a literal

val s = "ABC|12345|_0_1"
val split: List<String> = s.split(re)
// -> "ABC", "12345", "_0_1"

// limit to at most 37 splits
val split37 = s.split(re, limit = 37)
```

Note   For splitting up a big string including line breaks into lines you probably
don't want to use regular expressions for performance reasons. It is much easier
to use the lines() function, which can be applied on any string: val s = "big
string... "; s.lines().forEach { ln -> ... }

Extracting Substrings

Finding patterns in a string and actually extracting them happens via functions of the Regex class:

```
// a number pattern
val re = Regex("""
    -?  # possibly a "-"
    \d+ # one or more digits
    (
      \.    # a dot
      \d+   # one or more digits
    )?      # possibly
 """, RegexOption.COMMENTS)

val s = "x = 37.5, y = 3.14, z = -100.0"

val firstNumber:MatchResult? = re.find(s)
// start at a certain index instead:
// val firstNumber = re.find(s, 5)

val notFound = firstNumber == null
firstNumber?.run {
    val num = groupValues[0]
    // do something with num...
}

val allNumbers:Sequence<MatchResult> = re.findAll(s)
allNumbers.forEach { mr ->
    val num = mr.groupValues[0]
    // do something with num...
}
```

This is fine if we want to assign each pattern match to a local property. There is more to this, though: We can acquire match *groups* that belong to subpatterns defined by ( ) pairs. Consider the number matcher slightly rewritten:

```
val re = Regex("""
    (
      (
        -?  # possibly a "-"
        \d+ # one or more digits
      )
      (
        \.   # a dot
        (
          \d+  # one or more digits
        )
      )?       # possibly
    )
  """, RegexOption.COMMENTS)
```

It still matches the same patterns, but introduces subpatterns by various ( ) groups. If we apply this pattern to a number like, for example, -3.14, we can add the corresponding groups for illustration purposes, which gives us $((-3)(.(14)))$. Such groups can easily be addressed independently in the MatchResult:

```
// The pattern from the last listing compressed
val re = Regex("""((-?\d+)(\.(\d+))?)""")

val s = "x = 37.5, y = 3.14, z = -100.0"

val firstNumber:MatchResult? = re.find(s)

val notFound = firstNumber == null
firstNumber?.run {
    val (num, nf, f1, f2) = destructured

    // <- "37.5", "37", ".5", "5"
    // the same:
    //    val num = groupValues[1]
    //    val nf = groupValues[2]
    //    val f1 = groupValues[3]
    //    val f2 = groupValues[4]
```

```
    val wholeMatch = groupValues[0]   // 37.5
    // ...
}
val allNumbers:Sequence<MatchResult> = re.findAll(s)
allNumbers.forEach { mr ->
    val (num, nf, f1, f2) = mr.destructured
    // the same:
    //    val num = mr.groupValues[1]
    //    val nf = mr.groupValues[2]
    //    val f1 = mr.groupValues[3]
    //    val f2 = mr.groupValues[4]
    val wholeMatch = mr.groupValues[0]
    // ... wholeMatch is: 37.5, 3.14 or -100.0
    // ... num is: 37.5, 3.14 or -100.0
    // ... nf is: 37, 3, -100
    // ... f1 is: .5, .14, .0
    // ... f2 is 5, 14, 0
}
```

You can see that inside the groupValues property of the MatchResult instance the index 0 element always refers to the whole match, whereas all other indexes refer to ( ) groups. The destructured property instead starts with the first ( ) group. Only because we added one big surrounding ( ) embracing everything, the first member of destructured contains the same string as groupValues[0].

Caution   The destructured property, although easy to use, only can handle up to ten groups. The property groupValues is potentially unlimited.

Replacing

Replacing patterns in strings is similar to finding patterns. We have a function replaceFirst() that only replaces the first occurrence of a pattern, and replace(), which replaces all occurrences:

```
// again the number pattern:
val re = Regex("""((-?\d+)(\.(\d+))?)""")

val s = "x = 37.5, y = 3.14, z = -100.0"


// replace the first number by 22.22
val s2 = re.replaceFirst(s, "22.22")
// -> "x = 22.22, y = 3.14, z = -100.0"

// replace all numbers by 22.22
val s3 = re.replace(s, "22.22")
// -> "x = 22.22, y = 22.22, z = 22.22"
```

There is more to these two replace functions, though. With the second argument replaced by a lambda function we can do real magic during replacement (shown only for replace(); for replaceFirst() use the appropriate equivalent):

```
// again the number pattern:
val re = Regex("""((-?\d+)(\.(\d+))?)""")

val s = "x = 37.5, y = 3.14, z = -100.0"


// double all numbers
val s2 = re.replace(s, { mr:MatchResult ->
    val theNum = mr.groupValues[1].toDouble()
    (theNum * 2).toString() // <- replacement
})
// -> "x = 75.0, y = 6.28, z = -200.0"

// zero all fractions
val s3 = re.replace(s, { mr:MatchResult ->
    val (num, nf, f1, f2) = mr.destructured
    nf + ".0" // <- replacement
})
// -> "x = 37.0, y = 3.0, z = -100.0"
```

CHAPTER 18

Working in Parallel: Multithreading

Modern computers and modern smartphones have several CPUs able to work in parallel. You probably think of several apps running at the same time, but there is more to concurrency; you can have several "actors" do work in parallel in one app, noticeably speeding up program execution. I deliberately say "actors" because simply saying that several CPUs work in parallel only covers part of the story. In fact, software developers prefer to think of *threads,* which are program sequences that can potentially run independent of each other. Which CPU actually runs a thread is left to the process scheduling managed by the operating system. We adopt that thread notion and by that abstract from operation system process handling and hardware execution internals.

Within one app, having several threads running concurrently is commonly referred to as *multithreading.* Multithreading has been a prominent part of Java for years now, and you can find Java's relevant interfaces and classes inside packages `java.lang` and `java.util.concurrent` and subpackages. These are also included within Kotlin for Android. However, Kotlin has its own idea about multithreading and introduces a technique called *coroutines.* You can use both features, and in this chapter we discuss both of them.

Basic Multithreading the Java Way

Without any further preparation, when you start a Kotlin (or Java) app the program gets run in the *main* thread. However, you can define and start other threads that can be worked through concurrently while the main thread is running.

© Peter Späth 2019
P. Späth, *Learn Kotlin for Android Development*, https://doi.org/10.1007/978-1-4842-4467-8_18

Note   The Java multithreading classes are automatically available to Kotlin in an Android development environment.

The most important multithreading-related class in Java is java.util.Thread. You can create one using its constructor, but Kotlin has a function that simplifies thread creation: thread(). Its synopsis reads like this:

```
fun thread(
    start: Boolean = true,
    isDaemon: Boolean = false,
    contextClassLoader: ClassLoader? = null,
    name: String? = null,
    priority: Int = -1,
    block: () -> Unit
)
```

You use it as follows, for example:

```
val thr:Thread = thread(start = true) {
    ... do something ...
}
```

The thread() function creates a Thread using the following characteristics:

- If you don't explicitly specify the start parameter to read false, the Thread.start() function gets called immediately after thread creation.

- If you set isDaemon to true, a running thread will not prevent the runtime engine from shutting down when the main thread has finished its work. In an Android environment, however, undaemonized threads will not make an app continue being active when the system decides to shut down or suspend an app, so this flag has no noticeable implications for Android.

- Specifying a separate class loader is an advanced feature you can use if you want the thread to use a class loader different from the system class loader. In this book we don't talk about class loading issues; usually you can safely ignore class loading issues in an Android environment.

- Specifying a separate name for your thread helps troubleshooting if problems arise. The thread's name could show up in log files.

- Specifying a priority gives the system a hint for how a thread should be prioritized in relation to other threads. Values range from `Thread.MIN_PRIORITY` to `Thread.MAX_PRIORITY`. The default value is `Thread.NORM_PRIORITY`. For your first experiments you don't have to be concerned with this value.

- The `block` contains statements that get executed when the thread runs. The `thread()` function always exits immediately no matter what the `block` does and how long it runs.

The most basic thread example for an Android app might read (remember that a function as a last invocation parameter can go outside parentheses):

```
// inside an activity:
override fun onCreate(savedInstanceState: Bundle?) {
    ...
    thread {
        while(true) {
            Thread.sleep(1000L)
             Log.e("LOG", Date().toString())
        }
    }
}
```

For your experiments you can use the `NumberGuess` sample app we developed in earlier chapters. This thread starts an infinite loop (`while( true ){ }`), each iteration sleeps for 1,000 milliseconds and then writes the current date and time to the logging console. The `thread()` function returns the `Thread` instance, so if we need to later do more things with the thread we can also write

```
val thr:Thread = thread {
    while(true) {
        Thread.sleep(1000L)
        Log.e("LOG", Date().toString())
    }
}
```

Because of the default start = true the thread immediately starts its work in the background. If, however, you want to start the thread yourself, you write

```
val thr = thread(start = false) {
    while(true) {
        Thread.sleep(1000L)
        Log.e("LOG", Date().toString())
    }
}
...
thr.start()
```

This sounds easy so far, doesn't it? There is a reason we talk about multithreading in a later chapter of this book, though. Consider the following example:

```
val l = mutableListOf(1,2,3)
var i = 0
thread {
    while(true) {
        Thread.sleep(10L)
        i++
        if(i % 2 == 0) { l.add(i) }
            else { l.remove(l.first()) }
    }
}
thread {
    while(true) {
        Thread.sleep(1000L)
        Log.e("LOG", l.joinToString())
    }
}
```

Here we let one thread alter a list every 10 milliseconds, and another thread print the list to the logging console.

Once you start this it shouldn't take longer than a few milliseconds before your app crashes. What happened? The logs say (abbreviated):

```
2018-12-29 09:40:52.570 14961-14983/
     android.kotlin.book.numberguess
     E/AndroidRuntime: FATAL EXCEPTION: Thread-5
   Process: android.kotlin.book.numberguess, PID: 14961
   java.util.ConcurrentModificationException
       at java.util.ArrayList$Itr.next(...)
       at ...CollectionsKt.joinTo(...)
       at ...CollectionsKt.joinToString(...)
       at ...CollectionsKt.joinToString...
       at ...MainActivity$onCreate$2.invoke...
       at ...MainActivity$onCreate$2.invoke...
       at ...ThreadsKt....run()
```

The important parts are the two lines at `java.util.ConcurrentModificationException` and `java.util.ArrayList$Itr.next(...)`. The latter says something happens while we are iterating through the list. This iteration is needed to construct the string for the `joinToString()` function. The main clue comes from the exception name:

`ConcurrentModificationException`

It basically says that we are iterating through a list while it is being modified by another thread, and this is the problem: We have a list data inconsistency if we let several threads at the same time modify a list's structure and iterate through it.

Another issue that comes up when we talk about multithreading is that we need to find a clever way to synchronize threads. For example, one thread needs to wait for another thread to finish some work before it can start running.

These two issues—data consistency and synchronization—make multithreading kind of an art, and until now no final universal solution has been found. That is why, concerning multithreading, new ideas are constantly born and several approaches exist at the same time, all with mutual advantages and disadvantages over the others.

Before we talk about advanced approaches that Java and Kotlin follow, we finish our investigation of Java's basic multithreading solutions, so we get an understanding of the problem sphere. If we consider that concurrent modification exception example again, wouldn't it help if we could avoid multiple threads working on a shared list at the same time? This is possible, and the way we can do this is by wrapping the relevant code examples inside synchronized(){ } blocks as follows:

```
val l = mutableListOf(1,2,3)
var i = 0
thread {
    while(true) {
        Thread.sleep(10L)
        i++
        synchronized(l) {
          if(i % 2 == 0) { l.add(i) }
                else { l.remove(l.first()) }
        }
    }
}
thread {
    while(true) {
        Thread.sleep(1000L)
        synchronized(l) {
          Log.e("LOG", l.joinToString())
        }
    }
}
```

Here the synchronized(l) blocks in all threads accessing the list make sure that no thread accessing the list can enter the code inside synchronized while another thread is inside any other synchronized block for the same list. Instead the thread that arrives first makes all the other threads wait until it has finished its synchronized block.

It is also possible to add more parameters to the synchronized instruction. Just make it a comma-separated list as in

```
synchronized(l1, l2) {
    ...
}
```

where the synchronization makes sure that it is safe to let multiple threads work on both l1 and l2.

We still need a way to let one thread wait until another thread has finished its work. For this aim, the `join` instruction exists. Say you want to achieve the following:

```
val l = mutableListOf(1,2,3)
var i = 0
val thr1 = thread {
    for(i in 1..100) {
        l.add(i)
        Thread.sleep(10)
    }
}
thread {
    // Here we want to wait until thread thr1 is done.
    // How can this be achieved?
    ...
    Log.e("LOG", l.joinToString())
}
```

Now, tell the second thread to explicitly wait for thread `thr1` to finish its work via `thr1.join()`:

```
val l = mutableListOf(1,2,3)
var i = 0
val thr1 = thread {
    ...
}
thread {
    thr1.join()
    Log.e("LOG", l.joinToString())
}
```

Now the instructions after `thr1.join()` only start after thread `thr1` has finished its work.

These keywords and functions, and more interesting functions and constructs for basic multithreading the Java way, are listed in Table 18-1.

Table 18-1. *Basic Multithreading the Java Way*

Construct/Function	Description
thread(...)	Creates and possibly starts a thread. Parameters are: • start: Immediately start the thread after construction. Default: true. • isDaemon: If true, a running thread will not prevent the runtime engine from shutting down when the main thread has finished its work. Has no effect in Android. Default: false. • contextClassLoader: Specify a different class loader. Default is null, which signifies the system class loader. For Android you usually go with the default. • name: The name of the thread. Shows up in log files. Default: Use a default string with consecutive numbering. • priority: Specifying a priority gives the system a hint for how a thread should be prioritized in relation to other threads. Possible values: Between Thread.MIN_PRIORITY and Thread.MAX_PRIORITY, with Thread.NORM_PRIORITY being the default. • block: Contains the thread's code. If you don't need any special parameters you just write thread { [thread_code] }.
synchronized(object1, object2, ...) { }	The block inside the { } gets entered only if no other thread currently executes in a synchronized block with at least one of the same objects in its parameter list. Otherwise the thread will be put in a waiting state until the other relevant synchronized blocks have finished their work.
Thread.sleep (millis: Long)	Makes the current thread wait for the specified number of milliseconds. Can be interrupted, in which case the statement terminates immediately and an InterruptedException gets thrown.
Thread.sleep(millis: Long, nanos:Int)	Same as Thread.sleep(Long), but makes the function additionally sleep nanos nanoseconds.

(continued)

Table 18-1. (*continued*)

Construct/Function	Description
`thread.join()`	Makes the current thread wait until thread `thread` has finished its work.
`thread.interrupt()`	The current thread interrupts thread `thread`. The interrupted thread gets terminated and throws an `InterruptedException`. The interrupted thread must support interruption. It does so by invoking interruptible methods like `Thread.sleep()` or by periodically checking its own `Thread.interrupted` flag to see whether it is supposed to exit.
`@Volatile var` `varName = ...`	Only for class or object properties. Marks the backing field (the data behind the property) as `volatile`. The runtime engine (Java virtual machine) makes sure that updates to volatile variables get immediately communicated to all threads. Otherwise the cross-thread state under the circumstances might be inconsistent. The performance overhead is smaller compared to `synchronized` blocks.
`Any.wait()`	Only from inside a `synchronized` block. Suspends the synchronization such that other threads can continue their work. At the same time, it makes this thread wait for an unspecified time, until `notify()` or `notifyAll()` gets called.
`Any.wait( timeout:Long )`	Same as `wait()`, but waits at most for the specified number of milliseconds.
`Any.wait( timeout:Long, nanos:Int )`	Same as `wait()`, but waits at most for the specified number of milliseconds and nanoseconds.
`Any.notify()`	Only from inside a `synchronized` block. Wakes up one of the waiting threads. The waiting thread starts to work once the current thread leaves its `synchronized` block.
`Any.notifyAll()`	Only from inside a `synchronized` block. Wakes up all of the waiting threads. The waiting threads start to work once the current thread leaves its `synchronized` block.

For all other functions of class `java.lang.Thread`, consult the API documentation.

Advanced Multithreading the Java Way

Scattering `synchronized` blocks and `join` functions throughout your code poses a couple of problems: First, it makes your code hard to understand; understanding multithreaded state handling is anything but easy for nontrivial programs. Second, having several threads and `synchronized` blocks might end up in a deadlock: Some thread A waits for thread B while thread B is waiting for thread A. Third, writing too many `join` functions for gathering the threads' calculation results might result in too many threads just waiting, thwarting the advantages of multithreading. Fourth, using `synchronized` blocks for any collection handling might also end up in too many threads just waiting.

At some point in the history of Java's evolution, advanced higher level multithreading constructs were introduced, namely the interfaces and classes inside the `java.util.concurrent` package and subpackages. Without claiming completeness in this section, we cover some of these constructs, because they are also included within Kotlin and you can use them to any extent you wish.

Special Concurrency Collections

Wrapping any list or set access into `synchronized` blocks just for the sake of proper concurrent accessibility, or *thread safety*, leaves a feeling of discontent. If collections and maps are important for your app, it almost seems like thinking about multithreading is not worth the effort. Fortunately the `java.util.concurrency` package contains some list, set, and map implementations that help to avoid putting everything into a `synchronized` block.

- `CopyOnWriteArrayList`: A list implementation where any mutation operations happen on a fresh copy of the complete list. At the same time, any iteration uses exactly the state of the list it had when the iterator got created, so a `ConcurrentModificationException` cannot happen. Copying the complete list is costly, so this implementation usually helps only where reading operations vastly outnumber writing operations. In such cases, however, no `synchronized` blocks are needed for thread safety.

- `CopyOnWriteArraySet`: A set implementation where any mutation operations happen on a fresh copy of the complete set. What we said earlier for `CopyOnWriteArrayList` also holds for `CopyOnWriteArraySet` instances.

- `ConcurrentLinkedDeque`: A thread-safe `Deque` where iteration operations are *weakly consistent*, meaning read elements reflect the deque's state at some point at or since the creation of the iterator. No `ConcurrentModificationException` will be thrown.

- `ConcurrentLinkedQueue`: A thread-safe `Queue` implementation. What was said for the `ConcurrentLinkedDeque` earlier concerning thread safety also holds for this class. No `ConcurrentModificationException` will be thrown.

- `ConcurrentSkipListSet`: A thread-safe `Set` implementation. Iteration operations are *weakly consistent*, meaning read elements reflect the set's state at some point at or since the creation of the iterator. No `ConcurrentModificationException` will be thrown. Other than the type specification the API documentation suggests, the elements must implement the `Comparable` interface.

- `ConcurrentSkipListMap`: A thread-safe `Map` implementation. Iteration operations are *weakly consistent*, meaning read elements reflect the map's state at some point at or since the creation of the iterator. No `ConcurrentModificationException` will be thrown. Other than the type specification the API documentation suggests, the keys must implement the `Comparable` interface.

Locks

In the section "Basic Multithreading the Java Way" earlier in this chapter, we learned that `synchronized` blocks make sure program parts cannot be worked at the same time by different threads:

```
val obj = ...
thread {
    synchronized(obj) {
```

```
        ... synchronized code
    }
}
```

Such a `synchronized` block is a language construct; we can, however, achieve the same thing in a more object-oriented way by using a `lock` object as follows:

```
import java.util.concurrent.lock.*
...
val lock:Lock = ...
...
lock.lock()
try {
        ... synchronized code
} finally {
    lock.unlock()
}
```

More precisely, `synchronized` has its equivalent in a so-called *reentrant lock*, and the corresponding lock class accordingly reads `ReentrantLock`. In the preceding code we would therefore use

```
val lock:Lock = ReentrantLock()
```

as a `Lock` implementation.

The name *reentrant lock* comes from the lock's ability to be acquired by the same thread several times, so a thread would not fall into a waiting state when it already has acquired the lock via `lock.lock()` and tries to acquire the same lock again before an `unlock()` happens.

A `Lock` has more options compared to `synchronized`. Using a `Lock` you can, for example, avoid trying to lock while the current thread recently entered an *interrupted* state or does so while waiting for a lock. This can be achieved by writing

```
val lock:Lock = ReentrantLock()
...
try {
    lock.lockInterruptibly()
} catch(e: InterruptedException) {
```

```
    ... do things if we were interrupted
    return
}
try {
    ... synchronized code
} finally {
    lock.unlock()
}
```

You can also first check the lock, whether it can be acquired now or within some time before it actually gets acquired. The corresponding code reads

```
val lock:Lock = ReentrantLock()
...
if(lock.tryLock()) {
    try {
        ... synchronized code
    } finally {
        lock.unlock()
    }
} else {
    ... no lock acquired
    ... do other things
}
```

or in a variant that waits for a specific amount of time:

```
...
if(lock.tryLock(time:Long, unit:TimeUnit)) {
    // lock was acquired within that time span
    ...
} else {
    ...
}
```

A different lock interface is called `ReadWriteLock`. Compared to a normal `Lock` it has the ability to distinguish between read and write operations. This could be helpful in cases where several threads would be able to use variables in a read-only manner without any problem, whereas writing must block read operations and in addition must be confined to a single thread. A corresponding implementation reads `ReentrantReadWriteLock`. Its usage details are available in the API documentation.

Atomic Variable Types

Consider the following example:

```
class Counter {
    var c = 0
    fun increment() { c++ }
    fun decrement() { c-- }
}
```

Because the runtime engine (Java virtual machine JVM) internally decomposes c++ into (1) get the value of c, (2) increment what we just retrieved, and (3) write back the altered value to c, the following might happen:

```
Thread-A calls increment
Thread-B calls decrement
Thread-A retrieves c
Thread-B retrieves c
Thread-A increments its version of c
Thread-A updates c, c is now +1
Thread-B decrements its version of c
Thread-B updates c, c is now -1
```

The work of thread A therefore got lost entirely. This effect is commonly referred to as *thread interference*.

We saw in the previous section that synchronization via `synchronized` helps:

```
class Counter {
    var c = 0
    fun increment() { synchronized(c){ c++ } }
    fun decrement() { synchronized(c){ c-- } }
}
```

The updating of c by virtue of synchronized now can no longer be influenced by other threads. However, we might have a different solution. If we had a variable type that handles modification and retrieval in an *atomic* manner, without the chance of another thread interfering and destroying consistency, we could reduce the overhead a synchronized imposes. Such atomic data types do exist, and they are called AtomicInteger, AtomicLong, and AtomicBoolean. They are all from the java.util. concurrent.atomic package.

Using an AtomicInteger we can get rid of the synchronized blocks. A solution for the Counter class will then read:

```
import java.util.concurrent.atomic.*
...
class Counter {
    var c:AtomicInteger = AtomicInteger(0)
    fun increment() { c.incrementAndGet() }
    fun decrement() { c.decrementAndGet() }
}
```

Note   The package java.util.concurrent.atomic has a few more atomic types that are for special use cases. Have a look at the documentation if you are interested.

Executors, Futures, and Callables

Inside the java.util.concurrent package you will find a couple of interfaces and classes that handle multithreading on a higher level. The following list shows the main interfaces and classes important for high-level multithreading.

- Callable

  This is something that can be invoked, possibly by another thread, and returns a result.

- Runnable

  This one is not in package java.util.concurrent, but in package java.lang. It is something that can be invoked, possibly by another thread. No result is returned.

- Executors

  This is an important utility class for, among other things, obtaining ExecutorService and ScheduledExecutorService implementations.

- ExecutorService

  This is an interface for objects that allows invoking Runnables or Callables and gathering their results.

- ScheduledExecutorService

  This is an interface for objects that allows invoking Runnables or Callables and gathering their results. The invocation happens after some delay, or in a repeated manner.

- Future

  This is an object you can use to fetch the result from a Callable.

- ScheduledFuture

  This is an object you can use to fetch the result from a Callable submitted to a ScheduledExecutorService.

The primary usage pattern for these interfaces and classes goes as follows:

1. Use one of the functions starting with new from the singleton object Executors to get an ExecutorService or ScheduledExecutorService. Save it in a property; for our purposes we call it srvc or schedSrvc.

2. For registering tasks that need to be done concurrently, use any of the functions starting with invoke or submit for srvc, or any of the functions starting with schedule for schedSrvc.

3. Wait for termination, as signaled by suitable functions from ExecutorService or ScheduledExecutorService, or by the Futures or ScheduledFutures you might have received in the previous step.

As you can see, these interfaces, classes, and functions mainly orchestrate threads and their calculation results. They do not control the usage of shared data; for that you need to follow the techniques presented in the preceding sections.

As an example, we develop a multithreaded program that calculates π. The idea is simple: Obtain a pair of random numbers from the $[0; 1] \times [0; 1]$ plane. Calculate the distance to the origin and count the number of points with distances smaller than 1.0 and those with distances 1.0 or higher. Call the number of all points n and the number of points inside the quarter unit circle p. Because the area of a $[0; 1] \times [0; 1]$ plane is 1.0, but the area of the region within the quarter unit circle is $\pi/4$, we have $\dfrac{p}{n} = \pi/4$ or $\pi = 4 \cdot \dfrac{p}{n}$ (see Figure 18-1).

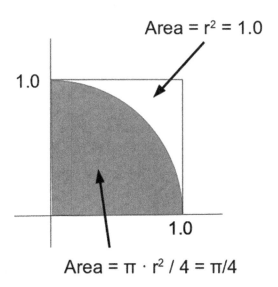

Figure 18-1. *Pi calculation*

Note   This is definitely not the cleverest way to calculate π, but it is easy to understand and you can easily distribute the workload among multiple threads.

In Android Studio, start a new app, and proceed as described in Chapter 1 for your first Kotlin app, renaming the app and packages accordingly. For the activity, create a layout with the following elements:

- Any labels, as shown in Figure 18-2.

- A TextView with ID @+id/procs next to the Processors label.

- An EditText with ID @+id/iters next to the Iterations label. Add attribute android:text="1000000".

- An EditText with ID @+id/threads next to the Threads label. Add attribute android:text="4".

- A TextView with ID @+id/cumulIters next to the Cumul Iters label.

- A TextView with ID @+id/pi next to the Current Pi label.

- A TextView with ID @+id/calcTime next to the Calc Time label.

- A Button with text CALC and attribute android:onClick="calc".

- A Button with text RESET and attribute android:onClick="reset".

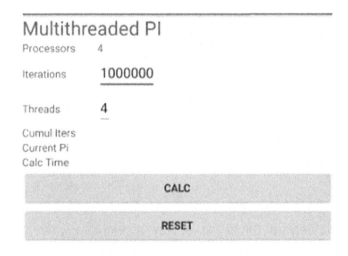

Figure 18-2. *Pi user interface*

We leave the the details of the layout up to you. For the actual calculation, the view IDs and the onClick handlers shown in the list are important. The calculation is not too complicated, so we do everything in the activity class. For more complex projects you should outsource the calculation to one or more dedicated calculation classes. In our case, let the activity class read

```
class MainActivity : AppCompatActivity() {
    var points = 0L
    var insideCircle = 0L
    var totalIters = 0L

override
fun onCreate(savedInstanceState: Bundle?) {
    super.onCreate(savedInstanceState)
    setContentView(R.layout.activity_main)

    savedInstanceState?.run {
        points = getLong("points")
        insideCircle = getLong("insideCircle")
        totalIters = getLong("totalIter")
    }

    val cores = Runtime.getRuntime().
        availableProcessors()
    procs.setText(cores.toString())
}

override
fun onSaveInstanceState(outState: Bundle?) {
    super.onSaveInstanceState(outState)
    outState?.run {
        putLong("points",points)
        putLong("insideCircle",insideCircle)
        putLong("totalIter", totalIters)
        report()
    }
}
}
```

```kotlin
fun calc(v:View) {
    val t1 = System.currentTimeMillis()
    val nThreads = threads.text.toString().
        takeIf { it != "" }?.toInt()?:1
    val itersNum = iters.text.toString().
        takeIf { it != "" }?.toInt()?:10000
    val itersPerThread = itersNum / nThreads
    val srvc = Executors.newFixedThreadPool(nThreads)
    val callables = (1..nThreads).map {
        object : Callable<Pair<Int,Int>> {
            override fun call(): Pair<Int, Int> {
                var i = 0
                var p = 0
                    (1..itersPerThread).forEach {
                        val x = Math.random()
                        val y = Math.random()
                        val r = x*x + y*y
                        i++
                        if(r < 1.0) p++
                    }
                    return Pair(i, p)
            }
        }
    }
    val futures = srvc.invokeAll(callables)
    futures.forEach{ f ->
        val p = f.get()
        points += p.first
        insideCircle += p.second
    }

    val t2 = System.currentTimeMillis()
    calcTime.setText((t2-t1).toString())

    report()
}
```

```kotlin
fun reset(v:View) {
    points = 0
    insideCircle = 0
    report()
}

private fun report() {
    cumulIters.setText(points.toString())
    if(points > 0) {
        val pipi = 1.0 * insideCircle / points * 4
        pi.setText(pipi.toString())
    } else {
        pi.setText("")
    }
}
```

The characteristics are as follows:

- The class has as state the total number of points in points, the number of points inside the quarter unit circle in insideCircle, and the total number of iterations in totalIters.

- In onSaveInstanceState() and onCreate() we make sure the state gets saved and restored whenever Android decides to suspend the app.

- Also in onCreate() we determine the number of CPUs the device has and write it to the user interface.

- Inside reset(), the algorithm gets reinitialized.

- Inside report(), we calculate π according to the preceding formula and write it to the user interface.

- The multithreading happens inside calc(). We read the number of threads and iterations to use from the user interface, distribute the iteration number evenly among the threads, obtain a thread pool from Executors, define and register the calculation algorithm, and eventually gather the results from all threads.

- At the end of `calc()`, we determine the time needed for the calculation and write it to the user interface.

You can play around with the thread and iteration numbers to see the impact of multithreading. On most devices you should see a noticeable difference between running on one and two or more threads. By the way, pressing the CALC button several times improves the accuracy of the calculated π as the numbers get accumulated.

Exercise 1

Implement the multithreaded π calculation app as described in this section.

Kotlin Coroutines

Kotlin has its own idea of how to handle multithreading. It uses a concept that has been around for a while in older computer languages, *coroutines*. Here the idea is implemented to write functions that can get suspended and later resumed at certain locations during their inner program flow. This happens in a *nonpreemptive* way, which means during running a program in a multithreaded way the program flow context doesn't get switched by the operating system, but rather by language constructs, library calls, or both.

Coroutines are not by default included within Kotlin. To install them, open the "app" module's `build.gradle` file and add to the "dependencies" section:

```
implementation
  'org.jetbrains.kotlinx:kotlinx-coroutines-core:1.1.0'
```

(one line).

Before we continue to discuss coroutines for Kotlin, we first present an extended glossary to help you get used to coroutines programming. You can quickly scan over it or entirely skip it for now and come back later, as after the list we give a more comprehensive introduction to coroutines.

- *Coroutine scope:* Any coroutine functionality runs within a *coroutine scope*. A scope is like a bracket around a multithreading ensemble, and scopes can have a parent scope defining a scope hierarchy. The root of the scope hierarchy can either be the

GlobalScope or it can be obtained by the function runBlocking
{ } where inside the { } block you entered a new blocking scope.
The blocking here means that the runBlocking() invocation only
finishes after all included scopes finished their work. Because
CoroutineScope is an interface, you can also define any class to
spawn a coroutine scope. A very prominent example is to have an
activity also represent a coroutine scope:

```
class MyActivity : AppCompatActivity(),
      CoroutineScope by MainScope() {
  ...
  override fun onDestroy() {
    super.onDestroy()
    cancel() // CoroutineScope.cancel
  }
  ...
}
```

The CoroutineScope by MainScope() refers to *delegation*: Any CoroutineScope
function gets forwarded to an instance of MainScope, which is a scope especially tailored
for user interface activities. Here, because of the cancel() on the root of the scope
hierarchy, any currently active scope inside the hierarchy gets shut down in the activity's
onDestroy().

- *Coroutine context:* A CoroutineContext object is a data container
  associated with a coroutine scope. It contains the objects that are
  necessary for a coroutine scope to properly do its work. Without any
  further intervention in a scope hierarchy, scope children inherit the
  context from their parents.

- *Global scope:* The GlobalScope is a singleton object with a lifetime
  determined by the application as a whole. Although it is tempting to
  use the global scope as a basis for the most important coroutines, it
  is generally not recommended that you use it for the sake of properly
  structuring the multithreading aspects of your app. Use a dedicated
  coroutine builder instead.

- *Job:* A job is a task that possibly runs in its own thread.

- *Coroutine builder:* These are functions that start a coroutine either in a blocking or nonblocking manner. Examples for builders are:

  - `runBlocking()`: This defines and runs a blocking coroutine. If `runBlocking()` gets used inside a coroutine scope, the block defined by `runBlocking{ }` spawns a new child scope.

  - `launch()`: This defines and runs a nonblocking coroutine. It cannot be used outside a coroutine scope. It immediately returns a `Job` object and runs its block in the background.

  - `async()`: This defines and runs a nonblocking coroutine that returns a value. It cannot be used outside a coroutine scope. It immediately returns a `Deferred` object and runs its block in the background.

  - `coroutineScope()`: This creates a new scope with the context inherited from the outer scope, except for a new `Job` object. It calls the specified block in the new scope.

  - `supervisorScope()`: This creates a new scope with a `SupervisorJob`. It calls the specified block in the new scope. Supervisor jobs are special jobs that can fail independently of each other.

All of them expect a lambda function as a last parameter, which serves as the block of instructions to run. Because such parameters can be noted outside the parentheses, you'll most often use them as in `launch { ..instructions.. }`.

- *Joining:* If you get the result of invoking `launch()` in a property: `val job = launch{ ... }`, you can later call `job.join()` to block the program execution until the job has finished.

- *Suspending function:* The keyword `suspend` is the only coroutine-related keyword you will find in the Kotlin language. All other coroutine material is available via the coroutines library. You need to add the `suspend` to functions that you want to be callable from inside a scope and that you want to be able to use with coroutines. For example, `suspend fun theFun() { }`. Consider the `suspend` as a coroutine scope forwarder.

- *Cancellation:* Once you have a Job object, you can invoke cancel() on it to signal canceling the job. Note that the job usually doesn't immediately quit its work, so you have to wait for the actual termination via a join() invocation, or you use cancelAndJoin(). You must ensure the coroutine you want to cancel is *cancelable.* To meet this aim you can either let the code call a suspending function like yield(), or you can periodically check for the isActive property you automatically have inside a coroutines scope.

- *Timeout:* To explicitly specify a timeout for a block of statements you use

```
withTimeout(3000L) { // milliseconds
    ... code here
}
```

Once the timeout limit is reached, a TimeoutCancellationException gets thrown, which is a subclass of CancellationException and gets ignored if you don't use a custom exception handler. A variant of withTimeout() reads withTimeoutOrNull(); it does not throw a TimeoutCancellationException but returns the value of the last expression in its block if no timeout happened, or otherwise null:

```
val res = withTimeoutOrNull(3000L) {
  ... code here
  "Done."
}
// -> res is null if timeout happened
```

- *Coroutine exception handler:* Coroutines have their own idea about how to handle exceptions. For example, if you do not provide a separate CoroutineExceptionHandler in the coroutine context, while canceling a job a CancellationException gets thrown, but that is ignored. What you still can do is wrap your code in a try { } finally { } block if you need to perform cleanup actions once a job gets canceled:

```
runBlocking {
  val job = launch {
    try {
```

```
      ... do work
   } finally {
      ... cleanup if canceled
   }
 }
 ...
 job.cancelAndJoin()
}
```

- *Delay:* Use `delay(timeMillis)` to specify a temporary suspension. The API documentation here speaks of a nonblocking suspension, as the thread running behind the coroutines actually is allowed to do other work. After the delay, the program flow can continue with the instructions behind the `delay` function.

- *Blocking:* You use

```
runBlocking {
    ...
}
```

to initiate a blocking execution of the statements inside the { } block. You usually apply it in the main function of your program to have a first coroutine scope that you can use for coroutines.

- *Coroutine dispatcher:* An instance of a `CoroutineDispatcher` is part of the coroutine context you find in the property `coroutineContext` of each scope.

```
runBlocking {
    val ctx:CoroutineContext =
            coroutineContext
    ...
}
```

The dispatcher controls what thread a coroutine is running in. This could be a specific thread, a thread pool, or the caller's thread (until the first suspension point) if an unconfined dispatcher gets used (not for general use).

- *Structured concurrency:* This describes the dependencies of job concurrency characteristics mirrored in a structure depicted by a hierarchy of { ... } constructs. Kotlin's coroutines strongly favor a structured concurrency style of setting up concurrency.

- *Channel:* Channels provide a means to communicate a data stream between coroutines. As of Kotlin version 1.3, this API is considered experimental. Check the official documentation to learn about the current state of this API.

- *Actor:* An actor is both a coroutine launcher and a channel endpoint. As of Kotlin version 1.3, this API is considered experimental. Check the official documentation to learn about the current state of this API.

The following paragraphs outline basic and advanced coroutine usage patterns.

Basic Coroutines

The most important thing to know about coroutines is that we need a *coroutine scope* before we can use the coroutine way of multithreading. For simplicity it would be nice if we had a construct like this:

```
openScope {
    // Scope now automatically available
    ...
}
```

Kotlin knows how to do that by virtue of functions with receivers. Look, for example, at the coroutines-related function runBlocking(). In the source code you'll basically find this:

```
fun <T> runBlocking(context: CoroutineContext =
            EmptyCoroutineContext,
        block: suspend CoroutineScope.() -> T): T
{
    // code to run block in a blocking thread
    ...
}
```

In the block: suspend CoroutineScope.() -> T you can see the block runs inside an object that extends CoroutineScope. Such a CoroutineScope is an interface with a val named coroutineContext of type CoroutineContext. See later for details about the context.

Caution   Interfaces can have vals. We didn't mention this feature in the object orientation introductory chapters, and during the runtime engine evolution it was primarily introduced for technical reasons. Here it gets used to make coroutines handling easier. Using vals and vars in your app's interfaces is discouraged though, because variables usually belong to implementation aspects, not to declaration aspects, which is what interfaces are for. Use variables in interfaces with caution!

Your options to use an existing scope if we already are running inside a coroutine or to generate a new scope are as follows:

- runBlocking { ... }

  This enters a new blocking scope. Blocking here means the runBlocking() invocation will only return after all activities inside the { ... } lambda finished their work. The runBlocking() can be started from inside and outside a coroutine scope, although using it from inside a coroutine scope is discouraged. In both cases a fresh context is created that includes using the currently running thread for the job.

- runBlocking(context:CoroutineContext) { ... }

  This is the same as runBlocking(), but with a base context as given by the parameter.

- GlobalScope

  Use of this is discouraged. Use this singleton object if you want to use a scope that is tied to the application itself and its life cycle. You can, for example, use GlobalScope.launch{ ... } or GlobalScope.async{ ... }. Normally you should start from a runBlocking{ ... } instead. Not explicitly using GlobalScope improves the structuring of your app.

- `coroutineScope { ... }`

  This creates a new coroutine scope that inherits the context from the outer coroutine scope; that is, the scope in which the `coroutineScope()` gets invoked. However, it overwrites the job and uses its own job derived from the contents of its lambda function parameter (the content of `{ ... }`). This function can only be called from inside a scope. Using `coroutineScope()` is a prominent example for *structured concurrency*: Once any child inside the `{ ... }` fails, all the rest of the children will fail as well and eventually the whole `coroutineScope()` will fail.

- `supervisorScope { ... }`

  This is the same as coroutineScope(), but lets its child scopes run independent of each other. In particular, if any of the children get canceled, the other children and the supervisor scope do not get canceled.

- `launch { ... }`

  This defines a background job. The `launch()` invocation returns immediately while the background job defined by the `{ ... }` lambda starts doing its work in the background. The `launch()` returns an instance of class `Job`. You can use the `join()` function from `Job` to wait for the job to finish.

- `async { ... }`

  This is the same as `launch()`, but allows for the background job to produce a result. For this aim `launch()` returns an instance of class `Deferred`. You can use its `await()` function to retrieve the result; of course, this implies waiting for the job to have finished.

- `Implement CoroutineScope`

  In any of your classes, you can implement class `CoroutineScope`: `class MyClass : CoroutineScope { ... }`. The problem with this approach is that, because `CoroutineScope` is just an interface, we need to implement the coroutine functionality by filling the coroutine context with sensible objects. A simple way to do that is using delegation: `class MyClass : CoroutineScope by MainScope() { ... }`, which delegates all coroutine builders to a `MainScope` object.

> That one is particularly useful for user interfaces. Once this is done we can freely use builders like launch() and async(), and also control functions like cancel(), from anywhere inside MyClass.

The launch() function has a couple of default parameters. Its complete synopsis reads as follows:

```
public fun CoroutineScope.launch(
  context: CoroutineContext = EmptyCoroutineContext,
  start: CoroutineStart = CoroutineStart.DEFAULT,
  block: suspend CoroutineScope.() -> Unit
): Job
```

You can use the context parameter to set the context name, for example, as in

```
launch(context = coroutineContext +
                  CoroutineName("CoRou1")) {
    ...
)
```

The start parameter can be used to tweak the way the coroutine starts. See the API documentation for details (enter "CoroutineStart" in Android Studio, then press Ctrl+B).

The async() function has the same default parameters as launch(), so you can also tweak the async() startup characteristics.

Consider the following example code. For Android you could test it directly inside the onCreate() function inside an activity.

```
runBlocking {
    // This starts in the current thread.
    // We are now inside a coroutine scope. This means
    // we have a
    //      val coroutineContext:CoroutineContext
    // for the context. The runBlocking() ends
    // after all work is done.
    Log.d("LOG", "1. Started inside runBlocking()")

    coroutineScope {
        Log.d("LOG", "2. coroutineScope()")
        delay(500L)
        Log.d("LOG", "3. coroutineScope()")
```

```kotlin
    coroutineScope {
        Log.d("LOG", "4. coroutineScope() II")
        // If you add this, both coroutineScope()
        // fail and runBlocking() prematurely ends:
        // throw CancellationException("4.")

        // Also, because runBlocking transports the
        // exception to the outside world, (15.)
        // below will not be reached.
    }
    Log.d("LOG", "5. inner done")
}

val job1 = launch {
    // This runs in the background, so
    // (8.) happens before (7.)
    Log.d("LOG", "6. inside launch()")
    delay(500)
    Log.d("LOG", "7. done with launch()")
}
Log.d("LOG", "8. returned from launch()")

val deferr1 = async {
    // This runs in the background as well, but it
    // returns something
    Log.d("LOG", "9. inside async()")
    delay(500)
    Log.d("LOG", "10. done with async()")
    "Result"
}
Log.d("LOG", "11. returned from async()")

job1.join()
Log.d("LOG", "12. launch finish")

val res1 = deferr1.await()
Log.d("LOG", "13. async finish")
```

```
    Log.d("LOG", "14. End of runBlocking()")
}
Log.d("LOG", "15. Returned from runBlocking()")
```

It has the following characteristics.

- Running the code, the logs will show this:

```
1.  Started inside runBlocking()
2.  coroutineScope()
3.  coroutineScope() - 0.5secs later
4.  coroutineScope() II
5.  inner done
8.  returned from launch()
11. returned from async()
6.  inside launch()
9.  inside async()
7.  done with launch()
10. done with async()
12. launch finish
13. async finish
14. End of runBlocking()
15. Returned from runBlocking()
```

Items 6, 9, 7, and 10 might show up in a different order because they belong to background processing.

- The outer runBlocking() introduces a root in the coroutine scope hierarchy.

- The runBlocking() only returns if all its children finish their work or a cancellation of their work occurs.

- If a CancellationException gets thrown (uncomment the throw to see that happen), it gets transported up the scope hierarchy and consequentially 15 will not be reached.

- Both async() and launch() introduce asynchronicity (concurrency); they return immediately while their { ... } lambdas do their work in the background.

- The job1.join() and deferr1.await() synchronize the background jobs; both wait for the corresponding job to finish.

Coroutine Context

A CoroutineContext holds the state of the coroutine scope as a set of context elements. Although the CoroutineContext does not implement the normal Set, List, or Map interface you'd normally use for such cases, you still can get its elements by one of these methods.

- coroutineContext[Job]

  This retrieves the Job instance that holds the instructions of which the coroutine consists.

- coroutineContext[CoroutineName]

  Optionally, this retrieves the name of the coroutine. You can specify the name via coroutineContext + CoroutineName("My FancyCoroutine") as the first parameter of a coroutine builder (e.g., launch() or async()) invocation.

- coroutineContext[CoroutineExceptionHandler]

  This is an optional dedicated exception handler. We'll talk about exceptions later.

- coroutineContext[ContinuationInterceptor]

  This internal item holds the object that is responsible for correctly continuing a coroutine after it was suspended and resumes its work.

Although any scope builder like runBlocking(), launch(), or async() spawns a new coroutine context that gets forwarded to other coroutine functions invoked from inside, you can temporarily tweak the context by using

```
withContext(context: CoroutineContext) {
    ...
}
```

As a parameter you are free to build your own context, or use + to change dedicated elements of the current context. For example, to temporarily set the coroutine name you'd write

```
... we are inside a coroutine scope

withContext(context = coroutineContext +
        CoroutineName("TmpName")) {
    ... here we have a scope with a tweaked context
}
```

In the same way, you can alter or redefine other context elements.

What a delay() Does

At first glance the delay(timeMillis:Long) function has the same use as the basic Thread.sleep(millis:Long) function from the Java way of using concurrency: Let the program flow wait for some time before it can continue with the instructions after the delay() or sleep() statement. However, there is a major difference between the two: The function Thread.sleep() actually blocks the current thread and lets other threads do their work, whereas delay() calls a suspending function that does not block the current thread but instead schedules a resumption of the program flow after the specified time elapses.

From a use-case view you use both for the same purpose: to continue with the program flow only after the specified time has elapsed. Knowing that for coroutines the thread does not get blocked, however, helps to tailor concurrency for maximum stability and performance.

What Is a Suspending Function?

A suspending function is a function that might or might not execute immediately or be suspended once invocation starts, and then eventually ends. It does not block a thread, even when it or parts of it are suspended.

From a coding point of view, you must make your own functions suspendable if you extract functions from a coroutine:

```
runBlocking {
    ...
    launch {
        ...
    }
}
```

converts to

```
runBlocking {
    ...
    doLaunch()
}
suspend fun doLaunch() {
    launch {
        ...
    }
}
```

Internally the suspend keyword leads to adding a hidden parameter for the coroutine context.

Waiting for Jobs

Dispatching work to several concurrently acting coroutines is one part of the story. First, if the coroutines calculated something, after the coroutines do their work we need to make sure we can gather the results before we continue with the program flow. Second, we must make sure the program as a big state machine is in a consistent state before we can continue doing more work after the coroutines finish. Here we are talking about *result gathering* and *concertation* or *synchronization*.

For synchronization, to make sure a Job or a Deferred has finished its work, use join() as in

```
val job = launch { ... }
val deferr = async { ... }

job.join() // suspend until job finished
deferr.join() // suspend until deferr finished
```

We can do this also for the Deferred, because it is a subclass of Job. In both cases it ensures that all the coroutine children of the jobs also finished their work. For the Deferred, however, we actually want to get the result of the calculation, which leads us to coroutines result gathering. You do so by writing

```
val deferr1 = async { ... }
val deferr2 = async { ... }

val deferr1Res = deferr1.await()
val deferr2Res = deferr2.await()
```

Again the `await()` function invocations suspend the program flow until the `Deferred`s finish their work. Again, the coroutine children of the `async` jobs also will have finished their work.

For a `Deferred` there is also a function `getCompleted()` you can use to get an already calculated result:

```
val deferr1Res = deferr1.getCompleted()
```

Here you must have made sure, though, that the `Deferred` actually finished its calculation, otherwise you'll get an `IllegalStateException`. You can read the `isCompleted` property to check whether a `Deferred` or a `Job` has completed.

In a hierarchical setup of coroutines with parent–child relationships, the coroutines library makes sure that children will finish their work before a parent quits, so we don't have to write

```
runBlocking {
    val job1 = launch {
    }
    job1.join() // unnecessary!
}
```

The join will happen automatically.

Canceling Coroutines

To cancel any job, invoke the `cancel()` function on the `Job` or `Deferred` object.

```
val job = launch { ... }
val deferr = async { ... }
...
job.cancel() // or deferr.cancel()
```

Canceling does not mean a job immediately quits its work. Instead it is marked and stops working at a feasible time.

- Inside a canceled job, any invocation of a suspend function will lead to the job finishing its execution. An example is delay(); inside the delay() function a cancellation check will occur and if the job was canceled, the job will immediately quit.

- If there are no suspend function calls or not enough of them, you can use the yield() function to initiate such a cancellation check.

- Inside your code you can regularly check whether the isActive property gives false. If this is the case, you know the job was canceled and you can finish the job execution.

Because a cancellation does not normally lead to an immediate job termination, you must append a join():

```
val job = launch { ... }
...
job.cancel()
job.join()
```

Another option is to use

```
val job = launch { ... }
...
job.cancelAndJoin()
```

which combines those two.

What a cancellation leads to concerning the coroutine scope hierarchy is discussed in the section "Exception Handling" later in this chapter.

Timeouts

You can specify timeouts to instructions inside a coroutine via

```
withTimeout(1000L) { // milliseconds

    ...

}
```

This throws a TimeoutCancellationException (a subclass of CancellationException) if the timeout limit gets reached, or

```
val res = withTimeoutOrNull(1000L) { // milliseconds
    ...
    [result expression]
}
```

which does not throw an exception but instead assigns null to the result if the elapsed time exceeds the given time. Because of Kotlin's idiomatic ?: operator for null value handling, we can also throw our own exceptions as in

```
withTimeoutOrNull(1000L) { // milliseconds
    ...
    "OK"
} ?: throw Exception("Timeout Exception")
```

Dispatchers

A coroutine dispatcher actually tells where and how a job gets run. More precisely, it describes which thread the coroutine runs in and how a thread gets created or looked up (e.g., from a thread pool). You can get hold of the current dispatcher with

```
coroutineContext[ContinuationInterceptor]
```

If you don't want to go with the defaults that a builder like launch() or async() uses, you can explicitly prescribe a dispatcher. Remember we can give launch() or async() the context as a first parameter. If we have a dispatcher, then, we can write

```
val myDispatcher = ...
runBlocking {
    val job = launch(coroutineContext + myDispatcher) {
        ...
    }
    job.join()
}
```

You don't have to develop such a dispatcher on your own, because some dispatchers are provided by the coroutines library:

- Dispatchers.Default

    This is the default dispatcher used if the context does not yet contain a dispatcher. It uses a thread pool with at least two threads, and the maximum number of threads is the number of CPUs the current device has minus 1. You can, however, overwrite that number by writing `System.setProperty( "kotlinx.coroutines.default.parallelism", 12 )` early in your app (before any coroutine gets built).

- `Dispatchers.Main`

  This is a dispatcher tied to user interface processing. For Android, if you want to use the main dispatcher, you must add library `kotlinx-coroutinesandroid` to the dependencies section inside `build.gradle`. If you route your coroutines structure like

  ```
  class MyClass :
      CoroutineScope by MainScope()
  {
      ...
  }
  ```

  the `Dispatchers.Main` gets used automatically.

- `Dispatchers.IO`

  This is a dispatcher especially tailored for blocking IO functionality. It is similar to the `Dispatchers.Default` dispatcher, but if necessary creates up to 64 threads.

- `newSingleThreadContext("MyThreadName)"`

  This starts a dedicated new thread. You should finish using it by applying `close()` at the end or otherwise store the instance returned by the `newSingleThreadContext()` function call at some global place for reuse.

- `Dispatchers.Unconfined`

  This is not for general use. An unconfined dispatcher is a dispatcher that uses the surrounding context's thread until the first suspending function gets called. It resumes from the first suspending function in the thread that got used *there*.

Exception Handling

During a coroutine's execution, we basically have three kinds of exceptions, and unless further precautions are taken, the following will happen:

- *For* `CancellationException` *exceptions and* `launch()`: Remember that cancellation exceptions occur when you explicitly invoke `cancel()` on a `Job` element. If a `CancellationException` gets thrown, it will lead to a quitting of the current coroutine, but not to a quitting of any of the parents; they will just ignore it. The hierarchy's root coroutine will just as well ignore the exception, so outside the coroutine machinery such an exception will not be detected.

- *For* `CancellationException` *exceptions and* `async()`: Other than for `launch()`, a cancellation of a `Deferred` job by invoking `cancel()` on the `Deferred` element will not lead to the exception being ignored. Instead, we must react on the exception, which will show up in the `await()` function.

- *For* `TimeoutCancellationException` *exceptions*: If a timeout in a `withTimeout( timeMillis:Long ) { ... }` happens, a `TimeoutCancellationException` gets thrown. This is a subclass of `CancellationException` and receives no special treatment, so what is true for normal cancellation exceptions holds for timeouts as well.

- *Any other exception:* Normal exceptions lead to an immediate quitting of any running job in the coroutines hierarchy, and will also be thrown by the root coroutine. If you expect such an exception, you must, for example, wrap a root `runBlocking()` into a try-catch clause. You can, of course, add try-catch clauses inside the jobs to catch such exceptions early.

To see what happens with a cancellation exception and how it gets propagated through the coroutines hierarchy, try the following code:

```
var l1:Job? = null
var l11:Job? = null
var l111:Job? = null
```

```
runBlocking {
    Log.d("LOG", "A")
    l1 = launch {
        Log.d("LOG", "B")
        l111 = launch {
            Log.d("LOG", "C")
            delay(1000L)
            Log.d("LOG", "D")
            l1111 = launch {
                Log.d("LOG", "E")
                delay(1000L)
                Log.d("LOG", "F")
                delay(1000L)
                Log.d("LOG", "G")
            }
            delay(2500L)
            Log.d("LOG", "H")
        }
        delay(1000L)
        Log.d("LOG", "I")
    }

    Log.d("LOG", "X1")
    delay(1500L)
    Log.d("LOG", "X2")
    l1111?.cancel()
    Log.d("LOG", "X3")
}
```

If you run this the logging will look like this:

```
10:05:31.295: A
10:05:31.295: X1
10:05:31.299: B
10:05:31.301: C
10:05:32.300: I
10:05:32.302: D
```

```
10:05:32.302: E
10:05:32.796: X2
10:05:32.796: X3
10:05:34.802: H
```

We observe the following characteristics:

- The runBlocking() does not forward the cancellation exception to the outside world. This exception thus is a somewhat "expected" exception.

- Label X1 gets reached immediately after A. This is not a surprise, as all launch() invocations lead to background processing.

- Labels B and C get reached shortly after A, because other than background processing startup, no delays are specified.

- Label I gets reached 1 second later, because of the delay(1000L) immediately in front of it. At that time the delay after label C has almost passed by. A few milliseconds later D and E get reached.

- While label E gets reached, the delay after X1 has not yet passed by completely, but half a second later X2 gets reached and we fire a cancellation on job l111. At that time we are in the middle of the delay(1000L) after E.

- Because of the cancellation, the delay after E is quit immediately and job l111 prematurely exits. Labels F and G thus never get reached.

- The parent coroutines of l111 continue with their work, they just ignore the cancellation of job l111. That is why a little later label H gets reached.

- Label X3 happens before H. We know that runBlocking() continues its work while any noncanceled child is still running. Job l111 was canceled, but neither job l11 nor l1 have been canceled, so both H and I get reached.

If in the latter example you replace l111.cancel() by l11.cancel(), the following output is produced:

```
11:40:35.893: A
11:40:35.894: X1
11:40:35.894: B
```

```
11:40:35.896: C
11:40:36.896: I
11:40:36.898: D
11:40:36.899: E
11:40:37.394: X2
11:40:37.395: X3
```

Here we can see both the parent job 111 and its children (job 1111) get canceled; labels F, G, and H never get reached.

Exercise 2

In the preceding example, remove the cancel() statement and instead add a timeout of 0.5 seconds to the delay() immediately after label E. What do you expect? Will the logging differ from the logging with the cancel() statement?

If you want to make sure a passage of the code cannot be canceled despite it containing suspending function calls, you can wrap it into a special new context:

```
...
withContext(NonCancellable) {
    // uncancellable code here
    ...
}
...
```

If you need to tailor the exception handling, it is possible to explicitly register an ExceptionHandler with a builder invocation:

```
val handler = CoroutineExceptionHandler {
    _, exception ->
    Log.e("LOG", "Caught $exception")
}

runBlocking(handler) {
    ...
}
```

or

```
val handler = ...
runBlocking {
    ...
    launch(coroutineContext + handler) {
        ...
    }
}
```

Note that despite it starting with a capital letter, the `CoroutineExceptionHandler()` actually is a function invocation. There is also an interface using the same name `CoroutineExceptionHandler` if you want to write a class for handling exceptions.

Such an exception handler only handles exceptions that do not otherwise get caught by the coroutines. We know that for `launch()` jobs a `CancellationException` does not get transported up the coroutines hierarchy; in this case and for this particular exception type, the exception handler does not get invoked either.

If you don't want all that exception propagation stuff, you can either use a *supervisor* job as in

```
// we are inside a coroutine scope

val supervisor = SupervisorJob()
withContext(coroutineContext + supervisor) {
    // the coroutines hierarchy here
    ...
}
```

or you use a `supervisor` scope:

```
// we are inside a coroutine scope

supervisorScope {
    // the coroutines hierarchy here
    ...
}
```

A supervisor leads to all coroutines handling their exceptions independent of each other. No child will, however, live longer than its parent.

CHAPTER 19

Using External Libraries

External libraries are collections of interfaces and classes that are of general use and thus can be reused in various projects. You won't find many Kotlin libraries yet, but because it is easy for Kotlin to interface with Java classes and interfaces, in your projects you can use one or some of the plethora of Java libraries published by other developers and development teams.

Example fields for external libraries are encoding and decoding, compression, CSV file handling, e-mailers, higher level math and statistics, databases, extended logging facilities, XML and JSON file handling, and many more. You will learn more about XML and JSON in Chapter 20.

The rest of this chapter talks about ways to add external libraries to your Android project, dives into peculiarities concerning nullability if you add external Java libraries, and describes how to build your own libraries.

Adding External Libraries

The first step in adding external libraries is specifying where the libraries come from. The places where libraries can be loaded or included from are called *repositories*. Once you start a new Android project, the project's `build.gradle` script contains the repositories at two places, inside the `buildscript` section and inside the `allprojects` section:

```
buildscript {
    ...
    repositories {
        google()
        jcenter()
    }
    ...
}
```

© Peter Späth 2019
P. Späth, *Learn Kotlin for Android Development*, https://doi.org/10.1007/978-1-4842-4467-8_19

```
allprojects {
    ...
    repositories {
        google()
        jcenter()
    }
    ...
}
...
```

Application dependencies use the repositories from the `allprojects` section. The repositories from the `buildscript` section instead refer to plug-ins and dependencies for the *build process*. We want to add application libraries, not tweak the build process, so the place to look at is the `allprojects` section. Here the following repositories can be specified:

- `google()`: This is a repository from which Android-specific libraries get loaded. This is always included and always necessary for Android projects, but it is usually not the place where you'd look up application-specific libraries. In other words, this is not the place we'd use for *external* libraries.

- `mavenCentral()`: This is the original Maven repository located at `https://repo1.maven.org/maven2`. In talking of the Maven build system, most developers first think of this repository for adding libraries. For Android, however, the first choice is to use `jcenter` instead.

- `jcenter()`: This references an alternative Maven repository at `http://jcenter.bintray.com`. It normally doesn't hurt to favor `jcenter` over `mavenCentral`, but in many cases both will work and it is even possible to specify both. Differences might show up in different performance for downloading libraries, and different "latest" library versions. The `jcenter` people claim that their repository is bigger and faster compared to `mavenCentral`.

- `mavenLocal()`: No matter how you use Maven as a build system, on your development machine a cache will be built up and perpetually filled with libraries you downloaded from any Maven repository (including jcenter). Also, if you create a Maven library project and install it, the library will show up in this cache even when you never plan to upload it to an official public repository. The mavenLocal() repository looks into that cache for library dependencies. Note that you'd usually find that cache under .m2 in your PC user's home folder.

- maven { url 'http://example.com/maven' }: You can use this to add a custom Maven repository. This is handy if you use your private or your company's Maven repository. Note that the google() and jcenter() repositories are just shortcuts for maven { url 'https://dl.google.com/dl/android/maven2/' } and maven { url 'https://jcenter.bintray.com/' }.

- ivy { url 'http://example.com/ivy' }: You can use this to add an Apache Ivy repository.

In most cases you will be fine with the default setting: Use google() and jcenter() as shown. You can try these and add new repositories only if necessary.

With the repositories set up, we can now add actual libraries in the form of dependencies. This works best in the module's build.gradle file. With a new project, the dependencies section of this file probably reads like this:

```
dependencies {
    implementation
        fileTree(dir: 'libs', include: ['*.jar'])
    implementation
        "org.jetbrains.kotlin:kotlin-stdlib-jdk7:
        $kotlin_version"
    implementation
        "com.android.support:appcompat-v7:28.0.0"
    implementation
        "com.android.support.constraint:
        constraint-layout:1.1.3"
    testImplementation
        "junit:junit:4.12"
    androidTestImplementation
        "com.android.support.test:runner:1.0.2"
```

```
    androidTestImplementation
        "com.android.support.test.espresso:
        espresso-core:3.0.2"
}
```

(Each item is on one line.) The details are not interesting here; what you need to know is that for new external libraries we have to add another line starting with implementation. The precise syntax for this new entry adheres to the following format:

```
implementation "MAVEN_GROUP_ID:MAVEN_ARTIFACT_ID:VERSION"
```

or

```
implementation 'MAVEN_GROUP_ID:MAVEN_ARTIFACT_ID:VERSION'
```

This triple of group ID, artifact ID, and version is also known as the *Maven coordinates*.

An equivalent approach consists of using a parameterized form (write it on one line without line breaks):

```
implementation group: "MAVEN_GROUP_ID",
    name: "MAVEN_ARTIFACT_ID",
    version "VERSION"
```

Again, you can also use single quotation marks.

This is best explained by an example. Say you want to add the Apache Commons Math library that allows for sophisticated mathematical calculations. We first need to determine the Maven coordinates for the library. There are several ways to get those coordinates.

- The library might have its own web site where, for example, the Maven coordinates are available under Downloads.

- Look directly at the web site of the repository and use a search facility provided there.

- Use a search engine of your choice and enter a search string like "apache commons math maven."

In most cases you will get the Maven coordinates as an XML string in the form

```
<!-- https://mvnrepository.com/artifact/
     org.apache.commons/commons-math3 -->
<dependency>
  <groupId>org.apache.commons</groupId>
  <artifactId>commons-math3</artifactId>
  <version>3.2</version>
</dependency>
```

Inside the dependency element you can see the group ID, the artifact ID, and the version. The Gradle equivalent can thus be easily deduced from the XML by looking at the tag names. Here the transcription reads

```
implementation "org.apache.commons:commons-math3:3.2"
```

or

```
implementation group: "org.apache.commons",
    name : "commons-math3",
    version : "3.2"
```

(one line).

Note   Sometimes you also get the Gradle syntax. Even if it reads `compile` `'org.apache.commons:commons-math3:3.2'` do not use `compile` but `implementation` instead. The `compile` keyword belongs to an older version of Gradle.

Android Studio then asks you to synchronize your project. Do so, and after that you can use the new library from inside your code.

Dependency Management

Libraries can depend on other libraries. This happens quite often, and it could develop into a real nightmare if we have to manually add all the dependencies a library exposes. Another Apache Commons library called Apache Commons Configuration in version 2.4, for example, depends on three more libraries, and those three in turn might depend on other libraries, and so on. Fortunately, Maven automatically resolves such dependencies, including all transitive dependencies, so we do not have to do anything.

We mention this here so you are aware that such dependencies and transitive dependencies could considerably blow up our app. If, for example, you add an unsuspicious library of size 100 kb, due to dependencies it could easily blow up to several megabytes. On modern devices this hardly ever poses a real problem, but it is good to know why the app file gets so big under certain circumstances.

Unresolved Local Dependencies

If you create a new project using Android Studio the first line inside the `dependencies` section of the module's `build.gradle` file reads

```
fileTree(dir: 'libs', include: ['*.jar'])
```

This means any `.jar` file you put into the `libs` folder will be added as a library to your app. No automatic dependency resolution will happen and you have to download the libraries yourself. This somewhat conflicts with the Maven method of dependency inclusion, so try to avoid using this technique.

External Libraries and Nullability

We know that in Kotlin the nullability of properties plays an important role in improving program stability. If we include external Java libraries the story is different. Java as a language does not draw the same precise distinction between nullable and non-nullable variables as Kotlin does. To be able to use external Java libraries, Kotlin assumes all function invocation parameters and function return values to be nullable.

If the API documentation of an external library says a function return value cannot be `null`, the only way to tell Kotlin about this fact is to use the Elvis operator and throw an exception if the return value is `null`:

```
val res = javaObject.function() ?:
        throw Exception("Cannot happen")
```

Creating Your Own Library

You can create a library in whatever way you want, including using the command line or other IDEs such as Eclipse. In this section we cover how to create and use libraries using Android Studio.

In Android Studio, a library project actually is more than just a `.jar` file that could be included in other projects. It is almost an app on its own because it can include Android configuration files and files that describe the user interface. No one hinders us from using Android libraries just for defining interfaces and classes that could be used from other projects, though.

As an example, we define a library named StringRegex that just extends the `String` class by an operator function for checking regular expression matches, so we can write

```
val s = "The big brown fox jumps over the creek."
val containsOnlyLetters = s % "[A-Za-z ]*"
// -> false because of the "."
```

For the definition of this extension function we overload the % operator `rem()`. The code for this reads

```
package org.foo.stringregex
```

```
operator fun String.rem(re:String):Boolean =
      this.matches(Regex(re))
```

where for the `package` you could, of course, use something different.

We first start a new library project in Android Studio. To do so go to File ➤ New ➤ New Project and select Add No Activity. As a project name, enter `StringRegexApp`, and as a package name enter `org.foo.stringregex`. As a Save location, enter whatever you like. Make you have Kotlin selected as the Language setting, and as a Minimum API level select anything that seems appropriate to you. Inside the new Android Studio project window that then opens go to File ➤ New ➤ New Module. Select Java Library. Enter `StringRegex` as the Library name. The other settings are not important here. The Project view will now look similar to Figure 19-1.

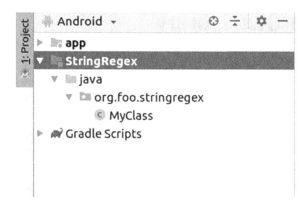

Figure 19-1   *StringRegex Android library*

Delete the Java class MyClass, as we don't need it. Inside the package `org.foo.`
`stringregex`, create a new Kotlin file. Right-click, and select New ➤ Kotlin File/Class. As
the name enter `stringregex` and as Kind select File.

Android Studio then might show a warning stating that Kotlin is not configured. If
this is the case, click Configure, select Java with Gradle from the menu, and in the dialog
box asking you for which modules to enable Kotlin, select All modules.

Note   For Android Studio 3.3 there is a bug in the Kotlin configuration wizard.
Inside the Stringregex module's `build.gradle` file you might have to comment
out the plug-in version inside `plugins`:

```
id 'org.jetbrains.kotlin.jvm' //version '1.3.20'
```

Open the `stringregex` file and enter the extension function code shown in the
preceding listing. You can now close the window, as we will be making a reference to it
from a client project.

From any app open in Android Studio, you can choose one of the apps we created for
this book, open the `settings.gradle` file, and add two statements.

```
include ':StringRegex'
project(':StringRegex').projectDir =
      new File('../StringRegexApp/StringRegex')
```

where the string inside File() must point to the library module we just created. We still need to declare the module dependency. To do this, open the client app module's build.gradle file and inside the dependencies section add

```
implementation project(":StringRegex")
```

This procedure can be repeated for as many apps referring to this library as you wish. You can now import the extension function and use it from inside the client code.

```
import org.foo.stringregex.rem

...
val s = "The big brown fox jumps over the creek."
val containsOnlyLetters = s % "[A-Za-z ]*"
// -> false because of the "."
```

To see or use the .jar file generated from the library, in the file system explorer of your operating system go to StringRegexApp / StringRegex / build / libs.

CHAPTER 20

XML and JSON

In Chapter 19 we learned how to include external libraries in our Android projects. Kotlin doesn't have dedicated XML and JSON processing classes included in its standard library, so to achieve XML- and JSON-related tasks we use appropriate external libraries and add some convenience functions in the form of extension functions.

Note Both XML and JSON are format specifications for structured data. You will frequently use them if your Android app communicates with the outside world for receiving or sending data in a standardized format.

This chapter assumes you have a sample app you can use to test the code snippets provided. Use whatever app you like or one of the apps we developed in this book. You could, for example, add some sample code providing Log output for testing inside the activity's onCreate() function, or you could use a test class using one of Android's test methodologies. Choose a method that best suits your needs.

XML Processing

XML files are at their simplest files of a form similar to this:

```
<?xml version="1.0" encoding="UTF-8"?>
<ProbeMsg>
  <TimeStamp>2016-10-30T19:07:07Z</TimeStamp>
  <ProbeId>1A6G</ProbeId>
  <ProbeValue ScaleUnit="cm">37.4</ProbeValue>
```

© Peter Späth 2019
P. Späth, *Learn Kotlin for Android Development*, https://doi.org/10.1007/978-1-4842-4467-8_20

```
<Meta>
  <Generator>045</Generator>
  <Priority>-3</Priority>
  <Actor>P. Rosengaard</Actor>
</Meta>
</ProbeMsg>
```

Note   XML allows for more elaborate constructs like schema validation and namespaces. In this chapter we only describe XML tags, attributes, and text contents. You are free to extend the samples and utility functions presented in this chapter to also include such extended features.

For XML processing one or a combination of the following paradigms gets used.

- *DOM Model: Complete tree handling:* In the Document Object Model (DOM) the XML data get treated as a whole represented by an in-memory, tree-like structure.

- *SAX: Event-based processing:* Here an XML file gets parsed and with each element or attribute an appropriate event is fired. The events are received by callback functions that have to be registered with the SAX processor. Such a "tell me what you are doing" style of processing is commonly called *push parsing.*

- *StAX: Stream-based processing:* Here you perform operations like "Give me the next XML element" and the like. In contrast to SAX, where we have a push parsing, for StAX we tell the parser what it has to do: "I tell you what you do." This therefore is called *pull parsing.*

On Android you typically handle small to medium-size XML files. For this reason in this chapter we use the DOM. For reading, we first parse the complete XML file and store the data in a DOM tree in memory. Here operations on them like deleting, changing, or adding elements are easy to accomplish and happen in memory; thus they are very fast. For writing we take the complete DOM tree from memory and generate an XML character stream from it, perhaps writing the result back to a file.

For XML handling we add the Java reference implementation *Xerces* as an external library. Inside Android Studio, open the module's build.gradle file and inside the dependencies section add:

```
implementation 'xerces:xercesImpl:2.12.0'
```

Note   Xerces also implements the SAX and StAX APIs, although we will use only its DOM implementation.

Reading XML Data

The DOM implementation we can use by virtue of the Xerces implementation already contains everything needed to read XML elements. We will, however, add a couple of extension functions that greatly improve the DOM API's usability. For this aim, create a package com.example.domext, or you can also use any other suitable package name. Add a Kotlin file dom.kt inside this package, and as its contents write:

```
package com.example.domext

import org.apache.xerces.parsers.DOMParser
import org.w3c.dom.Document
import org.w3c.dom.Node
import org.xml.sax.InputSource
import java.io.StringReader
import java.io.StringWriter
import javax.xml.transform.OutputKeys
import javax.xml.transform.TransformerFactory
import javax.xml.transform.dom.DOMSource
import javax.xml.transform.stream.StreamResult

fun parseXmlToDOM(s:String) : Document {
  val parser: DOMParser = DOMParser()
  return parser.let {
      it.parse(InputSource(StringReader(s)))
      it.document
  }
}
```

```
fun Node.fetchChildren(withText:Boolean = false) =
  (0..(this.childNodes.length - 1)).
  map { this.childNodes.item(it) }.
  filter { withText || it.nodeType != Node.TEXT_NODE }

fun Node.childCount() = fetchChildren().count()

fun Node.forEach(withText:Boolean = false,
                 f:(Node) -> Unit) {
  fetchChildren(withText).forEach { f(it) }
}

operator fun Node.get(i:Int) = fetchChildren()[i]
operator fun Node.invoke(s:String): Node =
  if(s.startsWith("@")) {
      this.attributes.getNamedItem(s.substring(1))
  }else{
      this.childNodes.let { nl ->
          val iter = object : Iterator<Node> {
              var i: Int = 0
              override fun next() = nl.item(i++)
              override fun hasNext() = i < nl.length
          }
          iter.asSequence().find { it.nodeName == s }!!
      }
  }
operator fun Node.invoke(vararg s:String): Node =
    s.fold(this, { acc, s1 -> acc(s1)  })

fun Node.text() = this.firstChild.nodeValue
fun Node.name() = this.nodeName
fun Node.type() = this.nodeType
```

Those are all package-level functions and extension functions for `org.w3c.dom.Node`, with the following characteristics:

- In the DOM API, each element in the tree (e.g., `ProbeValue` in the XML data from the beginning of this section) gets represented by a `Node` instance.

- We add a `parseXmlToDOM(s:String)` package-level function that converts an XML string to a `Document`.

- We add a `fetchChildren()` function to `Node` that returns all nontext children of a node that are disregarding text elements. If you add `with- Text=true` as a parameter, the text nodes of an element get included in the children list, even if they only contain spaces and line breaks. For example, in the XML data from the beginning of this section, the node `Meta` has three children: `Generator`, `Priority`, and `Actor`. With `withText=true` the spaces and line breaks between them would be returned as well.

- We add a `childCount()` function to `Node` that counts the number of children elements of a node, disregarding text elements. The official DOM API does not provide a function for that.

- We add a `forEach()` function to `Node` that allows us to iterate through a node's children the Kotlin way. The original DOM API does not provide such an iterator, as it only has functions and properties `hasChild-Nodes()`, `childNodes.length`, and `childNodes.item(index:Int)` to iterate through children. If you add `withText=true` as a parameter, the text nodes of an element are included in the children list, even if they only contain spaces and line breaks.

- We add a `get(i:Int)` function to `Node` to get a certain child from an element, disregarding text nodes.

- We overload the `invoke` operator of `Node`, which belongs to the parentheses `()`. The first variant with a `String` parameter navigates to a child by name: `node("cn")` = node → child with name "cn." If the parameter starts with a @ the attribute gets addressed: `node("@an")` = node → attribute with name "an." In the latter case, you still need to call `text()` to get the attribute value as a string.

- The second variant of the overloaded `invoke` operator allows us to specify several strings, which navigates to a child from a child from a child, and so on.

- We add functions to Node: first, text() gets the text contents of an element, then name()gives us the node name, and then type()evaluates to the node type (for possible values see the constant properties of the Node class).

Caution   For simplicity, the code snippets shown in this section for DOM processing do not handle exceptions in a sensible manner. You must add appropriate error handling before using the code for production projects.

This snippet provides examples of how to use the API and the extensions.

```
import ...
import com.example.domext.*

...
val xml = """<?xml version="1.0" encoding="UTF-8"?>
  <ProbeMsg>
    <TimeStamp>2016-10-30T19:07:07Z</TimeStamp>
    <ProbeId>1A6G</ProbeId>
    <ProbeValue ScaleUnit="cm">37.4</ProbeValue>
  <Meta>
    <Generator>045</Generator>
    <Priority>-3</Priority>
    <Actor>P. Rosengaard</Actor>
  </Meta>
</ProbeMsg>"""

try {
    // Parse the complete XML document
    val dom = parseXmlToDOM(xml)

    // Access an element
    val ts = dom("ProbeMsg")("TimeStamp").text()
    Log.d("LOG", ts) // 2001-11-30T09:08:07Z
```

```
    // Access an attribute
    val uni = dom("ProbeMsg")("ProbeValue")("@ScaleUnit")
    Log.d("LOG", uni.text()) // cm

    // Simplified XML tree navigation
    val uni2 = dom("ProbeMsg","ProbeValue","@ScaleUnit")
    Log.d("LOG", uni2.text()) // cm

    // Iterate through an element's children
    dom("ProbeMsg")("Meta").forEach { n ->
        Log.d("LOG", n.name() + ": " + n.text())
        //    Generator: 045
        //    Priority: -3
        //    Actor: P. Rosengaard
    }
}catch(e:Exception) {
    Log.e("LOG", "Cannot parse XML", e)
}
...
```

Altering XML Data

Once we have a DOM representation of an XML tree in memory, we can add elements. Although we could use the functions already provided by the DOM API, Kotlin allows us to improve the expressiveness. For this purpose, add the following code to our extension file dom.kt (I don't add new imports; press Alt+Enter to let Android Studio help you add necessary imports):

```
fun prettyFormatXml(document:Document): String {
  val format = OutputFormat(document).apply { lineWidth = 65
      indenting = true
      indent = 2
  }
  val out = StringWriter()
  val serializer = XMLSerializer(out, format)
  serializer.serialize(document)
  return out.toString()
}
```

```
fun prettyFormatXml(unformattedXml: String) =
      prettyFormatXml(parseXmlToDOM(unformattedXml))

fun Node.toXmlString():String {
  val transformerFact = TransformerFactory.newInstance()
  val transformer = transformerFact.newTransformer()
  transformer.setOutputProperty(OutputKeys.INDENT, "yes")
  val source = DOMSource(this)
  val writer = StringWriter()
  val result = StreamResult(writer)
  transformer.transform(source, result)
  return writer.toString()
}

operator fun Node.plusAssign(child:Node) {
  this.appendChild(child)
}

fun Node.addText(s:String): Node {
  val doc = ownerDocument
  val txt = doc.createTextNode(s)
  appendChild(txt)
  return this
}

fun Node.removeText() {
  if(hasChildNodes() && firstChild.nodeType == Node.TEXT_NODE)
      removeChild(firstChild)
}

fun Node.updateText(s:String) : Node { removeText()
  return addText(s)
}
```

```
fun Node.addAttribute(name:String, value:String): Node {
  (this as Element).setAttribute(name, value)
  return this
}

fun Node.removeAttribute(name:String) {
    this.attributes.removeNamedItem(name)
}
```

Here is a description of what we have in this case

- Functions prettyFormatXml(document: Document) and prettyFormatXml(unformattedXml: String) are utility functions mainly for diagnostic purposes. They create a pretty string given a Document or an unformatted XML string.

- Extension function Node.toXmlString() creates a string representation of the XML subtree starting from the current node. If you do this for the Document, the whole DOM structure will be converted.

- We overload the plusAssign operator (corresponding to +=) of Node to add a child node.

- We add an addText() extension to Node for adding text content to a node.

- We add a removeText() extension to Node for removing text content from a node.

- We add an updateText() extension to Node for altering the text content of a node.

- We add an addAttribute() extension to Node for adding an attribute to a node.

- We add a removeAttribute() extension to Node for removing an attribute from a node.

- We add an updateAttribute() extension to Node for altering an attribute of a node.

For example, use cases of these functions include the following code snippets. First we add an element plus attribute to a given node:

```
val xml = """<?xml version="1.0" encoding="UTF-8"?>
<ProbeMsg>
  <TimeStamp>2016-10-30T19:07:07Z</TimeStamp>
  <ProbeId>1A6G</ProbeId>
  <ProbeValue ScaleUnit="cm">37.4</ProbeValue>
  <Meta>
    <Generator>045</Generator>
    <Priority>-3</Priority>
    <Actor>P. Rosengaard</Actor>
  </Meta>
</ProbeMsg>"""

    try {
        val dom = parseXmlToDOM(xml)

        val msg = dom("ProbeMsg")
        val meta = msg("Meta")

        // Add a new element to "meta".
        meta += dom.createElement("NewMeta").
            addText("NewValue").
            addAttribute("SomeAttr", "AttrVal")

        Log.d("LOG", "\n\n" + prettyFormatXml(dom))

    }catch(e:Exception) { Log.e("LOG", "XML Error", e)
}
```

For this to work we also use the createElement() function from the Document class. At the end this code writes the altered XML to the logging console.

The following code samples explain how we can change and remove attributes and elements:

```
val xml = """<?xml version="1.0" encoding="UTF-8"?>
<ProbeMsg>
  <TimeStamp>2016-10-30T19:07:07Z</TimeStamp>
  <ProbeId>1A6G</ProbeId>
  <ProbeValue ScaleUnit="cm">37.4</ProbeValue>
  <Meta>
    <Generator>045</Generator>
    <Priority>-3</Priority>
    <Actor>P. Rosengaard</Actor>
  </Meta>
</ProbeMsg>"""

    try {
        val dom = parseXmlToDOM(xml)

        val msg = dom("ProbeMsg")
        val ts = msg("TimeStamp")
        val probeValue = msg("ProbeValue")

        // Update an attribute and the text contents of
        // an element.
        probeValue.updateAttribute("ScaleUnit", "dm")
        ts.updateText("1970-01-01T00:00:00Z")
        Log.d("LOG", "\n\n" + prettyFormatXml(dom))

        // Remove an attribute
        probeValue.removeAttribute("ScaleUnit")
        Log.d("LOG", "\n\n" + prettyFormatXml(dom))

        // Removing a node means removing it from
        // its parent node.
        msg.removeChild(probeValue)
        Log.d("LOG", "\n\n" + prettyFormatXml(dom))
}catch(e:Exception) {
    Log.e("LOG", "XML Error", e)
}
```

Creating New DOMs

If you need to write a DOM representation of an XML document from scratch, first create a Document instance. This one does not have a public constructor; instead you write:

```
val doc = DocumentBuilderFactory.
    newInstance().newDocumentBuilder().newDocument()
```

From there you can add elements as described previously. Note that to see any output from our prettyFormatXml() utility function you must add at least one child element to doc.

Exercise 1

Add a createXmlDocument() function to the dom.kt file to simplify document creation.

JSON Processing

JavaScript Object Notation (JSON) is the little sister of XML. Data written in the JSON format require less space compared those same data using the XML format. In addition, JSON data almost naturally map to JavaScript objects in a browser environment and JSON therefore has gained considerable attention during recent years.

Kotlin's standard library doesn't know how to handle JSON data, so, similar to XML processing, we add a suitable external library. From several possibilities we use the widely adopted Jackson library. To add it to an Android project, inside the module's build.gradle file in the dependencies section add

```
implementation
    'com.fasterxml.jackson.core:jackson-core:2.9.8'
implementation
    'com.fasterxml.jackson.core:jackson-databind:2.9.8'
```

(on two lines, remove the line breaks).

Several paradigms exist for JSON processing. The most commonly used are a tree-like structure with JSON-specific objects, and a mapping between Kotlin and JSON objects with various semiautomatic conversion mechanisms. We leave the mapping methodology for your further research; it contains a couple of highly involved peculiarities, mostly for JSON collection mapping. The Jackson home page gives you more information about it. We instead describe mechanisms to handle an in-memory tree representation of JSON data.

For the rest of this section we use the following JSON data to explain the functions used inside the examples:

```
val json = """{
    "id":27,
    "name":"Roger Rabbit",
    "permanent":true,
    "address":{
        "street":"El Camino Real",
        "city":"New York",
        "zipcode":95014
    },
    "phoneNumbers":[9945678, 123456781],
    "role":"President"
}"""
```

JSON Helper Functions

The Jackson library for JSON processing contains all that is needed to write, update, and delete JSON elements. The library is quite extensive and contains an enormous amount of classes and functions. To simplify the development and to include Kotlin goodies we use a couple of package-level functions and extension functions to improve the JSON code readability. These are best located in a Kotlin file json.kt inside some package com.whatever.ext.

We start with the imports, add an invoke operator so we can easily fetch a child from a node, and add a remove and a forEach function for removing a node and traversing through the children of a node:

```
import com.fasterxml.jackson.core.JsonFactory
import com.fasterxml.jackson.core.util.DefaultPrettyPrinter
import com.fasterxml.jackson.databind.JsonNode
import com.fasterxml.jackson.databind.ObjectMapper
```

```
import com.fasterxml.jackson.databind.node.*
import java.io.ByteArrayOutputStream
import java.math.BigInteger

operator fun JsonNode.invoke(s:String) = this.get(s)
operator fun JsonNode.invoke(vararg s:String) =
    s.fold(this, { acc, s -> acc(s) })
fun JsonNode.remove(name:String) {
    val on = (this as? ObjectNode)?:
        throw Exception("This is not an object node")
    on.remove(name) }
fun JsonNode.forEach(iter: (JsonNode) -> Unit ) {
    when(this) {
        is ArrayNode -> this.forEach(iter)
        is ObjectNode -> this.forEach(iter)
        else -> throw Exception("Cannot iterate over " +
                this::class)
    }
}
```

Next we add simple alias text() for asText()to streamline text extraction:

```
fun JsonNode.text() = this.asText()
```

Another iterator traverses through the children of an object node. This time we take care of the children's names as well:

```
fun JsonNode.forEach(iter: (String, JsonNode) -> Unit ) {
    if(this !is ObjectNode)
        throw Exception(
        "Cannot iterate (key,val) over " + this::class)
    this.fields().forEach{
        (name, value) -> iter(name, value) }
}
```

To write a child of an object node we define a put() function, so we can write node.
put("childName", 42):

```
// Works only if the node is an ObjectNode!
fun JsonNode.put(name:String, value:Any?) : JsonNode {
    if(this !is ObjectNode)
        throw Exception("Cannot put() on none-object node")
    when(value) {
        null -> this.putNull(name)
        is Int -> this.put(name, value)
        is Long -> this.put(name, value)
        is Short -> this.put(name, value)
        is Float -> this.put(name, value)
        is Double -> this.put(name, value)
        is Boolean -> this.put(name, value)
        is String -> this.put(name, value)
        is JsonNode -> this.put(name, value)
        else -> throw Exception(
            "Illegal value type: ${value::class}")
    }
    return this
}
```

For appending a value to an array object we define an add() function, which works
for various types:

```
// Add a value to an array, works only if this is an
// ArrayNode
fun JsonNode.add(value:Any?) : JsonNode {
    if(this !is ArrayNode)
        throw Exception("Cannot add() on none-array node")
    when(value) {
        null -> this.addNull()
        is Int -> this.add(value)
        is Long -> this.add(value)
        is Float -> this.add(value)
        is Double -> this.add(value)
```

```
        is Boolean -> this.add(value)
        is String -> this.add(value)
        is JsonNode -> this.add(value)
        else -> throw Exception(
            "Illegal value type: ${value::class}")
    }
    return this
}
```

For JSON object creation we define various createSomething() style functions, and we also add a couple of Kotlin-like builder functions:

```
// Node creators
fun createJsonTextNode(text:String) = TextNode.valueOf(text)
fun createJsonIntNode(i:Int) = IntNode.valueOf(i)
fun createJsonLongNode(l:Long) = LongNode.valueOf(l)
fun createJsonShortNode(s:Short) = ShortNode.valueOf(s)
fun createJsonFloatNode(f:Float) = FloatNode.valueOf(f)
fun createJsonDoubleNode(d:Double) = DoubleNode.valueOf(d)
fun createJsonBooleanNode(b:Boolean) = BooleanNode.valueOf(b)
fun createJsonBigIntegerNode(b: BigInteger) = BigIntegerNode.valueOf(b)
fun createJsonNullNode() = NullNode.instance

fun jsonObjectNodeOf(
    children: Map<String,JsonNode> = HashMap()) :
    ObjectNode {
  return ObjectNode(JsonNodeFactory.instance, children)
}

fun jsonObjectNodeOf(
    vararg children: Pair<String,Any?>) :
    ObjectNode {
  return children.fold(
      ObjectNode(JsonNodeFactory.instance), { acc, v ->
    acc.put(v.first, v.second)
    acc
  })
}
```

```
fun jsonArrayNodeOf(elements: Array<JsonNode> =
        emptyArray()) : ArrayNode {
    return ArrayNode(JsonNodeFactory.instance,
                        elements.asList())
}
fun jsonArrayNodeOf(elements: List<JsonNode> =
        emptyList()) : ArrayNode {
    return ArrayNode(JsonNodeFactory.instance,
                        elements)
}
fun jsonEmptyArrayNode() : ArrayNode {
    return ArrayNode(JsonNodeFactory.instance)
}
fun jsonArrayNodeOf(vararg elements: Any?) : ArrayNode {
    return elements.fold(
            ArrayNode(JsonNodeFactory.instance), { acc, v ->
        acc.add(v)
        acc
    })
}
```

Extension functions toPrettyString() and toJsonString() can be used to generate a string representation of any JSON node:

```
// JSON output as pretty string
fun JsonNode.toPrettyString(
        prettyPrinter:PrettyPrinter? =
        DefaultPrettyPrinter()) : String {
    var res:String? = null
    ByteArrayOutputStream().use { os ->
        val gen = JsonFactory().createGenerator(os).apply {
            if(prettyPrinter != null) this.prettyPrinter = prettyPrinter
        }
        val mapper = ObjectMapper()
        mapper.writeTree(gen, this)
```

```
        res = String(os.toByteArray())
    }
    return res!!
}

// JSON output as simple string
fun JsonNode.toJsonString() : String =
        toPrettyString(prettyPrinter = null)
```

The main idea of all these extension functions is to improve conciseness by adding JSON object-related and JSON array-related functions to the base node class JsonNode and perform class casts during runtime. Although it makes the JSON code smaller and more expressive, the risk of getting exceptions during runtime is increased.

Reading and Writing JSON Data

To read in JSON data, all you have to do is to write:

```
val json = ... // see section beginning
val mapper = ObjectMapper()
val root = mapper.readTree(json)
```

From here we can investigate JSON elements, iterate through and fetch JSON object members, and extract JSON array elements:

```
try {
    val json = ... // see section beginning
    val mapper = ObjectMapper()
    val root = mapper.readTree(json)

    // see what we got
    Log.d("LOG", root.toPrettyString())

    // type of the node
    Log.d("LOG", root.nodeType.toString())
    // <- OBJECT
    // is it a container?
```

```
    Log.d("LOG", root.isContainerNode.toString())
    // <- true

    root.forEach { k,v ->
        Log.d("LOG",
          "Key:${k} -> val:${v} (${v.nodeType})")
        Log.d("LOG",
          "    <- " + v::class.toString())
    }

    val phones = root("phoneNumbers")
    phones.forEach { ph ->
        Log.d("LOG", "Phone: " + ph.text())
    }
    Log.d("LOG", "Phone[0]: " + phones[0].text())

    val street = root("address")("street").text()
    Log.d("LOG", "Street: " + street)
    Log.d("LOG", "Zip: " + root("address", "zipcode").asInt())

}catch(e:Exception) {
    Log.e("LOG", "JSON error", e)
}
```

The following code snippet shows how to alter a JSON tree by adding, changing, or deleting nodes or JSON object members.

```
// add it to the "try" statements from the
// last listing

// remove an entry
root("address").remove("zipcode")
Log.d("LOG", root.toPrettyString())

// update an entry
root("address").put("street", "Fake Street 42")
Log.d("LOG", root.toPrettyString())
```

```
root("address").put("country", createJsonTextNode("Argentina"))
Log.d("LOG", root.toPrettyString())

// create a new object node
root.put("obj", jsonObjectNodeOf(
        "abc1" to 23,
        "abc2" to "Hallo",
        "someNull" to null
))
Log.d("LOG", root.toPrettyString())

// create a new array node
root.put("arr", jsonArrayNodeOf(
        23,
        null,
        "Hallo"
))
Log.d("LOG", root.toPrettyString())

// write without spaces or line breaks
Log.d("LOG", root.toJsonString())
```

Creating New JSON Trees

To create a new JSON tree in memory you use:

```
val root = jsonObjectNodeOf()
```

From there you can add JSON elements as described previously.

Exercise 2

Create a JSON document corresponding to:

```
{
  "firstName": "Arthur",
  "lastName": "Doyle",
  "dateOfBirth": "03/04/1997",
  "address": {
```

```
    "streetAddress": "21 3rd Street",
    "city": "New York",
    "state": "NY",
    "postalCode": "10021-1234"
  },
  "phoneNumbers": [
    {
      "type": "home",
      "number": "212 555-1234"
    },
    {
      "type": "mobile",
      "number": "123 456-7890"
    }
  ],
  "children": [],
  "spouse": null
}
```

Appendix

Solutions to the Exercises

The following are the solutions to the exercises given in the chapters.

Chapter 2

Exercise 1: Only (2) is correct. Version (1) uses round brackets for the body, but curly brackets are needed. Version (3) is technically correct but does not use camelcase notation for the class name, and Version (4) tries to use a space in the class name.

Exercise 2: Only (4) is correct. Version (1) uses an undefined "`variable`" keyword. Version (2) uses an undefined "`property`" keyword. Version (3) does not yield to the `propertyName:PropertyType` property notation. Version (5) does not specify a mutability keyword (`var` or `val`).

Exercise 3: A `val` corresponds to an immutable (unchangeable) variable. Setting it to `0.0` means it will never have a different value, which makes no sense for an invoice. This can be fixed by using `var` instead of `val`.

Exercise 4: It is not allowed to change a `val` property. The property gets first set by the parameter declaration part of the class declaration and cannot be changed afterward.

Exercise 5: The property `blue` must be initialized as well, either in the property declaration or inside the `init{ }` block.

Exercise 6: The class reads:

```
class Invoice(val buyerFirstName:String,
    val buyerLastName:String,
    val date:String,
    val goodName:String,
```

© Peter Späth 2019
P. Späth, *Learn Kotlin for Android Development*, https://doi.org/10.1007/978-1-4842-4467-8

```
      val amount:Int,
      val pricePerItem:Double)
{
      val buyerFullName:String =
          buyerFirstName + " " + buyerLastName
      val totalPrice:Double =
          amount * pricePerItem
}
```

Exercise 7: The method reads:

```
fun goodInfo():String {
    return amount.toString() + " pieces of "
          + goodName
}
```

or

```
fun goodInfo():String =
    amount.toString() + " pieces of " + goodName
```

Using string interpolation you can also use

```
fun goodInfo():String =
    "${amount} pieces of ${goodName}"
```

Here the .toString() is implied.

Exercise 8: The class reads:

```
class Person(var firstName:String,
             var lastName:String,
             var ssn:String,
             var dateOfBirth:String,
             var gender:Char)
```

An empty body { } can be added, but because it is empty it is optional.

Exercise 9: The class instantiation reads:

```
val person1 = Person("John", "Smith", "0123456789", "1997-10-23", 'M')
```

Exercise 10: Either add

```
class GameUser(val firstName:String,
      val lastName:String,
      val birthday:String,
      val userName:String,
      val registrationNumber:Int,
      val userRank:Double) {
}
```

to the end of the `MainActivity.kt` file, or create a file `GameUser.kt` inside the same folder as file `MainActivity.kt`. As its contents, you must repeat the `package` declaration.

```
package kotlinforandroid.book.numberguess
```

```
class GameUser(val firstName:String,
      val lastName:String,
      val birthday:String,
      val userName:String,
      val registrationNumber:Int,
      val userRank:Double) {
}
```

Exercise 11: The class instantiation using named parameters reads:

```
val person1 = Person("firstName = John",
      lastName = "Smith",
      ssn = "0123456789",
      dateOfBirth = "1997-10-23",
      gender = 'M')
```

The argument sort order is free.

Exercise 12: Add

```
var gameUser = GameUser(lastName = "Doe",
      firstName = "John",
      userName = "jdoe",
      birthday = "1900-01-01",
```

```
        registrationNumber = 0,
        userRank = 0.0 )
```

right underneath var tries = 0

Exercise 13: The new class with default SSN parameter in the constructor reads:

```
class Person(var firstName:String,
             var lastName:String,
             var ssn:String = "",
             var dateOfBirth:String,
             var gender:Char)
```

An instantiation using this default value would read:

```
val person1 = Person("firstName = John",
     lastName = "Smith",
     dateOfBirth = "1997-10-23",
     gender = 'M')
```

where the sort order of the arguments is free.

Exercise 14: The class declaration now reads:

```
class GameUser(val firstName:String,
               val lastName:String,
               val userName:String,
               val registrationNumber:Int,
               val birthday:String = "",
               val userRank:Double = 0.0) {
}
```

Exercise 15: The class with the secondary constructor added reads:

```
class Person(var firstName:String,
             var lastName:String,
             var ssn:String,
             var dateOfBirth:String,
             var gender:Char)
```

```
{
    constructor(firstName:String,
        lastName:String,
        ssn:String,
        gender:Char) : this(firstName,
            lastName, ssn, "000-00-00", gender)
}
```

To perform an instantiation, for example, write:

```
val person1 = Person("John", "Smith",
    "0123456789", 'M')
```

But you can also use named parameters:

```
val person1 = Person(firstName = "John",
    lastName = "Smith",
    ssn = "0123456789",
    gender = 'M')
```

Exercise 16: None.

Exercise 17: The object declaration reads:

```
object Constants {
    val numberOfTabs = 5
    val windowTitle = "Astaria"
    val prefsFile = "prefs.properties"
}
```

Property types are not needed; Kotlin can infer them from the literals right of the "="
sign. The diagnostic code looks like this:

```
fun main(args:Array<String>) {
    println(
        "Number of tabs: " +
            Constants.numberOfTabs +
        "\nWindow title: " +
            Constants.windowTitle +
```

```
        "\nPrefs file: " +
            Constants.prefsFile
    )
}
```

The formatting is, of course, up to you.

Exercise 18: The class at a bare minimum reads

```
class Triangle() {
    companion object {
        val NUMBER_OF_CORNERS = 3
    }
    fun info() {
        println("Number of corners: " +
            NUMBER_OF_CORNERS)
    }
}
```

Exercise 19: The code reads:

```
fun main(args:Array<String>) {
    val triangle = Triangle()
    val numberOfCorners =
        Triangle.NUMBER_OF_CORNERS
}
```

Exercise 20: The code reads:

```
interface ElementaryParticle {
    fun mass():Double
    fun charge():Double
    fun spin():Double
}

class Electron : ElementaryParticle {
    override fun mass() = 9.11e-31
    override fun charge() = -1.0
    override fun spin() = 0.5
}
```

```kotlin
class Proton : ElementaryParticle {
    override fun mass() = 1.67e-27
    override fun charge() = 1.0
    override fun spin() = 0.5
}
```

Exercise 21: (2), (3), (4), and (5) are true; (1) and (6) are false. For (1): Interfaces can never be instantiated. For (6): An electron is not a proton. (5) is possible because both are ElementaryParticles and we have a var that allows reassignment.

Exercise 22: The interface plus implementations code reads:

```kotlin
interface RandomNumberGenerator {
    fun rnd(minInt:Int, maxInt:Int)
}
class StdRandom : RandomNumberGenerator {
    override fun rnd(minInt: Int, maxInt: Int):Int {
        val span = maxInt - minInt + 1
        return minInt + Math.floor(Math.random()*span).toInt()
    }
}
class RandomRandom : RandomNumberGenerator {
    val rnd:Random = Random()
    override fun rnd(minInt: Int, maxInt: Int):Int {
        val span = maxInt - minInt + 1
        return minInt + rnd.nextInt(span)
    }
}
```

Put that at the end of MainActivity.kt, or put it into a new file using, for example, the name random.kt.

The new property in the activity reads

```kotlin
val rnd:RandomNumberGenerator = StdRandom()
// or ... = RandomRandom()
```

The new code in method `start(…)` reads

```
number = rnd.rnd(Constants.LOWER_BOUND, Constants. UPPER_BOUND)
```

(the `val span = …` line can be removed).

Exercise 23: Over the "java" item on the left-side pane (Android view), press mouse-right and then New → Kotlin File/Class for classes, interface, or singleton objects. Or choose New → Package for packages (folders). If asked, select the "main/java" branch. For all classes, interfaces, and singleton objects you can always first create a "class" type file and then accordingly adapt its contents.

Exercise 24: The listings read:

MainActivity.kt

```kotlin
package kotlinforandroid.book.numberguess


import android.content.Context
import android.support.v7.app.AppCompatActivity
import android.os.Bundle
import android.util.AttributeSet
import android.util.Log
import android.view.View
import android.widget.ScrollView
import android.widget.TextView
import kotlinforandroid.book.numberguess.common.Constants
import kotlinforandroid.book.numberguess.model.GameUser
import kotlinforandroid.book.numberguess.random.RandomNumberGenerator
import kotlinforandroid.book.numberguess.random.impl.StdRandom
import kotlinx.android.synthetic.main.activity_main.*
import java.util.*

class MainActivity : AppCompatActivity() {
    val rnd: RandomNumberGenerator = StdRandom()
    // or ... = RandomRandom()
    var started = false var number = 0
    var tries = 0
```

```kotlin
var gameUser = GameUser(
    lastName = "Doe",
    firstName = "John",
    userName = "jdoe",
    birthday = "1900-01-01",
    registrationNumber = 0,
    userRank = 0.0
)

override
fun onCreate(savedInstanceState: Bundle?) {
    super.onCreate(savedInstanceState)
    setContentView(R.layout.activity_main)

    fetchSavedInstanceData(savedInstanceState)
    doGuess.setEnabled(started)
}

override
fun onSaveInstanceState(outState: Bundle?) {
    super.onSaveInstanceState(outState)
    putInstanceData(outState)
}

fun start(v: View) {
    log("Game started")
    num.setText("")
    started = true
    doGuess.setEnabled(true)
    status.text = getString(R.string.guess_hint,
            Constants.LOWER_BOUND,
            Constants.UPPER_BOUND)

    number = rnd.rnd(Constants.LOWER_BOUND, Constants.UPPER_BOUND)
    tries = 0
    val r = Random()
    r.nextInt(7)
}
```

```kotlin
fun guess(v:View) {
    if(num.text.toString() == "") return
    tries++
    log("Guessed " + num.text +
            " (tries:" + tries + ")")
    val g = num.text.toString().toInt()
    if(g < number) {
        status.setText(R.string.status_too_low)
        num.setText("")
    } else if(g > number){
        status.setText(R.string.status_too_high) num.setText("")
    } else {
        status.text = getString( R.string.status_hit, tries)
        started = false
        doGuess.setEnabled(false)
    }
}

//////////////////////////////////////////////////
//////////////////////////////////////////////////

private
fun putInstanceData(outState: Bundle?) {
    if (outState != null) with(outState) {
        putBoolean("started", started) putInt("number", number)
        putInt("tries", tries)
        putString("statusMsg", status.text.toString())
        putStringArrayList("logs", ArrayList(console.text.split("\n")))
    }
}
private
fun fetchSavedInstanceData(
        savedInstanceState: Bundle?) {
    if (savedInstanceState != null)
    with(savedInstanceState) {
        started = getBoolean("started")
```

```
            number = getInt("number")
            tries = getInt("tries")
            status.text = getString("statusMsg")
            console.text =
                getStringArrayList("logs")!!.
                joinToString("\n")
        }
    }

    private fun log(msg:String) {
        Log.d("LOG", msg)
        console.log(msg)
    }
}
```

Constants.kt

```
package kotlinforandroid.book.numberguess.common

object Constants {
    val LOWER_BOUND = 1
    val UPPER_BOUND = 7
}
```

Console.kt

```
package kotlinforandroid.book.numberguess.gui

    import android.content.Context
    import android.util.AttributeSet
    import android.widget.ScrollView
    import android.widget.TextView

    class Console(ctx: Context, aset: AttributeSet? = null) :
        ScrollView(ctx, aset) {
        companion object {
            val BACKGROUND_COLOR = 0x40FFFF00
            val MAX_LINES = 100
```

```
    }
    val tv = TextView(ctx)
    var text:String
        get() = tv.text.toString()
        set(value) { tv.setText(value) }
    init {
        setBackgroundColor(BACKGROUND_COLOR)
        addView(tv)
    }
    fun log(msg:String) {
        val l = tv.text.let {
            if(it == "") listOf() else it.split("\n")
        }.takeLast(MAX_LINES) + msg
        tv.text = l.joinToString("\n")
        post(object : Runnable {
            override fun run() {
                fullScroll(ScrollView.FOCUS_DOWN)
            }
        })
    }
}
```

You also must adapt the element in activity_main.xml:

```
...
<kotlinforandroid.book.numberguess.gui.Console
        android:id="@+id/console"
        android:layout_height="100sp"
        android:layout_width="match_parent" />
...
```

GameUser.kt

```
package kotlinforandroid.book.numberguess.model

class GameUser(val firstName:String,
               val lastName:String,
```

```kotlin
            val userName:String,
            val registrationNumber:Int,
            val birthday:String = "",
            val userRank:Double = 0.0) {
}
```

RandomNumberGenerator.kt

```kotlin
package kotlinforandroid.book.numberguess.random
interface RandomNumberGenerator {
    fun rnd(minInt:Int, maxInt:Int):Int
}
```

RandomRandom.kt

```kotlin
package kotlinforandroid.book.numberguess.random.impl

import kotlinforandroid.book.numberguess.random.
      RandomNumberGenerator
import java.util.*

class RandomRandom : RandomNumberGenerator {
    val rnd: Random = Random()
    override fun rnd(minInt: Int, maxInt: Int):Int {
        val span = maxInt - minInt + 1
        return minInt + rnd.nextInt(span)
    }
}
```

StdRandom.kt

```kotlin
package kotlinforandroid.book.numberguess.random.impl

import kotlinforandroid.book.numberguess.random.
      RandomNumberGenerator

class StdRandom : RandomNumberGenerator {
    override fun rnd(minInt: Int, maxInt: Int):Int {
        val span = maxInt - minInt + 1
```

```
        return minInt +
                Math.floor(Math.random()*span).toInt()
    }
}
```

Chapter 3

Exercise 1: The var or val in the constructor parameter is missing, so the color is not transported to a property. In this case we have to use var, because we want to change it:

```
class Triangle(var color: String) {
    fun changeColor(newColor:String) {
        color = newColor
    }
}
```

Exercise 2: The code reads:

```
class A {
    var a:Int = 1 // A
    init {
        a = 2      // B
    }
    fun b() {
        a = 3      // C
    }
}
fun main(args:Array<String>) {
    val a = A()
    a.a = 4         // D
}
```

Exercise 3: Write

```
val a = 42
val s = "If we add 4 to a we get ${a+4}"
```

Exercise 4: Only (4) is allowed.

Exercise 5: It is not allowed to change method parameter variables.

Exercise 6: A `return` without argument is allowed for methods not returning anything, so the method is valid. The `return` at the end is superfluous though.

Exercise 7: Yes.

Exercise 8: Use the expression variant:

```
class A(val a:Int) {
    fun add(b:Int) = a + b
    fun mult(b:Int) = a * b
}
```

Exercise 9: The interface reads:

```
interface AInterface {
    fun add(b:Int):Int
    fun mult(b:Int):Int
}
```

Exercise 10: The output is `meth1: 42 7`

Exercise 11: The code reads:

```
println(A.x(42))
```

For using companion objects an instance of the class is not needed!

Exercise 12: The code reads:

```
val p = Person()
p.setName(lName = "Doe", fName = "John")
// or
p.setName(fName = "John", lName = "Doe")
```

Exercise 13: The method declaration reads:

```
fun set(lastName:String = "",
    firstName:String = "",
    birthDay?:String = null,
    ssn:String? = null) { ... }
```

And for the invocation write:

```
set(lastName = "Smith", ssn = "1234567890")
```

or

```
set(ssn = "1234567890", lastName = "Smith")
```

Exercise 14: The code reads:

```
class Club {
    fun addMembers(vararg names:String) {
        println(names.size)
        println(names.joinToString(" : "))
    }
}

fun main(args:Array<String>) {
    var club = Club()
    club.addMembers("Hughes, John",
                    "Smith, Alina",
                    "Curtis, Solange")
}
```

Exercise 15: The output will be:

```
B.y() -> a = 7
A.q() -> a = 7
```

Exercise 16: The output will be:

```
A.x() : g = 99
B.y() : g = 8
A.q() : g = 99
```

The property needs to be declared private, otherwise g from class A will be visible in the subclass B as well, and then we have two declarations of one property, which the language does not allow.

Exercise 17: The code then reads:

```
open class A() {
    open var g:Int = 99
    fun x() {
        println("A.x() : g = ${g}")
    }
    fun q() {
        println("A.q() : g = ${g}")
    }
}

class B : A() {
    override var g:Int = 8
    fun y() {
        println("B.y() : g = ${g}") q()
    }
}

    fun main(args:Array<String>) {
        val b = B()
        b.x()
        b.y()
    }
```

And the output will be

```
A.x() : g = 8
B.y() : g = 8
A.q() : g = 8
```

Exercise 18: Class (3) is invalid, because the local variable gets used before it is declared. Class (5) is invalid, because the declaration of a is valid only inside method1(). All the other classes are valid.

Exercise 19: The method calls itself, calls itself, calls itself, and so on, forever. This is called *recursion* and here leads to an error.

Chapter 4

Exercise 1: Write

```
package com.example.util

fun add10(a:Int) = a + 10
fun add100(a:Int) = a + 100
```

Maybe rename the file util.kt to avoid the impression that it contained a class or a singleton object. The file name, in fact, no longer plays a role.

The client code then reads:

```
package com.example

import com.example.util.*

class A(q:Int) {
    val x10:Int = add10(q)
    val x100:Int = add100(q)
}
```

Exercise 2: Write

```
package com.example
import java.lang.Math.log
class A {
  fun calc(a:Double) = log(a)
}
```

Exercise 3: (1) is not true, as the coordinates x and y cannot be swapped. (2) is not true, because the classes don't match. (3) is true, because the extracted x coordinates match. (4) is true, because the 1 automatically gets converted to 1.0 and after that all coordinates match. (5) is true, as the class and all coordinates match.

Exercise 4: The GameUser class is a good candidate for a data class. Just prepend data to the class declaration: data class GameUser ....

Exercise 5: Write

```kotlin
data class GameUser(val firstName:String,
                val lastName:String,
                val userName:String,
                val registrationNumber:Int,
                val gender:Gender = Gender.X,
                val birthday:String = "",
                val userRank:Double = 0.0) {
    enum class Gender{F,M,X}

    val fullName:String
    val initials:String
    init {
        fullName = firstName + " " + lastName
        initials = firstName.toUpperCase() +
                lastName.toUpperCase()
    }
}
```

The enumeration class could also be placed outside the GameUser class. Also, for this exercise whether you use vals or vars does not play a role.

Exercise 6: A set(value) … does not make sense, because vals are immutable. Other than that, for the getters you can do the same as for vars

Exercise 7: Write

```kotlin
val str:String get() = toString()
```

or

```kotlin
val str get() = toString()
```

because Kotlin can infer the return type. Do not use var instead of val, as setting here makes no sense.

Exercise 8: Write

```
data class GameUser(var firstName:String,
             var lastName:String,
             var userName:String,
             var registrationNumber:Int,
             var gender:Gender = Gender.X,
             var birthday:String = "",
             var userRank:Double = 0.0) {
    enum class Gender{F,M,X}

    val fullName:String
        get() = firstName + " " + lastName

    val initials:String
        get() = firstName.toUpperCase() +
                    lastName.toUpperCase()
}
```

Both `fullName` and `initials` shouldn't be `vars`, because they provide derived values.

Exercise 9: Write

```
data class Point(val x:Double, val y:double) {
  operator fun minus(p2:Point) =
      Vector(p2.x-this.x, p2.y-this.y)
}

data class Vector(val dx:Double, val dy:Double) {
  operator fun plus(v2:Vector) =
      Vector(this.dx + v2.dx, this.dy + v2.dy)
  operator fun minus(v2:Vector) =
      Vector(this.dx - v2.dx, this.dy - v2.dy)
}
```

Chapter 5

Exercise 1: The code reads:

```
Math.sqrt(
    ( a + (b-x)/2 ) / ( b*b - 7*x )
)
```

You can also use `Math.pow(b, 2.0)` instead of `b * b`

Exercise 2: Write

```
class Concatenator {
  var string:String = ""
  fun add(s:String) { string += s }
  operator fun contains(other:String) =
      string.contains(other)
}
```

Chapter 6

Exercise 1: Texts and formatting are up to you.

Chapter 8

Exercise 1: The exception class reads:

```
package kotlinforandroid.book.numberguess.common
```

```
class GameException(msg:String) : Exception(msg)
```

The `guess()` function inside class `MainActivity` with the check added reads:

```
fun guess(v:View) {
    if(num.text.toString() == "") return

    try {
      if (num.text.toString().toInt() <
            Constants.LOWER_BOUND)
          throw GameException(
```

```
            "Must guess a number >= " +
            "${Constants.LOWER_BOUND}")
      if (num.text.toString().toInt() >
            Constants.UPPER_BOUND)
        throw GameException(
            "Must guess a number <= " +
            "${Constants.UPPER_BOUND}")

      // rest of the original function...
    } catch(e:GameException) {
        Toast.makeText(this,
          "Guessable numbers: " +
          "${Constants.LOWER_BOUND} to " +
          "${Constants.UPPER_BOUND} ",
          Toast.LENGTH_LONG).show()
    }
}
```

Chapter 9

Exercise 1: The code reads:

```
val arr = IntArray(101, { i -> 100 - i })
```

Exercise 2: The code reads:

```
booleanArrayOf(true, false, true)
```

Exercise 3: The code reads:

```
val fruits = mutableSetOf("Apple", "Banana",
    "Grape", "Engine")
fruits.remove("Engine")
fruits.add("Cherry")
val fruits5 = fruits.filter {
    element -> element.length == 5
}
```

Note In Kotlin you can remove the round brackets from ({ ... }). Also, you can substitute the element with any other name you like.

Exercise 4: You could write

```
val sorted = gul.sortedWith(
    compareBy(GameUser::lastName)
        then
    compareBy(GameUser::firstName))
```

Or, to be a little bit less expressive:

```
val sorted = gul.sortedWith(
    compareBy(GameUser::lastName,
              GameUser::firstName))
```

Exercise 5: The code reads:

```
gul.sortWith(
    compareBy(GameUser::lastName)
        then
    compareBy(GameUser::firstName))
```

or

```
gul.sortWith(
    compareBy(GameUser::lastName,
              GameUser::firstName))
```

Exercise 6: The code reads:

```
val groupedByManufacturer = cars.groupBy {
    car -> car.vin.substring(0,3)
}
val wxxCars = groupedByManufacturer["WXX"]
```

Exercise 7: The code reads:

```
(1..100).toList().reduce{ acc,v -> acc*v }
```

Actually the `toList()` can be omitted, as ranges have a `reduce()` as well:

```
(1..100).reduce{ acc,v -> acc*v }
```

Exercise 8: The code reads:

```
val fruits = listOf("Bananas", "apples",
    "Oranges")
val prices = listOf(1.69, 2.19, 2.79)
data class Fruit(
    val name:String, val price:Double)
val zipped = fruits.zip(prices,
      { a, b -> Fruit(a, b) })
```

Chapter 11

Exercise 1: (1) and (3) are true, and (2) is only true in cases where we implemented an appropriate `equals()` function.

Exercise 2: (1) and (2) are true. (3) is true only if function `hashCode()` is implemented appropriately. However, for == to work correctly, a `hashCode()` implementation is not needed. It *should* be provided, though, to avoid surprises if a class gets used as a map key.

Chapter 12

Exercise 1: One possible solution would be:

```
val f : (String, Int) -> String =
   { s:String, num:Int ->
     (1..num).map { s }.joinToString { it } }
```

We use the range operator `..` to get something that iterates `num` times over whatever, map each iteration to the parameter string, and then concatenate the `num` identical copies of the string.

Exercise 2: The code reads:

```
val f : (String) -> String = { it + "!" }
```

Exercise 3: The filter reads:

```
val startsWithL = employees.filter {
    it.firstName.startsWith("L") }.toList()
```

Chapter 13

Exercise 1: The code reads:

```
class Quadruple<A,B,C,D>(
    var p1:A, var p2:B, var p3:C, var p4:D)
val q1 = Quadruple(1, 2, 3.14, "Hello")
```

The type and property parameter names, of course, are up to you.

Note that we could have written this:

```
class Quadruple<A,B,C,D>(
    var p1:A, var p2:B, var p3:C, var p4:D)
val q1:Quadruple<Int, Int, Double, String> =
    Quadruple<Int, Int, Double, String>(
    1, 2, 3.14, "Hello")
```

but the explicit type parameters could be omitted because Kotlin can infer the type from the literals provided.

Exercise 2: The code reads:

```
class Sorter<T : Comparable<T>> {
    val list: MutableList<T> = mutableListOf()
    fun add(value:T) {
        list.add(value)
        list.sort()
    }
}
```

Chapter 14

Exercise 1: The annotation declaration reads:

```
@Target(AnnotationTarget.VALUE_PARAMETER)
@Retention(AnnotationRetention.RUNTIME)
annotation class NotNegative()
```

Inside the `Calculator.Operator` enumeration, add `SQRT("sqrt")`

Inside the `f?.valueParameters?.forEachIndexed { ...` loop, add

```
p.findAnnotation<NotNegative>()?.run {
    if (params[ind] < 0.0)
        throw RuntimeException(
        "Parameter ${ind} must be positive")
}
```

Finally, add a function:

```
fun sqrt(@NotNegative p:Double) : Double {
    return Math.sqrt(p)
}
```

Chapter 16

Exercise 1: Write

```
val sorted = l.sortedBy { empl -> empl.ssn }
```

or

```
val sorted = l.sortedBy { it.ssn }
```

Exercise 2: Let it read

```
val map = l.associateBy { empl -> empl.ssn }
```

or

```
val map = l.associateBy { Employee::ssn }
```

Exercise 3: The output is a list $[1, 2, 3, 4]$

Exercise 4: The output is a list $["1", "2", "3", "4"]$

Exercise 5: The code reads:

```
val filtered = l.filter { it.ssn.startsWith("0") }
```

Exercise 6: The check reads:

```
val l = listOf(1, 2, 3, 4)
val allGreaterThanZero = l.all { it > 0 }
```

Exercise 7: One possibility is

```
l.find{ it == 42 }?.run{
    throw Exception("42 found!") }
```

Another possibility reads:

```
l.contains(42).takeIf { it }?.run {
    throw Exception("42 found!") }
```

Exercise 8: The solution is

```
l.sumByDouble { it.weight }
```

Chapter 17

Exercise 1: There are several possibilities. We save the "now" instant on creation and deduce a Duration object with twice the elapsed time since that instant:

```
class  ClockTwiceAsFast : Clock() {
    val myStartInstant : Instant
    init {
        myStartInstant = Clock.systemUTC().instant()
    }

    override
    fun withZone(zone: ZoneId?): Clock = this
    override
    fun getZone(): ZoneId = ZoneId.of("Z")
```

```
    override fun instant(): Instant {

      val dur2 = Duration.between(myStartInstant,
        Clock.systemUTC().instant()).multipliedBy(2L)
      return myStartInstant.plus(dur2)
    }
}
```

Exercise 2: Write

```
operator fun String.rem(regex:String) = this.matches
  (Regex(regex))
```

Chapter 18

Exercise 1: Start creating the app as a "Basic Activity" app. Android Studio then builds a standard `activity_main.xml` file. The actual user interface elements get defined in `content_main.xml`:

```
<?xml version="1.0" encoding="utf-8"?>
<LinearLayout
      xmlns:android=
        "http://schemas.android.com/apk/res/android"
      xmlns:tools=
        "http://schemas.android.com/tools"
      xmlns:app=
        "http://schemas.android.com/apk/res-auto"
      android:orientation="vertical"
      android:layout_width="match_parent"
      android:layout_height="match_parent"
      app:layout_behavior=
        "@string/appbar_scrolling_view_behavior"
      tools:showIn="@layout/activity_main"
      tools:context=".MainActivity">
```

```
<TextView
        android:layout_width="wrap_content"
        android:layout_height="wrap_content"
        android:text="Multithreaded PI"
        android:textSize="25sp"/>

<LinearLayout android:layout_width="match_parent"
         android:layout_height="wrap_content"
         android:orientation="horizontal">
    <TextView android:layout_width="100dp"
         android:layout_height="wrap_content"
         android:text="Processors"/>
    <TextView android:id="@+id/procs"
         android:layout_width="wrap_content"
         android:layout_height="wrap_content"/>
</LinearLayout>

    <LinearLayout android:layout_width="match_parent"
         android:layout_height="wrap_content"
         android:orientation="horizontal">
    <TextView android:layout_width="100dp"
         android:layout_height="wrap_content"
         android:text="Iterations"/>
    <EditText android:id="@+id/iters"
         android:text="1000000"
         android:inputType="number"
         android:layout_width="wrap_content"
         android:layout_height="wrap_content"/>
</LinearLayout>

    <LinearLayout android:layout_width="match_parent"
         android:layout_height="wrap_content"
         android:orientation="horizontal">
    <TextView android:layout_width="100dp"
         android:layout_height="wrap_content"
         android:text="Threads"/>
```

```
        <EditText android:id="@+id/threads"
                android:text="4"
                android:inputType="number"
                android:layout_width="wrap_content"
                android:layout_height="wrap_content"/>
</LinearLayout>

<LinearLayout android:layout_width="match_parent"
                android:layout_height="wrap_content"
                android:orientation="horizontal">
        <TextView android:layout_width="100dp"
                android:layout_height="wrap_content"
                android:text="Cumul Iters"/>
        <TextView android:id="@+id/cumulIters"
                android:layout_width="wrap_content"
                android:layout_height="wrap_content"/>
</LinearLayout>

<LinearLayout android:layout_width="match_parent"
                android:layout_height="wrap_content"
                android:orientation="horizontal">
        <TextView android:layout_width="100dp"
                android:layout_height="wrap_content"
                android:text="Current Pi"/>
        <TextView android:id="@+id/pi"
                android:layout_width="wrap_content"
                android:layout_height="wrap_content"/>
</LinearLayout>

<LinearLayout android:layout_width="match_parent"
                android:layout_height="wrap_content"
                android:orientation="horizontal">
        <TextView android:layout_width="100dp"
                android:layout_height="wrap_content"
                android:text="Calc Time"/>
```

```
        <TextView android:id="@+id/calcTime"
                android:layout_width="wrap_content"
                android:layout_height="wrap_content"/>
    </LinearLayout>

    <Button android:text="CALC"
            android:onClick="calc"
            android:layout_width="match_parent"
            android:layout_height="wrap_content"/>
    <Button android:text="RESET"
            android:onClick="reset"
            android:layout_width="match_parent"
            android:layout_height="wrap_content"/>
</LinearLayout>
```

The corresponding activity class already got listed in the floating text. Note that for simplicity, label and button texts are directly entered in the layout file. Instead they should be exported to resource files.

Exercise 2: Write

```
...
l111 = launch {
    Log.d("LOG", "E")
    withTimeout(500L) {
        delay(1000L)
    }
    Log.d("LOG", "F")
    delay(1000L)
    Log.d("LOG", "G")
}
...
```

The logging will not differ from the logging with the cancel().

Chapter 20

Exercise 1: Write

```
fun createXmlDocument(): Document =
        DocumentBuilderFactory.newInstance().
        newDocumentBuilder().newDocument()
```

Exercise 2: A possible solution would be:

```
val root = jsonObjectNodeOf()
with(root) {
    put("firstName", "Arthur")
    put("lastName", "Doyle")
    put("dateOfBirth", "03/04/1997")
    put("address",
        jsonObjectNodeOf(
            "streetAddress" to "21 3rd Street",
            "city" to "New York",
            "state" to "NY",
            "postalCode" to "10021-1234"))
    put("phoneNumbers",
        jsonArrayNodeOf(
            jsonObjectNodeOf("type" to "home",
                "number" to "212 555-1234"),
            jsonObjectNodeOf("type" to "mobile",
                "number" to "123 456-7890")
        ))
    put("children", jsonEmptyArrayNode())
    putNull("spouse")
}
Log.d("LOG", root.toPrettyString())
```

Index

A

abs() function, 348

add() functions, 95, 275, 282

Aggregators function, 331–332

Android device, 3–4

Android Studio

    adding external libraries

        parameterized form, 440

        repositories, 437–439

    library creation, 443–445

    nullability, 442

Annotations

    applications, 296–297

    array, 297

    characteristics, 292–294

    custom, 302–304

    elements, 298–300

    KAPT, 298

    meta-information, 289–291

    operator classes, 291

    operator() function, 304

    reflection API, 298

    use-site targets, 294–295

Anonymous classes, 113

Any.notifyAll() function, 401

Any.notify() function, 401

Any.wait() function, 401

Apache Commons library, 441

API level 25 or less, 349–352

API level 26 or greater

clock, 366–367

Duration and Period classes, 362–365

instants, 357

LocalDate, 353–356

LocalDateTime, 353–356, 360–362

LocalTime, 353–356

minSdkVersion, 353

OffsetDateTime, 358–359

OffsetTime, 358–359

ZonedDateTime, 360–362

Application programming interface (API)

    documentation, 166

Array

    collections

        lists, 200, 205–211

        maps, 201, 212–214

        sets, 200–204

    constructors, 196–197

    empty array of object references, 198

    folding, 223–224

    grouping, 222–223

    lambda function, 196–197

    null object references, 198

    objects, 193–195

    operations, 198–200

    reducing, 224–225

    sorting, 217–220

    zipping, 225–227

async() function, 416, 422

atan2() function, 348

await() function, 421, 428, 432

© Peter Späth 2019

P. Späth, *Learn Kotlin for Android Development*, https://doi.org/10.1007/978-1-4842-4467-8

Printed in the United States
By Bookmasters